SPANISH
STEP BY STEP

CHARLES BERLITZ

Charles Berlitz, world-famous linguist and author of more than 100 language teaching books, is the grandson of the founder of the Berlitz Schools. Since 1967, Mr. Berlitz has not been connected with the Berlitz Schools in any way.

WYNWOOD™ Press
New York, New York

Library of Congress Cataloging-in-Publication Data
Berlitz, Charles Frambach, 1914–
    Spanish step-by-step / by Charles Berlitz.
        p.   cm.
    ISBN 0-922066-28-0
    1. Spanish language—Textbooks for foreign speakers—English.
I. Title.
PC4129.E5B4   1990
468.3′421—dc20   89-25104
                                                                    CIP

Copyright © 1990 by Charles Berlitz
Published by WYNWOOD™ Press
New York, New York
Printed in the United States of America

PREFACE

Spanish Step-By-Step is the first book of its kind and vastly different from other books designed to teach or review Spanish.

This book will guide you to a knowledge of Spanish step by easy step from first contact with the language to advanced conversation, including explanations that anyone can understand and conversational material that you can immediately use.

It will teach you to speak correct, colloquial Spanish as it is spoken today and will teach you easily, without lengthy and involved explanations. From the first page you will learn instant communication in Spanish.

This is because of the logical and unusual way that Spanish is presented in the *Step-By-Step* approach. Every phrase of Spanish construction, every use of Spanish verbs, every turn of modern Spanish idiom, and all sorts of situations that apply to everyday living and emotions are presented in short, easy-to-follow conversational patterns. These dialogues will not only hold your interest, but they will also stay in your memory, once you have used them, since it is relatively easy to remember words and phrases that you can readily use in conversations with Spanish-speaking people.

If you are a beginner, you will be surprised at the ease with which you can learn to speak Spanish and pronounce it so that Spanish people can understand you. If you already know some Spanish, you will find that this book will increase your understanding, your fluency, your ability to use the Spanish vocabulary you already know and, above all, your confidence in speaking Spanish.

There are 25 steps to Spanish in this book which, with a vocabulary selected on the basis of frequency in conversation, will take you from simple ordering in a café to an ability to understand what is said to you by Spanish-speaking people you may meet and, better still, to reply; and finally, to be able to discuss books, politics, art, science, business, history, and any general topic of conversation. In addition, these conversational teaching selections constitute an excursion into the culture patterns of the Spanish-speaking world—so that you will know not only what to say, but also when to say it. You will learn how to start conversations with people—how to tell a story—how people speak when they are excited—and you will even acquire the language of romance.

Along the way you will absorb a vocabulary of several thousand words—actually more than most people use in speaking any language. You will be taught the verb forms and idiomatic constructions through the situational dialogues mentioned above; in other words, you will develop an *instinct* for correct use according to the situation—the same way you did when you learned your own language.

Explanations of these special constructions are given at the very spot where they are needed. These easy-to-understand explanations on the right side of each page refer directly to each new point of Spanish idiom or construction.

At the end of each step, there is a section of instant conversation in the form of a short dialogue, the reading of which serves not only as a re-impression of the previous step, but also shows Spanish people talking naturally in situations that use the new material you have just learned in a normal, correct way. And, as you approach Spanish in this natural *Step-By-Step* way, you will find yourself speaking it fluently and understanding it easily and, most important, you will enjoy the experience of learning it.

CONTENTS

Contents

Contents

Contents

HOW TO PRONOUNCE SPANISH

Every sentence in the lessons and dialogues of this book is written three times — first in Spanish, then in easy-to-read syllables that show you how to pronounce it, and finally in English, so you can understand the meaning.

To read the Spanish correctly, say the second line out loud, pronouncing each separate syllable as if it were in English and ¡Olé! — it comes out Spanish.

Here is an example. Note that the syllables in capital letters are to be stressed:

¿Cómo está usted?
¿KO-mo ess-TA oos-TED?
How are you?

As you progress you should try to pronounce the Spanish without looking at the second line — but it will still be there if you need it.

The Spanish pronunciation of many letters and combinations of letters differs considerably from English. The following list will help you to remember the difference.

IN SPANISH	ENGLISH EQUIVALENT
a	ah
e	ay (a short sound, almost like "eh")
i	ee
o	oh
u	oo
ay (or) ai	eye (or) i
g (before e and i)	h (guttural)
g (before a, o, u)	g
h	(silent)

IN SPANISH	ENGLISH EQUIVALENT
j	h
ll	lli (as in million)
ñ	ny (as in canyon)
r	a rolled r
rr	a strongly rolled r
x	h (when beginning syllable)

In the phonetics, an "h" is added at the end of a syllable only to avoid confusion when the letter combinations already have an English meaning as "to," "do," "a," which are rendered *toh, doh, ah.*

In most of Spain the c before e or i, or z before any letter, is pronounced like the English th in think, and rather resembles a lisp. In southern Spain and in Latin America, however, these letters are generally sounded like an s. We have written them as s in the pronunciation line because this pronunciation is more widely used.

As Spanish is a phonetic language, meaning that its letters always have the same value, once you learn the sounds of the letters and their combinations you will be able to pronounce the language correctly. In this respect, Spanish is an easier language to pronounce than English.

A word of advice: after reading each lesson for the first time it is most important that you read the text and the "instant conversation" section aloud. Read it slowly at first, and then gradually increase your speed to that of a normal conversational level, reading the Spanish line instead of the pronunciation line. This is an excellent technique not only to help your pronunciation but also to imprint the vocabulary and expressions firmly in your mind. Whether you are studying alone or with someone else, try reading the different paragraphs or roles within the lesson, and especially the instant conversations, aloud, with expression and even gestures, and with increasing speed. By accustoming yourself to speaking normally and easily you will attain a natural flow and rhythm which is the essence of speaking Spanish as if it were your native language.

SPANISH

STEP BY STEP

INSTANT CONVERSATION: IN A CAFÉ

The following short conversation of a typical scene in a café could be used in any Spanish speaking country. The dashes in front of some of the sentences is a Spanish way of showing the changes in the identity of the speakers, rather than quotation marks.

— Buenos días, señor.
BWAY-nohs DEE-yahs, sen-YOR.
Good morning, sir.

The Important Second Line
The second line, which gives the Spanish pronunciation, is meant to be read as if you were reading English syllables, and the result will come out as understandable Spanish. For complete value of each Spanish letter see Preface.

— Buenos días.
BWAY-nohs DEE-yahs.
Good morning.

— ¿Está libre esta mesa?
¿Ess-TA LEE-bray ESS-ta MAY-sa?
Is this table free?

"Está" — for location
Está means *"is"* in the sense of where something is, and is used to indicate position or temporary condition. The word *esta* means "this" and is pronounced with a different emphasis because it does not have a written accent over the *a*.

The literal translation of *¿Está libre esta mesa?* is "Is free this table?" However, in the translations, we give the closest English approximation rather than a word-for-word translation.

— Sí, señor. Siéntese, por favor.
See, sen-YOR. S'YEN-tay-say, por fa-VOR.
Yes, sir. Sit down, please.

— Con su permiso.
Kohn soo pair-MEE-so.
With your permission.

— Oh, perdone, señora.
Oh, pair-DOH-nay, sen-YO-ra.
Oh, pardon me, madam.

— No es nada, señor.
No ess NA-da, sen-YOR.
It is nothing, sir.

"Es" for description
In the expression *No es nada* the lady is literally saying "It isn't nothing," which although a double negative is correct Spanish usage, "It isn't nothing" is equivalent to "Don't mention it" or "It's quite all right."

Es is another word for "is," used for describing or naming things. It means "he is," "she is," "it is" or "you are."

— Camarero, un café negro, por favor.
Ka-ma-RAY-ro, oon ka-FAY NAY-gro, por fa-VOR.
Waiter, one black coffee, please.

— Sí, señor, en seguida.
See, sen-YOR, en say-GHEE-da.
Yes, sir, right away.

— Ah, Ramón. ¿Cómo está usted?
Ah, Ra-MOHN. ¿KO-mo ess-TA oo-STED?
Ah, Raymond. How are you?

¿Cómo está usted?
Usted ("you") is generally shortened to the abbreviation *Ud.* when written. *Está* means "is" in the temporary sense, or for location.

4

— Muy bien, gracias, ¿y Ud.?
Mwee b'yen, GRA-s'yahs, ¿ee oo-STED?
Very well, thank you, and you?

— Así, así. Siéntese un momento, por favor.
Ah-SEE, ah-SEE. S'YEN-tay-say oon mo-MEN-toh, por fa-VOR.
So-so. Sit down a moment, please.

— Con mucho gusto.
Kohn MOO-cho GOOS-toh.
With much pleasure.

— Camarero, por favor, otro café.
Ka-ma-RAY-ro, por fa-VOR, OH-tro ka-FAY.
Waiter, please, another coffee.

— Muchas gracias.
MOO-chahs GRA-s'yahs.
Thank you very much.

— Este café está bueno, ¿no?
ESS-tay ka-FAY ess-TA BWAY-no, ¿no?
This coffee is good, isn't it?

¿No?
¿No? can be used as a question at the end of a statement, to ask agreement or assent to what one has said.

Reversed question marks appear at the beginning as well as at the end of a question, so that you can see, when reading, that a question is coming. This also applies to exclamation marks, as you will see later.

— Sí, no está malo.
See, no ess-TA MA-lo.
Yes, it's not bad.

— Camarero, la cuenta, por favor.
Ka-ma-RAY-ro, la KWEN-ta, por fa-VOR.
Waiter, the bill, please.

— Aquí está, señor.
Ah-KEE ess-TA, sen-YOR.
Here it is, sir.

All objects are masculine or feminine
In Spanish not only people and animals, but all things, animate or inanimate, are masculine or feminine. It is important to know whether a noun is masculine or feminine, because the word for "the," "a," and adjectives have masculine and feminine forms which must conform with the noun they refer to.

Among the nouns you see here, *café, momento* and *camarero* are masculine, while *mesa* and *cuenta* are feminine.

The masculine forms of "a," "the" and "this" are *un, el* and *este* and the feminine forms are *una, la* and *esta.*

> a moment — *un momento*
> the moment — *el momento*
> this moment — *este momento*
> a table — *una mesa*
> the table — *la mesa*
> this table — *esta mesa*

— Gracias por el café.
GRA-s'yahs por el ka-FAY.
Thank you for the coffee.

— De nada. Adiós.
Deh NA-da. Ah-D'YOHS.
You're welcome. Good-bye.

— ¡Adiós y hasta la vista!
¡Ah-D'YOHS ee AHS-ta la VEES-ta!
Good-bye and see you soon!

So long!
Hasta la vista literally means "until the sight" and is equivalent to "until soon" or "so long."

TEST YOUR SPANISH

Match up these phrases. Score 10 points for each correct answer. See answers below.

1. Good morning.   ____ Con su permiso.

2. Sit down, please.   ____ Perdone, señora.

3. With your permission.   ____ Buenos días.

4. Pardon me, madam.   ____ ¡Adiós, y hasta la vista!

5. It is nothing, sir.   ____ Siéntese, por favor.

6. Waiter, one black coffee, please.   ____ ¿Cómo está Ud?

7. Yes, sir, right away.   ____ Muy bien, gracias — ¿y Ud?

8. How are you?   ____ Camarero, un café negro, por favor.

9. Very well, thank you — and you?   ____ Sí, señor, en seguida.

10. Good-bye, and see you soon!   ____ No es nada, señor.

Answers: 3 4 1 10 2 8 9 6 7 5

SCORE ____%

Un hotel, un restaurante,
Oon oh-TELL, oon rest-ow-RAHN-tay,
A hotel, a restaurant,

un teatro, un banco.
oon tay-AH-tro, oon BAHN-ko.
a theater, a bank.

¿Es un restaurante?
¿Ess oon rest-ow-RAHN-tay?
Is it a restaurant?

Sí. Es un restaurante.
See. Ess oon rest-ow-RAHN-tay.
Yes. It's a restaurant.

¿Es un hotel?
¿Ess oon oh-TELL?
Is it a hotel?

No, señor. No es un hotel.
No, sen-YOR. No ess oon oh-TELL.
No, Sir. It is not a hotel.

> **"No" = "not"**
> The word for "not" — no comes before the
> verb. "It is not." — No es.

¿Qué es?
¿Kay ess?
What is it?

Es un teatro.
Ess oon tay-AH-tro.
It is a theatre.

Un taxi, un autobús.
Oon TAHK-see, oon ow-toh-BOOS.
A taxi, a bus.

¿Es un taxi o un autobús?
¿Ess oon TAHK-see oh oon ow-toh-BOOS?
Is it a taxi or a bus?

Es un taxi.
Ess oon TAHK-see.
It is a taxi.

Un cine, una tienda, un museo.
Oon SEE-nay, OO-na T'YEN-da, oon moo-SAY-oh.
A movie theater, a store, a museum.

¿Es una tienda? Sí, es una tienda.
¿Ess OO-na T'YEN-da? See, ess OO-na T'YEN-da.
Is it a store? Yes, it is a store.

¿Es un museo? No, no es un museo.
¿Ess oon moo-SAY-oh? No, no ess oon moo-SAY-oh.
Is it a museum? No, it is not a museum.

Es un cine.
Ess oon SEE-nay.
It is a movie theater.

Una calle, una plaza, una estatua.
OO-na KAHL-yay, OO-na PLA-sa, OO-na ess-TA-too-ah.
A street, a square, a statue.

¿Qué calle es ésta?
¿Kay KAHL-yeh ess ESS-ta?
What street is this?

"This" and "that"
The adjectives "this" and "that" are *este* and *ese* when referring to a masculine word, and *esta* and *esa* for a feminine word.

this taxi — *este taxi*   this shop — *esta tienda*
that taxi — *ese taxi*   that shop — *esa tienda*

9

When they are used as pronouns they bear a written accent.

this taxi — *este taxi*   this shop — *esta tienda*
this *one* — *éste*   this one — *ésta*
that street — *esa calle*
that one — *ésa*
What street is this?
¿Qué calle es ésta?

Es la calle Cervantes.
Ess la KAHL-yay Sehr-VAHN-tays.
It is Cervantes Street.

¿Qué plaza es ésta?
¿Kay PLA-sa ess ESS-ta?
What square is this?

Es la Plaza Bolívar.
Ess la PLA-sa Bo-LEE-var.
It is Bolivar Square.

¿Qué estatua es ésta?
¿Kay ess-TA-twa ess ESS-ta?
What statue is this?

Es la estatua de San Martín.
Ess la ess-TA-twa day Sahn Mar-TEEN.
It is the statue of San Martin.

¿Es éste el autobús para el aeropuerto?
¿Ess ESS-tay el ow-toh-BOOS PA-ra el ah-air-oh-PWAIR-toh?
Is this the bus for the airport?

INSTANT CONVERSATION: A RIDE IN A TAXI

— Taxi, ¿está libre?
TAHK-see, ¿ess-TA LEE-bray?
Taxi, are you free?

— Sí, señor. ¿Adónde va Ud.?
See, sen-YOR. ¿Ah-DOHN-day va oo-STED?
Yes, sir. Where are you going?

— Al Hotel Ávila. ¿Está lejos?
Ahl Oh-TELL AH-vee-la. ¿Ess-TA LAY-hohs?
To the Hotel Avila. Is it far?

> **A + el = al**
> A ("to") and *el* ("the," masculine) when used together form the contraction *al*. A and *la* ("the," feminine) do not contract. In like manner *de* ("of") combines with *el* to form *del* while *de* and *la* do not contract.

— No, señor. No está lejos. Está cerca.
No, sen-YOR. No ess-TA LAY-hohs. Ess-TA SAIR-ka.
No, sir. It is not far. It's near.

— Perdón. ¿Dónde está el Hotel Plaza?
Pair-DOHN. ¿DOHN-day ess-TA el Oh-TEL PLA-sa?
Pardon me. Where is the Plaza Hotel?

> **¿Dónde?**
> Note the difference: *¿Dónde?* — Where? *¿Adónde?* — Where to? *¿De dónde?* — From where?

11

— Allí, a la izquierda.
Ahl-YEE, ah la ees-K'YAIR-da.
Over there, on the left.

— ¿Es un hotel bueno?
¿Ess oon oh-TEL BWAY-no?
Is it a good hotel?

— Sí, señor, muy bueno . . . y muy caro.
See, sen-YOR, mwee BWAY-no . . . ee mwee KA-ro.
Yes, sir, very good . . . and very expensive.

— ¿Dónde está el museo nacional?
¿DOHN-day ess-TA el moo-SAY-oh na-s'yo-NAHL?
Where is the National Museum?

— Al final de esta calle, a la derecha.
Ahl fee-NAHL day ESS-ta KAHL-yay, ah la day-RAY-cha.
At the end of this street, on the right.

Ese edificio grande — allí.
EH-say ay-dee-FEE-s'yo GRAHN-day — ahl-YEE.
That big building — over there.

> **The adjective follows the noun**
> Spanish adjectives usually come after the noun
> they describe. *Edificio* ("building") is followed
> by *grande* ("big"), which describes it.

Éste es el Hotel Colón.
ESS-tay ess el oh-TEL Ko-LOHN.
This is the Hotel Colón (Columbus).

— Muy bien. Gracias. ¿Cuánto es?
Mwee b'yen. GRA-s'yahs. ¿KWAN-toh ess?
Very good. Thank you. How much is it?

— Cuatro pesos.
KWA-tro PAY-sohs.
Four pesos.

— Vamos a ver — uno, dos, tres, cuatro . . . y cinco.
VA-mohs ah vair — OO-no, dohs, trayss, KWA-tro . . . ee SEEN-ko.
Let's see — one, two, three, four . . . and five.

— Muchas gracias, caballero.
MOO-chahs GRA-s'yahs, ka-bahl-YAIR-ro.
Thank you very much, sir.

Caballero
Caballero, literally "man on horseback", was
originally used when speaking to a knight or a
noble, but is now a polite way of saying "sir."
In general, Spanish uses words like *señor, señora and señorita,* even without the person's
name following, more frequently than in English.

— De nada.
Day NA-da.
You're welcome.

It's nothing
De nada literally means "of nothing" and is
equivalent to "You are welcome."

When to use the written accent (´)
The written accent is used principally to show
that the normal rules of stress have been
changed. The normal rules are that if a word
ends in a vowel or *n* or *s* it is stressed on the
syllable before the last. If it ends with any other
letter it is stressed on the last syllable.

Camarero is stressed on the next to last syllable
and needs no accent, but *café* is written with an
accent because it breaks the normal rules.
Thus, *México* and *América* need accents but
Estados Unidos and *Portugal* don't.

Another reason for accents is to differentiate
between words which are spelled the same but
have different meanings:

> *el* — the; *él* — he
> *este* — this; *éste* — this one

In addition, accents are used over interrogative
pronouns and prepositions.

> *quien* — who; *¿quién?* — who?
> *donde* — where; *¿dónde?* — where?
> *¿adónde?* — where to?

13

TEST YOUR SPANISH

"Is" can be translated as *es* or *está*, *es* expressing a constant or permanent state of a person or object, and *está* denotes location or temporary condition. Fill in either es or *está* in the following sentences. Score 10 points for each correct answer. Answers below.

1. ¿Cómo _____ Ud.?

2. ¿Dónde _____ el teatro?

3. ¿Cuánto _____?

4. ¿Dónde _____ el Hotel Plaza?

5. ¿_____ un taxi o un autobús?

6. El Museo Nacional _____ a la derecha.

7. El restaurante _____ muy bueno y muy caro.

8. ¿_____ bueno el Hotel Bolívar?

9. ¿Dónde _____ el autobús?

10. ¿Cómo _____ Ramón?

SCORE _____%

14

THE PRESENT TENSE OF VERBS

Unos ejemplos del verbo *ser:*
OO-nohs ay-HEM-plohs del VAIR-bo *sair:*
Some examples of the verb *to be:*

¿Cuál es su nacionalidad?
¿Kwahl ess soo na-s'yohn-ah-lee-DAHD?
What is your nationality?

Yo soy español y mi esposa es española también.
Yo soy ess-pahn-YOHL ee mee ess-PO-sa ess ess-pahn-YO-la
                                          tahm-B'YEN.
I'm Spanish and my wife is Spanish also.

Adjectives change for gender and number
Spanish adjectives agree in gender and numbers with the nouns they describe. As *esposa* is feminine the adjective *español* must end in -a. Note also *un ejemplo* — "an example": *unos ejemplos* — "some examples."

Él es mexicano.
El ess may-hee-KA-no.
He is Mexican.

¿Quién es ella?
¿K'yen ess EL-ya?
Who is she?

Ella es su esposa: es inglesa.
EL-ya ess soo ess-PO-sa: ess een-GLAY-sa.
She is his wife: she is English.

Possessive pronouns
The possessive pronouns are:

15

mi — my
su — your, his, her, its, their
nuestro — our

Nuestro is the only one that changes for masculine or feminine. All three add an *s* when the object possessed is plural.

Eso es interesante.
Es-so ess een-tay-ray-SAHN-tay.
That's interesting.

A neuter form for "that"
Eso is a neuter form of "that" used to cover a fact or situation where the gender is not evident as being masculine or feminine.

Nosotros somos norteamericanos.
No-SO-trohs SO-mohs nor-tay-ah-may-ree-KA-nohs.
We are North American.

Nouns in the plural
The plural of nouns and adjectives is formed by adding an *s*, or sometimes — *es*. Adjectives agree in number with the nouns or pronouns they refer to. Incidentally, although *americano* means "American" it is more polite in the Spanish-speaking world to specify *norteamericano* — "North American," as inhabitants of Latin American countries are geographically Americans too.

¿Quiénes son ellos?
¿K'YAY-nays sohn EL-yohs?
Who are they?

Ellos son amigos de Carlos.
EL-yohs sohn ah-MEE-gohs day KAR-lohs.
They are friends of Charles

"De" as a possessive
The genitive or possessive is formed by the use of *de* — "of." Both "Julio's friends" and "the friends of Julio" are translated by *los amigos de Julio.*

El verbo *estar:*
El VAIR-bo *ess-TAR:*
The verb "to be":

Estoy aquí de visita.
Ess-TOY ah-KEE day vee-SEE-ta.
I'm here on a visit.

¿Dónde está el teléfono?
¿DOHN-day ess-TA el tay-LAY-fo-no?
Where is the telephone?

El Sr. Blanco no está en su oficina.
El sen-YOR BLAHN-ko no ess-TA en soo oh-fee-SEE-na.
Mr. Blanco is not in his office.

Está enfermo.
Ess-TA en-FAIR-mo.
He's ill.

A temporary state
Está is used to indicate that Mr. Blanco is ill because it is a temporary, not permanent, condition.

Está en casa.
Ess-TA en KA-sa.
He's at home.

Estamos aquí por una semana.
Ess-TA-mohs ah-KEE por OO-na say-MA-na.
We are here for a week.

¿Dónde están mis maletas?
¿DOHN-day ess-TAHN mees ma-LAY-tahs?
Where are my bags?

"Ser" and "estar"
Here is a comparative table of the two verbs for "to be" — *ser* and *estar*. *Ser* and *estar* are the infinitives which you have already encountered forms of each on pp. 11 and 12, *ser* being the form of "to be" used for the constant or permanent state of a person or object while *estar*, a

17

completely different verb, is used for forms of "to be" for expressing a temporary condition or location.

When you look up a verb in the dictionary you will find it is given in its infinitive form.

	ser	*estar*
yo	*soy*	*estoy*
Ud., él, ella	*es*	*está*
nosotros, nosotras	*somos*	*estamos*
Uds., ellos, ellas	*son*	*están*

And remember that the verb can be used without the pronoun, as the form of the verb indicates the subject.

The three pronouns that can be used with the form *es* or *está* correspond to "you (singular) are," "he (or) she is," and also "it is." *Nosotros* is "we" when it refers to men and *nosotras* is "we" when it refers to women only. When it refers to men and women together the masculine form is used.

Uds. is "you" when it refers to several people. *Ellos and ellas* are the masculine and feminine forms for "they"; and, as in the case of *nosotros* you use the masculine form when it refers to men and women, even if the group consists of only one man and many women.

El verbo *hablar:*
El VAIR-bo *ah-BLAR:*
The verb "to speak":

Yo hablo español.
Yo AH-blo ess-pahn-YOHL.
I speak Spanish.

¿Habla Ud. inglés?
¿AH-bla oo-STED een-GLAYS?
Do you speak English?

Mi esposa no habla bien el español.
Mee ess-PO-sa no AH-bla b'yen el ess-pahn-YOHL.
My wife doesn't speak Spanish well.

No equivalent word for "do"
The auxiliary "do" or "does" for asking questions or "do not" or "does not" for making negative statements has no counterpart in Spanish.

To ask a question with "do" or "does" just reverse the position of the verb.

> *Ud. habla* — you speak
> *¿Habla Ud.?* — Do you speak?

To make a negative with "do not" or "does not" use *no:*

> *él habla* — he speaks
> *él no habla* — he does not speak

Hablamos español con nuestros amigos suramericanos.
Ah-BLA-mohs ess-pahn-YOHL kohn NWES-trohs ah-MEE-gohs
                                    soor-ah-may-ree-KA-nohs.
We speak Spanish with our South American friends.

Ellos no hablan inglés.
El-yohs no AH-blahn een-GLAYS.
They do not speak English.

Hablar = to speak
"To speak" is *hablar.* Here is how it is conjugated in the present tense:

> *yo hablo* — I speak
> *Ud., él, ella habla* — you speak, he, she speaks
> *nosotros, nosotras hablamos* — we speak (masculine and feminine)
> *Uds. ellos, ellas hablan* — you (plural) speak, they speak (masculine and feminine)

Remember that the pronouns are frequently dropped, as the form of the verb indicates who is doing the action.

Una presentación:
OO-na pray-sen-ta-S'YOHN:
An introduction:

— Señora Fuentes . . . mi amigo, Ramón López.
Sen-YO-ra FWEN-tays . . . mee ah-MEE-go, Ra-MOHN LO-pays.
Mrs. Fuentes . . . my friend, Raymond Lopez.

— Encantada, señor.
En-kahn-TA-da, sen-YOR.
Delighted (fem.), sir.

— Encantado, señora.
En-kahn-TA-doh, sen-YO-ra.
Delighted (masc.), madam.

On being introduced
Encantado, a polite way of acknowledging an
introduction, literally means "enchanted." If you
are a man you say *encantado* and if you are a
woman you say *encantada.* In case you forget
which form to use you can always say *mucho
gusto* — "much pleasure" — which is the
same for both masculine or feminine.

— Su nombre es español
Soo NOHM-bray ess ess-pahn-YOHL
Your name is Spanish

pero Ud. es americano, ¿verdad?
PAIR-ro oo-STED ess ah-may-ree-KA-no, ¿vair-DAHD?
but you are American, aren't you?

¿No es verdad?
Words asking agreement such as: "aren't you";
"don't you think so"; "isn't it true", etc., can
be expressed by *¿no es verdad?, ¿verdad?* or
simply *¿no? Verdad* means "truth."

— Sí, mis padres son de España.
See, mees PA-drays sohn day Ess-PAHN-ya.
Yes, my parents are from Spain.

Parents
"My parents" — *mis padres. Padre* when singular means "father," but in the plural it means "parents" or "fathers." The word for mother is *madre.* The Spanish word that resembles the English word "parents" is *parientes,* which means "relatives."

— ¡Qué interesante!
¡Kay een-tay-ray-SAHN-tay!
How interesting!

¿De qué parte son?
¿Day kay PAR-tay sohn?
What part are they from?

— Mi padre es de Barcelona.
Mee PA-dray ess day Bar-say-LO-na.
My father is from Barcelona.

Mi madre es de Sevilla.
Mee MA-dray ess day Say-VEEL-ya.
My mother is from Seville.

Yo soy de Nueva York,
Yo soy day NWAY-va York,
I'm from New York,

pero allí se habla mucho el español también
PAIR-ro ahl-YEE say AH-bla MOO-cho el ess-pahn-YOHL tahm-B'YEN.
but Spanish is spoken a lot there too.

One speaks Spanish
When *se* is used with the form of the verb which goes with *él* or *ella* it means "one." Here is a sign one sees with increasing frequency in many American cities:

Aquí se habla español. — Here one speaks Spanish. (or) Spanish is spoken here.

— Eso es verdad.
ES-so ess vair-DAHD.
That is true.

—Y ¿habla Ud. inglés, señora?
Ee ¿AH-bla oo-STED een-GLAYS, sen-YO-ra?
And do you speak English, madam?

—Un poco solamente.
Oon PO-ko so-la-MEN-tay.
Only a little.

El inglés es muy difícil.
El een-GLAYS ess mwee dee-FEE-seel.
English is very difficult.

Pero con Ud., señor, no es necesario
PAIR-ro kohn oo-STED, sen-YOR, no ess nay-say-SA-r'yo
But with you, sir, it is not necessary

hablar inglés.
ah-BLAR een-GLAYS.
to speak English.

Habla muy bien el español.
AH-bla mwee b'yen el ess-pahn-YOHL.
You speak Spanish very well.

> **¿Habla Ud. español?**
> The definite article is more frequently used in
> Spanish than in English. While it is correct to
> say *¿Habla Ud español?* "Do you speak Span-
> ish?," when the language is more specifically
> assessed the article is customary; *Él habla muy
> mal el inglés.* "He speaks English very badly."

Y con un acento muy bueno.
Ee kohn oon ah-SEN-toh mwee BWAY-no.
And with a very good accent.

—Muchas gracias, señora.
MOO-chahs GRA-s'yahs, sen-YO-ra.
Thank you very much, madam.

Ud. es muy amable.
Oo-STED ess mwee ah-MA-blay.
You are very kind.

INSTANT CONVERSATION: IN AN OFFICE

El Sr. Martín es de Nueva York.
El sen-YOR Mar-TEEN es day NWAY-va York.
Mr. Martin is from New York.

Es norteamericano, pero habla español.
Ess nor-tay-ah-may-ree-KA-no, PAIR-ro AH-bla ess-pahn-YOHL.
He is North American, but he speaks Spanish.

Está en la oficina del Sr. Gómez.
Ess-TA en la oh-fee-SEE-na del sen-YOR GO-mayss.
He is in Mr. Gomez' office.

El Sr. Martín habla
El sen-YOR Mar-TEEN AH-bla
Mr. Martin speaks

con la secretaria del Sr. Gómez.
kohn la say-kray-TA-r'ya del sen-YOR GO-mayss.
with Mr. Gomez' secretary.

> **De + el = del**
> The possessive case is expressed by *de* ("of")
> and when this is followed by *el* ("the"), *de* and
> *el* contract to *del*. *De* does not contract when
> used with the feminine *la* ("the") or when used
> with the plural *los* or *las*.

SR. MARTÍN:
Buenos días, señorita.
BWAY-nohs DEE-yahs, sen-yo-REE-ta.
Good morning, Miss.

¿Es ésta la oficina del Sr. Gómez?
¿Ess ESS-ta la oh-fee-SEE-na del sen-YOR GO-mayss?
Is this Mr. Gomez' office?

23

LA SECRETARIA:
Sí, señor. Yo soy su secretaria.
See, sen-YOR. Yo soy soo say-kray-TA-r'ya.
Yes, Sir. I am his secretary.

SR. MARTÍN:
Soy un amigo del Sr. Gómez.
Soy oon ah-MEE-go del Sen-YOR GO-mayss.
I am a friend of Mr. Gomez.

Ésta es mi tarjeta.
ESS-ta ess mee tar-HAY-ta.
This is my card.

Soy de Nueva York
Soy day NWAY-va York
I am from New York

y estoy aquí de visita.
ee ess-TOY ah-KEE day vee-SEE-ta.
and I am here on a visit.

¿Está él muy ocupado ahora?
¿Ess-TA el mwee oh-koo-PA-doh ah-OH-ra?
Is he very busy now?

LA SECRETARIA:
Un momento, por favor, señor.
Oon mo-MEN-toh, por fa-VOR, sen-YOR.
One moment, please sir.

(Ella habla por teléfono.)
(EL-ya AH-bla por tay-LAY-fo-no.)
(She speaks on the telephone.)

Hola, señor Gómez.
OH-la, sen-YOR GO-mayss.
Hello, Mr. Gomez.

¿Está Ud. muy ocupado ahora?
¿Ess-TA oo-STED mwee oh-koo-PA-doh ah-OH-ra?
Are you very busy now?

Está aquí un Sr. José Martín
Ess-TA ah-KEE oon sen-YOR Ho-SAY Mar-TEEN
There is a Mr. Joseph Martin here

Muy bien, señor Gómez.
Mwee b'yen, sen-YOR GO-mayss.
Very well, Mr. Gomez.

Inmediatamente.
Een-may-d'ya-ta-MEN-tay.
Immediately.

A vocabulary dividend
The ending -*mente* corresponds to the English
adverbial ending -"ly." Many Spanish adverbs
are easily recognizable if you remember this
point.

rápidamente — rapidly
generalmente — generally
usualmente — usually
posiblemente — possibly
frecuentemente — frequently
naturalmente — naturally
directamente — directly

Está bien, Sr. Martín.
Ess-TA b'yen, sen-YOR Mar-TEEN.
It's all right, Mr. Martin.

El señor Gómez está en su oficina.
El sen-YOR GO-mayss ess-TA en soo oh-fee-SEE-na.
Mr. Gomez is in his office.

Por aquí, por favor.
Por ah-KEE, por fa-VOR.
This way, please.

SR. MARTÍN:
Gracias, señorita.
GRA-s'yahs, sen-yo-REE-ta.
Thank you, Miss.

25

Ud. es muy amable.
Oo-STED ess mwee ah-MA-blay.
You are very kind.

LA SECRETARIA:

A sus órdenes, señor.
Ah soos OR-day-nays, sen-YOR.
At your orders, sir.

Spanish courtesy

A sus órdenes — "at your orders" is a very polite way of acknowledging thanks. It is often used by men when introduced, in place of the more usual *mucho gusto.* You will find, in general, that Spanish tends to emphasize courtesy and politeness.

Even the pronoun *yo* ("I") is written with a small *y* while *Ud.* ("you") is written with a capital *U.*

TEST YOUR SPANISH

Match up these phrases. Score 10 for each correct answer. See answers below.

1. Where are you from? _____ ¿Habla Ud. inglés?

2. We are North Americans. _____ Estamos aquí por una semana.

3. That's interesting. _____ Eso es verdad.

4. I am here on a visit. _____ Ud. es muy amable.

5. We are here for a week. _____ Nosotros somos norteamericanos.

6. Do you speak English? _____ Habla muy bien el español.

7. I speak only a little. _____ Estoy aquí de visita.

8. That is true. _____ Eso es interesante.

9. You speak Spanish very well. _____ Hablo un poco solamente.

10. You are very kind. _____ ¿De dónde es Ud?

Answers: 6 5 8 10 2 9 4 3 7 1

SCORE _____%

step 3　NUMBERS AND HOW TO USE THEM

Los números:
Lohs NOO-may-rohs:
The numbers:

1	2	3	
uno	dos	tres	
OO-no	**dohs**	**trayss**	

4	5	6	
cuatro	cinco	seis	
KWA-tro	**SEEN-ko**	**sayss**	

7	8	9	10
siete	ocho	nueve	diez
s'YAY-tay	**OH-cho**	**N'WAY-vay**	**d'yess**

De diez a quince:
Day d'yess ah KEEN-say:
From 10 to 15:

11	12	13	14
once	doce	trece	catorce
OHN-say	**DOH-say**	**TRAY-say**	**ka-TOR-say**

15
quince
KEEN-say

y, entonces:
ee, en-TOHN-says:
and then:

16	17	18
diez y seis	diez y siete	diez y ocho
d'yess ee sayss	**d'yess ee S'YAY-tay**	**d'yess ee OH-cho**

28

19
diez y nueve
d'yess ee N'Way-vay

20
veinte
VAIN-tay

Después de veinte:
Des-PWESS day VAIN-tay:
After 20 —:

21
veintiuno
vain-tee-OO-no

22
veintidós
vain-tee-DOHS

23
veintitrés
vain-tee-TRAYSS

21
Veintiuno - "twenty-one" is really *veinte y uno*
written as one word.

24
veinticuatro
vain-tee-KWA-tro

25
veinticinco
vain-tee-SEEN-ko

etcétera, hasta
et-SAY-teh-ra, AHS-ta
etc., until

30
treinta
TRAIN-ta

y, entonces:
ee, en-TOHN-sehs:
and then:

31
treinta y uno
TRAIN-ta ee OO-no

40
cuarenta
kwa-REN-ta

50
cincuenta
seen-KWEN-ta

60
sesenta
say-SEN-ta

70
setenta
say-TEN-ta

80
ochenta
oh-CHEN-ta

90
noventa
no-VEN-ta

100
cien
s'yen

De cien a mil:
day s'yen ah meel:
From 100 to 1000:

100
cien
s'yen

101
ciento uno
S'YEN-toh OO-no

200
doscientos
dohs-S'YEN-tohs

300	400	500
trescientos	cuatrocientos	quinientos
trayss-S'YEN-tohs	**kwa-tro-S'YEN-tohs**	**keen-YEN-tohs**

600	700	800
seiscientos	setecientos	ochocientos
sayss-S'YEN-tohs	**say-tay-S'YEN-tohs**	**oh-cho-S'YEN-tohs**

900	1000	100.000
novecientos	mil	cien mil
no-vay-S'YEN-tohs	**meel**	**s'yen meel**

1.000.000
un millón
oon meel-YOHN

Large numbers
Periods are used instead of commas for writing numbers. The comma is used as a decimal point.

Los números son importantes.
Lohs NOO-may-rohs sohn eem-por-TAHN-tays.
The numbers are important.

En las tiendas ...
En lahs T'YEN-dahs ...
In stores ...

> Un cliente: ¿Cuánto es?
> **Oon klee-EN-tay: ¿KWAN-toh ess?**
> A customer: How much is it?

> La vendedora: Seis pesos y medio, señor.
> **La ven-day-DOH-ra: Sayss PAY-sohs ee MAY-d'yo, sen-YOR.**
> The saleslady: Six and a half pesos, sir.

En el teléfono ...
En el tay-LAY-fo-no ...
On the telephone ...

> Una voz: Hola. ¿Quién habla?
> **OO-na vohs: OH-la. ¿K'yen AH-bla?**
> A voice: Hello. Who is speaking?

Segunda voz: ¿Es éste el 78-45-83?
**Say-GOON-da vohs: ¿Es ESS-tay el say-TEN-ta ee OH-cho, kwa-
REN-ta ee SEEN-ko, oh-CHEN-ta ee trayss?**
Second voice: Is this 78-45-83?

Primera voz: No señor. Éste es el 7,8,4,3,8,5.
**Pree-MAY-ra vohs: No sen-YOR. ESS-tay ess el S'YAY-tay, OH-cho,
KWA-tro, trayss, OH-cho, SEEN-ko.**
First voice: No sir. This is 7,8,4,3,8,5.

Telephone numbers
Spanish telephone numbers are generally given
in pairs, except for a case like "07," which
would be said: "zero seven" — *cero siete.*

Segunda voz: Oh. ¡Perdón!
Say-GOON-da vohs: Oh. ¡Pair-DOHN!
Second voice: Oh. Pardon!

Para las direcciones . . .
PA-ra lahs dee-rek-S'YO-nays . . .
For addresses . . .

Un caballero: ¿Cuál es su dirección, por favor?
Oon ka-bahl-YAY-ro: ¿Kwahl ess soo dee-rek-S'YOHN, por fa-VOR?
A gentleman: What is your address, please?

Una dama: Es el número 144
**OO-na DA-ma: Ess el NOO-may-ro S'YEN-toh kwa-REN-ta ee
KWA-tro**
A lady: It's number 144

de la Quinta Avenida,
day la KEEN-ta Ah-vay-NEE-da,
Fifth Avenue,

el segundo piso.
el say-GOON-doh PEE-so.
the second floor.

Primero, segundo, etc.

The ordinal numbers from 1 to 10 are:

first —	*primero*	sixth —	*sexto*
second —	*segundo*	seventh —	*séptimo*
third —	*tercero*	eighth —	*octavo*
fourth —	*cuarto*	ninth —	*noveno*
fifth —	*quinto*	tenth —	*décimo*

Para saber qué hora es . . .
PA-ra sa-BAIR kay OH-ra ess . . .
In order to know what time it is . . .

Infinitives

Saber is the infinitive of the verb "to know."
The infinitive is the basic verb form: The one you
will find in the dictionary, always ending in "r".

¿Qué hora es?
¿Kay OH-ra ess?
What time is it?

Son las siete.
Sohn lahs S'YAY-tay.
It's seven o'clock.

Telling Time

In telling time the feminine plural article *las* is
used with the number of the hour because *hora*,
the word for "hour" is feminine.

For "one o'clock," however, the singular is
used: "It's one o'clock," — *es la una*.

Son las siete y cinco . . . las siete y diez.
Sohn lahs S'YAY-tay ee SEEN-ko . . . lahs S'YAY-tay ee d'yess.
It's seven five . . . seven ten.

Son las siete y cuarto.
Sohn lahs S'YAY-tay ee KWAR-toh.
It's seven fifteen.

Son las siete y veinte . . . las siete y veinticinco.
**Sohn lahs S'YAY-tay ee VAIN-tay . . . lahs S'YAY-tay ee
vain-tee-SEEN-ko.**
it's seven twenty . . . seven twenty-five.

Son las siete y media.
Sohn lahs S'YAY-tay ee MAY-d'ya.
It's seven thirty.

Son las ocho menos veinticinco . . . las ocho menos veinte.
Sohn lahs OH-cho MAY-nohs vain-tee-SEEN-ko . . . lahs OH-cho
 MAY-nohs VAIN-tay.
It's twenty five to eight . . . twenty to eight.

> **After the half hour**
> For telling time after the half hour you will also
> hear para ("for") used as well as menos, such
> as:
>
> > twenty to eight — veinte para las ocho
> > ten to eight — diez para las ocho, etc.

Son las ocho menos cuarto.
Sohn lahs OH-cho MAY-nohs KWAR-toh.
It's a quarter to eight.

Son las ocho menos diez . . . las ocho menos cinco.
Sohn lahs OH-cho MAY-nohs d'yess . . . lahs OH-cho MAY-nohs
 SEEN-ko.
It's ten to eight . . . five to eight.

Son las ocho.
Sohn lahs OH-cho.
It's eight o'clock.

Las nueve en punto.
Lahs NWAY-vay en POON-toh.
Nine o'clock sharp.

Para hacer citas . . .
PA-ra ah-SAIR SEE-tahs . . .
To make appointments . . .

— ¿Está bien para mañana — a las seis?
¿Ess-TA b'yen PA-ra mahn-YA-na — ah lahs sayss?
Is it all right for tomorrow — at six?

Mañana
Mañana, the Spanish word that everyone knows, means "morning" as well as "tomorrow."

mañana — tomorrow
la mañana — the morning
mañana por la mañana — tomorrow morning

— ¿Cómo? ¿A qué hora?
¿KO-mo? ¿Ah kay OH-ra?
What? At what time?

— A las seis de la tarde.
Ah lahs sayss day la TAR-day.
At six in the afternoon.

— Sí, cómo no — pero ¿ dónde?
See, KO-mo no — PAIR-ro ¿ DOHN-day?
Yes, certainly — but where?

— En la Plaza de la Revolución —
En la PLA-sa day la Ray-vo-loo-S'YOHN —
In the Square of the Revolution —

Another vocabulary dividend
Many English words ending in -tion have exact counterparts in Spanish with the ending -*ción*, and are all feminine. You will have no trouble recognizing these:

nación	*admiración*
constitución	*selección*
administración	*construcción*
exploración	*revolución*
acción	*destrucción*

Directamente en frente del monumento.
Dee-rek-ta-MEN-tay en FREN-tay del mo-noo-MEN-toh.
Directly in front of the monument.

Muy bien. Pero si no estoy allí
Mwee b'yen. PAIR-ro see no ess-TOY ahl-YEE
Very well. But if I'm not there

a las seis en punto,
ah lahs sayss en POON-toh,
at exactly six,

sírvase esperar unos minutos, ¿no?
SEER-va-say ess-peh-RAR OO-nohs mee-NOO-tohs, ¿no?
please wait a few minutes, won't you?

Requests and Orders

An easy way to give a command is to use *sírvase* followed by the infinitive of the verb: "Please don't wait here" *Sírvase no esperar aquí*

INSTANT CONVERSATION: AT A UNIVERSITY

Un joven habla con una joven:
Oon HO-ven AH-bla kohn OO-na HO-ven:
A young man speaks to a young woman:

EL JOVEN:
Buenos días, señorita.
BWAY-nohs DEE-yahs, sen-yo-REE-ta.
Good morning, miss.

Ud. es una nueva estudiante aquí, ¿no es verdad?
Oo-STED ess OO-na NWAY-va ess-too-D'YAHN-tay ah-KEE, ¿no ess vair-DAHD?
You are a new student here, isn't that true?

LA JOVEN:
Sí, es mi primer año aquí.
See, ess mee pree-MAIR AHN-yo ah-KEE.
Yes, it's my first year here.

EL JOVEN:
Bueno. Yo soy el secretario
BWAY-no. Yo soy el say-kray-TA-r'yo
Good. I am the secretary

de la universidad.
day la oo-nee-vair-see-DAHD.
of the university.

Jaime Castillo Jiménez, a sus órdenes.
HI-may Kahs-TEEL-yo Hee-MAY-nays, ah soos OR-day-nays.
Jaime Castillo Jiménez, at your orders.

LA JOVEN:
Encantada, señor.
En-kahn-TA-da, sen-YOR.
Delighted, sir.

EL JOVEN:
El gusto es mío, señorita.
El GOOS-toh ess MEE-yo, sen-yo-REE-ta.
The pleasure is mine, miss.

> **Mi = my   mío = mine**
> *El gusto es mío* — "the pleasure is mine" — is
> another polite thing to say when acknowledging
> introductions. *Su* means "your" and *suyo*
> means "yours." Often when you admire some-
> thing a friend has, he will say *es suyo* —"it is
> yours" — but that does not necessarily mean
> that you should take it.

¿Cuál es su nombre y apellido?
¿Kwahl ess soo NOHM-bray ee ah-pel-YEE-doh?
What is your first and last name?

LA JOVEN:
María Gálvez Fuentes.
Ma-REE-ya GAHL-vays FWEN-tays.
María Gálvez Fuentes.

> **Family names**
> Spanish last names are usually double, the first
> part being the father's family name and the sec-
> ond part being the mother's maiden name. To il-
> lustrate: if your father's last name is
> Jiménez-López and your mother's maiden name
> is Fernádez-Toro, your last name would be Ji-
> ménez-Fernández. For most purposes the fa-
> ther's last name suffices, but for formal
> introductions and documents the double last
> name is used.

EL JOVEN:
Gracias. Y ¿cuál es su número de teléfono?
GRA-s'yahs. Ee ¿kwahl ess soo NOO-may-ro day tay-LAY-fo-no?
Thank you. And what is your telephone number?

LA JOVEN:
Mi teléfono es 31-94-69.
Mee teh-LAY-fo-no ess TRAIN-ta ee OO-no, no-VEN-ta ee KWA-tro, say-SEN-ta ee N'WAY-vay.
My telephone is 31-94-69.

EL JOVEN:
Muy bien. Y ¿su dirección?
Mwee b'yen. Ee ¿soo dee-rek-S'YOHN?
Very well. And your address?

LA JOVEN:
Mi dirección es Calle de la Independencia 73,
Mee dee-rek-S'YOHN ess KAHL-yay day la Een-day-pen-DEN-s'ya say-TEN-ta ee trayss,
My address is 73 Independence Street,

tercer piso.
tair-SAIR PEE-so.
third floor.

> **Adjectives before the noun**
> Some adjectives, like *primero, tercero, bueno*
> and *malo* drop their "o" when placed before a
> noun but not after it. "A good man" can be
> translated by *un buen hombre or un hombre*
> *bueno.*

EL JOVEN:
Excelente. Eso es todo.
Ek-say-LEN-tay. EH-so ess TOH-doh.
Excellent. That's all.

Gracias y ¡hasta pronto!
GRA-s'yahs ee ¡AHS-ta PROHN-toh!
Thanks and until soon!

UN AMIGO DE LA JOVEN: Y, ¿ese tipo?
Oon ah-MEE-go day la HO-ven: Ee, ¿ES-say TEE-po?
A FRIEND (MALE) OF THE YOUNG WOMAN: And that character?

LA JOVEN:
No es un tipo.
No ess oon TEE-po.
He isn't a character.

Él es el secretario
El ess el say-kray-TA-r'yo
He is the secretary

de la universidad.
day la oo-nee-vair-see-DAHD.
of the university.

EL AMIGO:
¡Qué broma!
¡Kay BRO-ma!
What a joke!

Eso no es verdad.
Es-so no ess vair-DAHD.
That's not true.

Él es un estudiante como nosotros.
El ess oon ess-too-D'YAHN-tay KO-mo no-SO-trohs.
He's a student like us.

Cuidado, ¿eh?
Kwee-DA-doh, ¿eh?
Careful, eh?

TEST YOUR SPANISH

Translate these sentences into English. Score 10 points for each correct translation. See answers below.

1. ¿Cuánto es? _____

2. Seis pesos y medio, señor. _____

3. ¿Quién habla? _____

4. ¿Cuál es su dirección? _____

5. ¿Qué hora es? _____

6. Son las ocho menos cuarto. _____

7. A las seis de la tarde. _____

8. ¿Cuál es su nombre y apellido? _____

9. ¿Cuál es su número de teléfono? _____

10. Eso no es verdad. _____

SCORE _____%

LOCATING THINGS AND PLACES

"Hay" es una palabra corta y muy útil.
"I" ess OO-na pa-LA-bra KOR-ta ee mwee OO-teel.
"There is" (there are) is a short and useful word.

Aquí hay unos ejemplos:
Ah-KEE I OO-nohs ay-HEM-plohs:
Here are some examples:

> **Hay**
> *Hay* is one of the most important words in
> Spanish and of great conversational frequency.
> Note that the pronunciation is simply that of the
> letter "I" or "eye" in English. *Hay* does not
> change for the singular or plural.

¿Hay alguien en esta oficina?
¿I AHL-gh'yen en ESS-ta oh-fee-SEE-na?
Is there anyone in this office?

Sí, hay alguien.
See, I AHL-gh'yen.
Yes, there is.

¿Cuántas personas hay?
¿KWAN-tahs pair-SO-nahs I?
How many people are there?

Hay tres personas.
I trayss pair-SO-nahs.
There are three people.

¿Cuántos escritorios hay en la pieza?
¿KWAN-tohs ess-kree-TOH-r'yohs I en la P'YAY-sa?
How many desks are there in the room?

Hay dos escritorios.
I dohs ess-kree-TOH-r'yohs.
There are two desks.

¿Cuántas sillas hay?
¿KWAN-tahs SEEL-yahs I?
How many chairs are there?

Hay tres sillas.
I trayss SEEL-yahs.
There are three chairs.

¿Qué hay en la pared?
¿Kay I en la pa-RED?
What is there on the wall?

En la pared hay cuadros y un reloj.
En la pa-RED I KWA-drohs ee oon ray-LO.
On the wall there are pictures and a clock.

Ahora son las cinco y media.
Ah-OH-ra sohn lahs SEEN-ko ee MAY-d'ya.
Now it's five thirty.

¿Hay alguien en la oficina?
¿I AHL-gh'yen en la of-fee-SEE-na?
Is there anyone in the office?

No, no hay nadie allí.
No, no I NA-d'hay ahl-YEE.
No, there is nobody there.

> **A choice for "here" and "there"**
> You will notice that there are several words for
> "here" and "there". *Aquí* and *acá* both mean
> "here"; *allí and allá* both mean "there"; *ahí*
> also means "there," but closer to the speaker.

¿Hay algo sobre la mesa grande?
¿I AHL-go SO-bray la MAY-sa GRAHN-day?
Is there anything on the large table?

Remember
In general, the modifying adjective follows the noun; with the gender and number of the noun it modifies:

> El gato negro — The black cat
> La casa blanca — The white house
> Los libros pequeños — The small books
> Las muchachas bonitas — The pretty girls

Sí, hay algo.
See, I AHL-go.
Yes, there is something.

¿Qué hay?
¿Kay I?
What is there?

Hay varias cosas —
I VA-r'yahs KO-sahs —
There are various things —

una lámpara, libros, flores y un cenicero.
OO-na LAHM-pa-ra, LEE-brohs, FLO-rays ee oon say-nee-SAY-ro.
a lamp, books, flowers and an ashtray.

¿Hay algo sobre la mesa pequeña?
¿I AHL-go SO-bray la MAY-sa peh-KEHN-ya?
Is there anything on the small table?

No, no hay nada.
No, no I NA-da.
No, there is nothing.

The double negative is correct
No hay nada — "There isn't anything" (literally "there isn't nothing") and No hay nadie — "there isn't anybody" (literally "there isn't nobody") are examples of the double negative, correct in Spanish, but not in English.

Hay es útil para hacer preguntas,
I ess OO-teel PA-ra ah-SAIR pray-GOON-tahs,
"There is (there are)" is useful for asking questions,

43

como, por ejemplo:
KO-mo, por ay-HEM-plo:
as, for example:

Dispense, señor. ¿Sabe Ud. . . .
Dees-PEN-say, sen-YOR. ¿SA-bay oo-STED. . .
Excuse me, sir. Do you know . . .

. . . dónde hay un buen restaurante?
. . . DOHN-day I oon bwen rest-ow-RAHN-tay?
. . . where there is a good restaurant?

. . . dónde hay un banco?
. . . DOHN-day I oon BAHN-ko?
. . . where there is a bank?

. . . dónde hay una farmacia?
. . . DOHN-day I OO-na far-MA-s'ya?
. . . where there is a drug store?

. . . dónde hay un teléfono público?
. . . DOHN-day I oon tay-LAY-fo-no POO-blee-ko?
. . . where there is a public telephone?

. . . dónde hay un buzón de correos?
. . . DOHN-day I oon boo-SOHN day ko-RRAY-ohs?
. . . where there is a mailbox?

Aquí hay otras expresiones útiles:
Ah-KEE I OH-trahs ess-pray-S'YO-nays OO-tee-lays:
Here are other useful expressions:

En la casa:
En la KA-sa:
In the house:

Niño: ¿Hay algo para comer?
NEEN-yo: ¿I AHL-go PA-ra ko-MAIR?
Boy: Is there anything to eat?

> **Para = in order to**
> *Para* means "for" in the sense of "for a purpose" or "in order to." *Comer* is "to eat"
> *para comer* means "to eat" in the sense of "in

order to eat''; ''for eating'' or ''for the purpose of eating.''

Madre: Sí, hay pan, mantequilla y jamón en la nevera.
MA-dray: See, I pahn, mahn-tay-KEEL-ya ee ha-MOHN en la nay-VAY-ra.
Mother: Yes, there's bread, butter and ham in the icebox.

En la oficina:
En la of-fee-SEE-na:
In the office:

El jefe: ¿Hay algo importante en el correo?
El HAY-fay: ¿I AHL-go eem-por-TAHN-tay en el ko-RRAY-oh?
The boss: Is there anything important in the mail?

La secretaria: No, no hay nada importante.
La seh-kray-TA-r'ya: No, no I NA-da eem-por-TAHN-tay.
The secretary: No, there is nothing important.

Entre amigos:
EN-tray ah-MEE-gohs:
Between friends:

Raúl: Hola, ¿qué hay de nuevo?
Ra-OOL: OH-la, ¿kay I day NWAY-vo?
Raúl: Hi, what's new?

Fidel: Nada de particular.
Fee-DEL: NA-da day par-tee-koo-LAR.
Fidel: Nothing in particular.

Una frase de cortesía:
OO-na FRA-say day kor-tay-SEE-ya:
A phrase of politeness:

Muchísimas gracias por el lindo regalo.
Moo-CHEE-see-mahs GRA-s'yahs por el LEEN-doh ray-GA-lo.
Very many thanks for the lovely present.

Importantísimo
The ending -ísimo (masculine) or -ísima (feminine) intensifies the adjective it is added to.

45

Una muchacha linda — a pretty girl.
Una muchacha lindísima — a very pretty girl.

Malo is "bad"; *malísimo* is "very bad."

No hay de qué.
No I day kay.
You're welcome.

You are welcome

No hay de qué means "You are welcome." It is a good example of how a language cannot be translated word for word, since its literal translation would be "there is not of what."

INSTANT CONVERSATION:
GETTING MAIL AND MESSAGES

UN HUÉSPED:
Oon WESS-ped:
A GUEST:

   Mi llave, por favor.
   Mee LYA-vay, por fa-VOR.
   My key, please.

   Perdone, tengo prisa.
   Pehr-DOH-nay, TEN-go PREE-sa.
   Pardon, I'm in a hurry.

   "To have" for "to be"
   Spanish frequently uses *tener* — "to have" for
   expressions where English uses "to be." *Tener*
   is an irregular verb of which we have just
   learned the form for "I have" — *tengo*, and the
   form for "you have" and "he" (or) "she has" is
   tiene. You should learn the following
   expressions:

   I'm in a hurry — *Tengo prisa.*
   I am hot. — *Tengo calor.*
   I am cold. — *Tengo frío.*
   I am hungry. — *Tengo hambre.*
   I am thirsty. — *Tengo sed.*
   Are you in a hurry? — *¿Tiene prisa?*
   Are you hot? — *¿Tiene calor?*
   Are you cold? — *¿Tiene frío?*
   Are you hungry? — *¿Tiene hambre?*
   Are you thirsty? — *¿Tiene sed?*

   ¿Hay cartas para mí?
   ¿I KAR-tahs PA-ra mee?
   Are there letters for me?

EL EMPLEADO:
El em-play-AH-doh:
THE EMPLOYEE:

Cómo no, señor. Hay dos cartas,
KO-mo no, sen-YOR. I dohs KAR-tahs,
Certainly, sir. There are two letters,

una tarjeta postal
OO-na tar-HAY-ta pos-TAHL
a postcard

y un paquete bastante grande.
ee oon pa-KAY-tay bahs-TAHN-tay GRAHN-day.
and a rather large package.

Una de las cartas es de Venezuela.
OO-na day lahs KAR-tahs ess day VAY-nay-SWAY-la.
One of the letters is from Venezuela.

Las estampillas son muy bonitas, ¿no?
Lahs ess-tahm-PEEL-yahs sohn mwee bo-NEE-tahs, ¿no?
The stamps are very pretty, aren't they?

EL HUÉSPED:
Bastante. ¿Eso es todo?
Bahs-TAHN-tay. ¿Es-so ess TOH-doh?
Rather. Is that all?

EL EMPLEADO:
No, señor. Hay más.
No, sen-YOR. I mahs.
No, sir. There's more.

Una carta certificada. Tenga.
OO-na KAR-ta sair-tee-fee-KA-da. TEN-ga.
A certified letter. Here.

Here it is
Tenga — literally "have (it)," in the sense of "here it is" is a form of *tener* in the imperative, and is a useful expression when handing something to someone.

EL HUÉSPED:
Gracias.
GRA-s'yahs.
Thank you.

EL EMPLEADO:
Hoy hay bastante correo para Ud.,
Oy I bahs-TAHN-tay ko-RRAY-oh PA-ra oo-STED,
There's a lot of mail for you today,

¿no es verdad?
¿no ess vair-DAHD?
isn't there?

EL HUÉSPED:
Es cierto.
Ess S'YAIR-toh.
That's certain.

EL EMPLEADO:
Oh, un momento.
Oh, oon mo-MEN-toh.
Oh, one moment.

Hay dos recados de teléfono.
I dohs ray-KA-dohs day teh-LAY-fo-no.
There are two telephone messages.

Todo está escrito en este papel.
TOH-doh ess-TA ess-KREE-toh en ESS-tay pa-PEL.
Everything is written on this paper.

EL HUÉSPED:
Gracias. ¿Hay algo más?
GRA-s'yahs. ¿I AHL-go mahs?
Thank you. Is there anything more?

EL EMPLEADO:
No, señor. No hay nada más.
No, sen-YOR. No I NA-da mahs.
No, sir. There's nothing more.

EL HUÉSPED:

Bueno. Y ahora, por favor,
BWAY-no. Ee ah-OH-ra, por fa-VOR,
Good. And now, please,

diez estampillas de cincuenta centavos cada una,
d'yess ess-tahm-PEEL-yahs day seen-KWEN-ta sen-TA-vohs KA-da OO-na,
ten stamps of fifty centavos each,

> **Cada uno = each one**
> *Cada* means "each" and is an adjective that does not change for masculine or feminine.
>
> > *cada hombre* — each man
> > *cada mujer* — each woman

y unos sobres para correo aéreo.
ee OO-nohs SO-brays PA-ra ko-RRAY-oh ah-AY-ray-oh.
and some air mail envelopes.

> **Before a noun, "uno" becomes "un"**
> *Uno* means "one" (masculine) and, when used before a noun, it is shortened to *un* meaning "a", "an" or "one". When used in the plural it means "some".
>
> > *unos amigos* — some friends (male)
> > *unas amigas* — some friends (female)
>
> and remember, if "some friends" include women, it is still *unos amigos*.

TEST YOUR SPANISH

Translate these sentences into English. Score 10 points for each correct translation. See answers below.

1. ¿Cuántas personas hay? _____

2. Hay tres personas. _____

3. ¿Dónde hay un buen restaurante? _____

4. ¿Dónde hay una farmacia? _____

5. Hola, ¿qué hay de nuevo? _____

6. Nada de particular. _____

7. ¿Hay cartas para mí? _____

8. Tengo prisa. _____

9. ¿Tiene Ud. frío? _____

10. No hay nada más. _____

Answers: 1. How many people are there? 2. There are three people. 3. Where is there a good restaurant? 4. Where is there a drug store? 5. Hi, what's new? 6. Nothing in particular. 7. Are there letters for me? 8. I'm in a hurry. 9. Are you cold? 10. There's nothing more.

SCORE _____%

step 5

HOW TO USE THE RIGHT VERB FORM

Hay tres grupos de verbos.
I trays GROO-pohs day VAIR-bohs.
There are three groups of verbs.

Verbos como *hablar, tomar,*
VAIR-bohs KO-mo *ah-BLAR, toh-MAR,*
Verbs like "to speak," "to take,"

estudiar, comenzar, terminar, durar
ess-too-D'YAR, ko-men-SAR, tair-mee-NAR, doo-RAR
"to study," "to begin," "to end," "to last"

son del primer grupo.
sohn del pree-MAIR GROO-po.
are of the first group.

Spanish through Spanish
You will notice that in the first part of each step we frequently use Spanish to explain verbs or other constructions. While this information is repeated more fully in the English notes, seeing it first in Spanish is a more natural and direct approach and,when you review the step without looking at the English, you will be learning Spanish through the use of Spanish.

Aquí hay unas frases útiles con *hablar:*
Ah-KEE I OO-nahs FRA-says OO-tee-lays kohn ah-BLAR:
Here are some useful phrases with *to speak:*

¿Con quién hablo?
¿Kohn k'yen AH-blo?
With whom am I speaking?

¿Habla Ud. inglés?
¿AH-bla oo-STED een-GLAYS?
Do you speak English?

¿Quién habla?
¿K'yen AH-bla?
Who is speaking?

> **¿Quién habla?**
> The above uses of *hablar* which you already met in Step 2 will serve as a review and also remind you that the present tense can also be translated by the progressive.
>
> *Hablo* means "I speak" or "I am speaking"
>
> The phrase *¿Quién habla?* — "Who is speaking?" is frequently used in answering the telephone.
>
> Another formula you will often hear is:
>
> > *¿De parte de quién?* — On whose behalf?
> > or: Who is speaking?

Habla el Sr. Serrano.
AH-bla el sen-YOR Seh-RRA-no.
Mr. Serrano is speaking.

¿De qué hablan?
¿Day kay AH-blahn?
What are they talking about?

Otros verbos del primer grupo:
OH-trohs VEHR-bohs del pree-MAIR GROO-po:
Other verbs of the first group:

— ¿Qué estudia Miguel?
¿Kay ess-TOO-d'ya Mee-GHELL?
What is Michael studying?

— Él estudia música.
El ess-TOO-d'ya MOO-see-ka.
He is studying music.

— Y Ud., ¿qué estudia?
Ee oo-STED, ¿kay ess-TOO-d'ya?
And you, what are you studying?

— Estudio arte.
Ess-TOO-d'yo AR-tay.
I am studying art.

Mi amiga Elena y yo
Mee ah-MEE-ga Ay-LAY-na ee yo
My friend Helen and I

tomamos una lección
toh-MA-mohs OO-na lek-S'YOHN
take a lesson

cada lunes.
KA-da LOO-nays.
each Monday.

La lección comienza a las nueve
La lek-S'YOHN ko-M'YEN-sa ah lahs N'WAY-vay
The lesson begins at nine

y termina a las doce.
ee tehr-MEE-na ah lahs DOH-say.
and ends at twelve.

The present tense: verb group I

As you have seen, the verbs ending in -ar, the 1st. group (or conjugation), all have exactly the same endings as hablar, as is the case with tomar — "to take," estudiar — "to study," terminar — "to end."

	tomar	estudiar	terminar
yo	tomo	estudio	termino
Ud., él, ella	-a	-a	-a
nosotros, -as	-amos	-amos	-amos
Uds., ellos, ellas	-an	-an	-an

A spelling change occurs in the middle of comenzar — "to begin" — in that the e changes to *ie* in three forms, but this does not affect the endings.

comienzo, comienza, comenzamos, comienzan

— Dura mucho tiempo, ¿no?
DOO-ra MOO-cho T'YEM-po, ¿no?
It lasts a long time, doesn't it?

Y María, ¿toma ella también
Ee Ma-REE-ya, ¿TOH-ma EL-ya tahm-B'YEN
And Mary, does she also take

lecciones de arte?
lek-S'YO-nays day AR-tay?
art lessons?

— No, ella y su hermana
No, EL-ya ee soo air-MA-na
No, she and her sister

toman clases de baile.
TOH-mahn KLA-says day BY-lay.
take dance lessons.

Possessive pronouns
Su is the possessive form for "his," "her," "your," "its," or "their." When the thing possessed is plural *su* becomes *sus.*

Mi — "my" becomes *mis* when the object possessed is plural.

Nuestro — "our" has a feminine form — *nuestra* and, in the plural, becomes *nuestros* and *nuestras.*

Mi casa — My house
Mis libros — My books
Su familia — Your (his, her, etc.) family
Sus ojos — Your eyes
Nuestro país — Our country
Nuestra ciudad — Our city
Nuestros hijos — Our sons
Nuestras hijas — Our daughters

— Y José, ¿qué curso toma?
Ee Ho-SAY, ¿kay KOOR-so TOH-ma?
And Joseph, what course does he take?

— No toma ningún curso.
No TOH-ma neen-GOON KOOR-so.
He isn't taking any course.

> **Ninguno**
> *ninguno* — (-a) means "no" or "not any". *Nin-*
> *guno is shortened to* ningún *before a masculine*
> *noun. Incidentally, the same meaning could be*
> *given by using* alguno *after* curso. *No toma*
> *curso alguno.*

Es un perezoso.
Ess oon pay-ray-SO-so.
He's a lazy one.

Verbos como *comprender,*
VAIR-bohs KO-mo *kohm-pren-DAIR,*
Verbs like "to understand,"

aprender y *leer*
ah-pren-DAIR ee *lay-AIR*
"to learn" and "to read"

son del segundo grupo.
sohn del say-GOON-doh GROO-po.
are of the second group.

Aquí hay unas frases útiles con *comprender:*
Ah-KEE I OO-nahs FRA-says OO-tee-lays kohn *kohm-pren-DAIR:*
Here are some useful phrases with "to understand:"

Yo no comprendo.
Yo no kohm-PREN-doh.
I don't understand.

¿Comprende Ud.?
¿Kohm-PREN-day oo-STED?
Do you understand?

Nosotros comprendemos español.
No-SO-trohs kohm-pren-DAY-mohs ess-pahn-YOHL.
We understand Spanish.

Ellos no comprenden mucho.
EL-yohs no kohm-PREN-den MOO-cho.
They do not understand very much.

Otros verbos del segundo grupo:
OH-trohs VAIR-bohs del say-GOON-doh GROO-po:
Other verbs of the second group:

— ¿Qué lee Ud.?
¿Kay lay oo-STED?
What are you reading?

— Leo un periódico en español.
LAY-oh oon pay-R'YO-dee-ko en ess-pahn-YOHL.
I'm reading a newspaper in Spanish.

— ¿Qué periódico lee?
¿Kay pay-R'YO-dee-ko lay?
What newspaper are you reading?

— Leo *El Mundo.*
LAY-oh *El MOON-doh.*
I'm reading The World.

Aprendo muchas palabras nuevas.
Ah-PREN-doh MOO-chahs pa-LA-brahs NWAY-vahs.
I am learning many new words.

— ¿Comprende todo?
¿Kohm-PREN-day TOH-doh?
Do you understand everything?

— No, no comprendo todo.
No, no kohm-PREN-doh TOH-doh.
No, I don't understand everything.

— ¿Y sus amigos, Raúl y Fidel?
¿Ee soos ah-MEE-gohs, Ra-OOL ee Fee-DELL?
And your friends, Raúl and Fidel?

¿Qué leen ellos en español?
¿KAY LAY-en EL-yohs en ess-pahn-YOHL?
What are they reading in Spanish?

— ¡Oh! Ellos están muy avanzados.
¡Oh! EL-yohs ess-TAHN mwee ah-vahn-SA-dohs.
Oh! They are very advanced.

Leen revistas y libros.
LAY-en ray-VEES-tahs ee LEE-brohs.
They read magazines and books.

Aprenden rápidamente
Ah-PREN-den RA-pee-da-MEN-tay
They learn quickly

y comprenden casi todo.
ee kohm-PREN-den KA-see TOH-doh.
and understand almost everything.

Present tense: verb group II
Verbs ending in *-er* such as the three we have given here and others you will find in later steps, are the 2nd. verb group and form their present tense for the four forms we are studying by taking off the *-er* ending of the infinitive and adding *-o, -e, -emos* or *-en*, according to the person:

	comprender	aprender	leer
yo	comprendo	aprendo	leo
Ud., él, ella	-e	-e	-e
nosotros, (-as)	-emos	-emos	-emos
Uds., ellos, ellas	-en	-en	-en

Verbos como *vivir, escribir,*
VAIR-bohs KO-mo *vee-VEER, ess-kree-BEER,*
Verbs like "to live," "to write,"

recibir y *partir*
ray-see-BEER ee par-TEER
"to receive" and "to leave"

son del tercer grupo.
sohn del tair-SAIR GROO-po.
are of the third group.

Unos ejemplos con *vivir:*
OO-nohs ay-HEM-plohs kohn *vee-VEER:*
Some examples with "to live:"

¿Dónde vive Ud.?
¿DOHN-day VEE-vay oo-STED?
Where do you live?

Yo vivo en la calle Mayor.
Yo VEE-vo en la KAHL-yay Ma-YOR.
I live on Main Street.

¿Vive la Sra. Martínez aquí?
¿VEE-vay la sen-YO-ra Mar-TEE-nays ah-KEE?
Does Mrs. Martinez live here?

Nosotros vivimos en México.
No-SO-trohs vee-VEE-mohs en MAY-hee-ko.
We live in Mexico.

Ellos viven cerca de mi casa.
EL-yohs VEE-ven SAIR-ka day mee KA-sa.
They live near my house.

Y otros verbos de este grupo . . .
Ee OH-trohs VAIR-bohs day ESS-tay GROO-po . . .
And other verbs of this group . . .

¿A qué hora reciben Uds. su correo?
¿Ah kay OH-ra reh-SEE-ben oo-STAY-days soo ko-RRAY-oh?
At what time do you (plural) receive your mail?

Recibimos el correo a las nueve y media.
Ray-see-BEE-mohs el ko-RRAY-oh ah lahs NWAY-vay ee MAY-d'ya.
We receive the mail at nine thirty.

Generalmente recibo muchas cartas.
Hay-nay-rahl-MEN-tay ray-SEE-bo MOO-chahs KAR-tahs.
I generally receive many letters.

¿Y escribe muchas también?
¿Ee ess-KREE-bay MOO-chahs tahm-B'YEN?
And do you also write many?

Sí, escribo muchas.
See, ess-KREE-bo MOO-chahs.
Yes, I write many.

Escribo frecuentemente a mis padres.
Ess-KREE-bo fray-kwen-tay-MEN-tay ah mees PA-drays.
I write to my parents frequently.

Viven en España.
VEE-ven en Ess-PAHN-ya.
They live in Spain.

Present tense: verb group III

The 3rd. verb group is almost exactly like the 2nd. group with the exception that the form for *nosotros* has an *i* instead of an *e*.

	vivir	escribir
yo	*vivo*	*escribo*
Ud., él, ella	*-e*	*-e*
nosotros (-as)	*-imos*	*-imos*
Uds., ellos, ellas	*-en*	*-en*

You now know how to find the most important forms of all Spanish verbs except some irregular ones. This term, irregular, simply means that the forms are somewhat different from the regular pattern, as you will now see.

El verbo *ir* es irregular.
El VAIR-bo *eer* ess ee-rray-goo-LAR.
The verb "to go" is irregular.

Yo voy a un restaurante.
Yo voy ah oon rest-ow-RAHN-tay.
I go to a restaurant.

¿A dónde va ella?
¿Ah DOHN-day va EL-ya?
Where is she going?

Nosotros vamos con ellos.
No-SO-trohs VA-mohs kohn EL-yohs.
We are going with them.

Ellos van primero a la tienda
EL-yohs vahn pree-MAY-ro ah la T'YEN-da
They are going to the store first

y después van al teatro.
ee dess-PWESS vahn ahl tay-AH-tro.
and afterwards they are going to the theater.

Some irregular (and important) verbs
The verb *ir* — "to go" is irregular, as are the verbs *ser* and *estar* from the previous steps. *Saber* — "to know" is irregular only in the form for *yo:*

ir	*saber*	*ser*	*estar*
voy	*sé*	*soy*	*estoy*
va	*sabe*	*es*	*está*
vamos	*sabemos*	*somos*	*estamos*
van	*saben*	*son*	*están*

Los verbos *poner, hacer, tener*
Lohs VAIR-bohs *po-NAIR, ah-SAIR, teh-NAIR*
The verbs "to put," "to do," "to have"

del segundo grupo,
del seh-GOON-doh GROO-po,
of the second group,

y *venir, salir* y *decir* del tercer grupo
ee *vay-NEER, sa-LEER* ee *day-SEER* del tair-SAIR GROO-po
and "to come," "to leave" and "to say" of the third group

son irregulares.
sohn ee-rray-goo-LA-rays.
are irregular.

La forma de *yo* termina en -*go:*
La FOR-ma day *yo* tair-MEE-na en -*go:*
The form of "I" ends in -*go:*

61

Yo vengo de San Francisco.
Yo VEN-go day Sahn Frahn-SEES-ko.
I come from San Francisco.

Tengo un pasaporte americano.
TEN-go oon pa-sa-POR-tay ah-may-ree-KA-no.
I have an American passport.

Hago un viaje a España.
AH-go oon V'YA-hay ah Ess-PAHN-ya.
I'm making a trip to Spain.

Salgo en el vuelo ciento cincuenta para Madrid.
**SAHL-go en el VWAY-lo S'YEN-toh seen-KWEN-ta PA-ra
Ma-DREED.**
I'm leaving on flight one hundred fifty to Madrid.

Perdón. ¿Dónde pongo mi maleta?
Pair-DOHN. ¿DOHN-day POHN-go mee ma-LAY-ta?
Excuse me. Where do I put my bag?

Tener y *venir* tienen otras formas irregulares:
Tay-NAIR ee vay-NEER **T'YAY-nen OH-trahs FOR-mahs
ee-rray-goo-LA-rays:**
"To have" and "to come" have other irregular forms:

Aquí hay unas frases útiles:
Ah-KEE I OO-nahs FRA-says OO-tee-lays:
Here are some useful phrases:

¿Tiene cerveza Bohemia?
¿T'YAY-nay sehr-VAY-sa Bo-AY-m'ya?
Have you Bohemia beer?

No, señor, no tenemos.
No, sen-YOR, no tay-NAY-mohs.
No, sir, we don't have it.

En la otra cantina tienen.
En la OH-tra kahn-TEE-na T'YAY-nen.
In the other bar they have it.

¿A qué hora viene Ud.?
¿Ah kay OH-ra V'YAY-nay oo-STED?
At what time are you coming?

Mi mujer y yo venimos a las cinco.
Mee moo-HAIR ee yo vay-NEE-mohs ah lahs SEEN-ko.
My wife and I are coming at five.

Los otros vienen más tarde.
Lohs OH-trohs V'YAY-nen mahs TAR-day.
The others are coming later.

> **First person verb form in -go**
> The irregularity in the verbs we have been examining is the ending for the 1st. person in -go, and occasional spelling changes in the middle of the verb, as in the case of venir, tener and decir, of which the four forms are:
>
> | venir | tener | decir |
> |---------|---------|----------|
> | vengo | tengo | digo |
> | viene | tiene | dice |
> | venimos | tenemos | decimos |
> | vienen | tienen | dicen |

¿Qué dice ella?
¿Kay DEE-say EL-ya?
What does she say?

Ella dice que no va.
EL-ya DEE-say kay no va.
She says that she's not going.

Pero sus amigas dicen que van.
PAY-ro soos ah-MEE-gahs DEE-sen kay vahn.
But her friends say that they are going.

63

INSTANT CONVERSATION:
AN INVITATION TO THE MOVIES

— ¡Hola muchachas! ¿Adónde van Uds.?
¡OH-la moo-CHA-chahs! ¿Ah DOHN-day vahn oo-STAY-dehs?
Hi, girls! Where are you going?

— Nosotras vamos al cine.
No-SO-trahs VA-mohs ahl SEE-nay.
We're going to the movies.

> **Nosotras**
> *Nosotras* is the feminine form of *nosotros*, al-
> though if there were males in their party they
> would have to say *nosotros* in the interests of
> grammar (if not equality).

— ¿A qué cine van?
¿Ah kay SEE-nay vahn?
What theater are you going to?

— Vamos al Capitolio.
VA-mohs ahl Ka-pee-TOH-l'yo.
We're going to the Capitol.

— ¿Qué película dan hoy?
¿Kay peh-LEE-koo-la dahn oy?
What movie are they giving today?

> **Dar = to give**
> *Dar* ("to give") is a 1st. conjugation verb with
> an irregular first form:
>
> *doy, da, damos, dan.*

— Una película nueva.
OO-na pay-LEE-koo-la NWAY-va.
A new picture.

Dicen que es muy divertida.
DEE-sen kay ess mwee dee-vair-TEE-da.
They say it's very funny.

¿No viene con nosotros?
¿No V'YAY-nay kohn no-SO-trohs?
Aren't you coming with us?

¿Qué dice?
¿Kay DEE-say?
What do you say?

— No sé si tengo tiempo.
No say see TEN-go T'YEM-po.
I don't know if I have time.

¿Cuándo comienza?
¿KWAN-doh ko-M'YEN-sa?
When does it start?

— Pronto. A las ocho y media.
PROHN-toh. Ah lahs OH-cho ee MAY-d'ya.
Soon. At eight thirty.

Tenemos quince minutos para llegar.
Teh-NAY-mohs KEEN-seh mee-NOO-tohs PA-ra l'yay-GAR.
We have fifteen minutes to get there.

— Y, ¿saben cuándo termina?
Ee, ¿SA-ben KWAN-doh tair-MEE-na?
And, do you know when it ends?

— Termina a las diez y media, más o menos.
Tair-MEE-na ah lahs d'yess ee MAY-d'ya, mahs oh MAY-nohs.
It ends at ten thirty, more or less.

— Eso no es tarde.
ES-so no ess TAR-day.
That's not late.

— Entonces tengo tiempo.
En-TOHN-sehs TEN-go T'YEM-po.
Then I have time.

Voy con Uds. y las invito a Uds. . . .
Voy kohn oo-STAY-dehs ee lahs een-VEE-toh ah oo-STAY-days. . . .
I'll go with you and I invite you. . .

> ### Invitar
> *Invitar* ("to invite") is a regular 1st. conjugation
> verb. *A* is used with *Uds.* because when a per-
> son is the object of a verb, as in this case, an *a*
> must precede it.

— ¡Hombre! No es necesario.
¡OHM-bray! No ess neh-seh-SA-r'yo.
Really! It isn't necessary.

> ### Hombre — "Man"
> *¡Hombre!* literally "man!" is used so much as
> an interjection to mean "Really!," "Well, now,"
> "Look!," "One moment!" and other things, that
> it can be considered part of the spoken idiom
> and not slang.

Somos muchas.
SO-mohs MOO-chahs.
We are too many.

Cada uno paga su parte.
KA-da OO-no PA-ga soo PAR-tay.
Each one pays his share.

> ### Influence of the masculine gender
> Although the group speaking with the generous
> young man are all girls, they say *cada uno* be-
> cause they are including him.

TEST YOUR SPANISH

Fill in the correct verb forms. Score 10 points for each correct answer. See answers below.

1. Do you understand?
   ¿—————Ud?

2. I don't understand.
   Yo no —————.

3. Where do you live?
   ¿Dónde ————— Ud?

4. I live on Main Street.
   Yo ————— en la calle Mayor.

5. We live in Mexico.
   Nosotros ————— en México.

6. They read magazines and books.
   Ellos ————— revistas y libros.

7. I come from San Francisco.
   Yo ————— de San Francisco.

8. I have an American passport.
   ————— un pasaporte americano.

9. I'll go with you.
   ————— con Uds.

10. We understand Spanish.
    Nosotros ————— español.

Answers: 1. Comprende; 2. comprendo; 3. vive; 4. vivo; 5. vivimos; 6. leen; 7. vengo; 8. Tengo; 9. voy; 10. comprendemos.

SCORE ——%

67

step 6 FAMILY RELATIONSHIPS

¿Quiénes son los miembros de una familia?
¿Kee-EN-ess sohn lohs mee-EM-brohs day OO-na fa-MEEL-ya?
Who are the members of a family?

marido y mujer
ma-REE-doh ee moo-HAIR
husband and wife

padres y niños
PA-drays ee NEEN-yohs
parents and children

padre e hijo
PA-dray ay EE-ho
father and son

madre e hija
MA-dray ay EE-ha
mother and daughter

"Y" becomes "e", "o" becomes "u"
Y — "and" changes to e for phonetic reasons
when the following word begins with i or hi (as
the h is always silent). Also, o — "or" changes
to u when the word following begins with an o,
as in siete u ocho — "seven or eight."

hermano y hermana
air-MA-no ee air-MA-na
brother and sister

abuelo y nieto
ah-BWAY-lo ee N'YAY-toh
grandfather and grandson

abuela y nieta
ah-BWAY-la ee N'YAY-ta
grandmother and
granddaughter

El señor Zavala es un hombre de negocios.
El sen-YOR Sa-VA-la ess oon OHM-bray day nay-GO-s'yohs.
Mr. Zavala is a businessman.

Tiene su oficina en Madrid.
T'YAY-nay soo oh-fee-SEE-na en Ma-DREED.
He has his office in Madrid.

Los Zavala tienen dos hijos,
Lohs Sa-VA-la T'YAY-nen dohs EE-hohs,
The Zavalas have two children,

Plural of family names
A family name is made plural by making its
article plural; no 's' is added to the name itself.

un hijo y una hija.
oon EE-ho ee OO-na EE-ha.
a son and a daughter.

Su hijo, Guillermo, es estudiante.
Soo EE-ho, Gheel-YAIR-mo, ess ess-too-D'YAHN-tay.
Their son, William, is a student.

Positions or jobs
In ascribing jobs or positions to people the *un*
or *una* is usually dropped.

Va a la escuela.
Va ah la ess-KWAY-la.
He goes to school.

Pilar, la hermana de Guillermo,
Pee-LAR, la air-MA-na day Gheel-YAIR-mo,
Pilar, William's sister,

estudia arte.
ess-TOO-d'ya AR-tay.
studies art.

Tiene novio, está comprometida.
T'YAY-nay NO-v'yo, ess-TA kohm-pro-may-TEE-da.
She has a fiancé, she is engaged.

Engaged
We say *está comprometida* because it is a temporary situation. But when a girl is married we
can say either *es casada* or *está casada*, de-
pending on whether we consider it a description
(*es*) or a condition (*está*), not necessarily
temporary.

69

Su novio es abogado.
Soo NO-v'yo ess ah-bo-GA-doh.
Her fiancé is a lawyer.

El padre del señor Zavala,
El PA-dray del sen-YOR Sa-VA-la,
Mr. Zavala's father,

el abuelo de Guillermo y Pilar,
el ah-BWAY-lo day Gheel-YAIR-mo ee Pee-LAR,
William's and Pilar's grandfather,

está retirado.
ess-TA ray-tee-RA-doh.
is retired.

Es un antiguo oficial del ejército.
Ess oon ahn-TEE-gwo oh-fee-S'YAHL del ay-HAIR-see-toh.
He is a former army officer.

En una familia también tenemos:
En OO-na fa-MEEL-ya tahm-B'YEN tay-NAY-mohs:
In a family we also have:

los tíos y las tías,
lohs TEE-yohs ee lahs TEE-yahs,
(the) uncles and (the) aunts,

los sobrinos y las sobrinas,
lohs so-BREE-nohs ee lahs so-BREE-nahs,
(the) nephews and (the) nieces,

los primos y las primas.
lohs PREE-mohs ee lahs PREE-mahs.
(the) cousins (masculine and feminine).

En la familia política tenemos:
En la fa-MEEL-ya po-LEE-tee-ka tay-NAY-mohs:
In the "in-law" family we have:

el suegro y la suegra,
el SWAY-gro ee la SWAY-gra,
the father-in-law and the mother-in-law,

el cuñado y la cuñada,
el koon-YA-doh ee la koon-YA-da,
the brother-in-law and the sister-in-law,

el yerno y la nuera.
el YAIR-no ee la N'WAY-ra.
the son-in-law and the daughter-in-law.

INSTANT CONVERSATION: TALKING ABOUT ONE'S FAMILY

— ¿Está Ud. casada?
¿Ess-TA oo-STED ka-SA-da?
Are you (fem.) married?

— Sí; aquel caballero es mi marido.
See; ah-KEL ka-bahl-YAY-ro ess mee ma-REE-doh.
Yes; that gentleman is my husband.

— ¿El de la barba?
¿El day la BAR-ba?
The (one) with the beard?

— No, el otro; el del bigote.
No, el OH-tro; el del bee-GO-tay.
No, the other one; the one with the moustache.

— ¿Tiene Ud. hijos?
¿T'YAY-nay oo-STED EE-hohs?
Do you have children?

— Tenemos cuatro —
Tay-NAY-mohs KWA-tro —
We have four —

tres hijos y una hija.
trayss EE-hohs ee OO-na EE-ha.
three sons and a daughter.

— ¿Y, usted?
¿Ee, oo-STED?
And you?

— No tengo hijos — soy soltero.
No TEN-go EE-hohs — soy sol-TAY-ro.
I don't have children — I'm single.

¿Están sus hijos aquí?
¿Ess-TAHN soos EE-hohs ah-KEE?
Are your children here?

— No. Uno de ellos vive en Inglaterra.
No. OO-no day EL-yohs VEE-vay en Een-gla-TAY-rra.
No. One of them lives in England.

Está casado con una inglesa.
Ess-TA ka-SA-doh kohn OO-na een-GLAY-sa.
He is married to an English woman.

Los otros muchachos y la niña
Lohs OH-trohs moo-CHA-chohs ee la NEEN-ya
The other boys and the girl

están todavía en el colegio.
ess-TAHN toh-da-VEE-ya en el ko-LAY-h'yo.
are still in school.

Aquí tiene una foto de ellos.
Ah-KEE T'YAY-nay OO-na FO-toh deh EL-yohs.
Here's a picture of them.

— ¡Qué niños tan hermosos!
¡Kay NEEN-yohs tahn air-MO-sohs!
What beautiful children!

¿Cuántos años tienen?
¿KWAN-tohs AHN-yohs T'YAY-nen?
How old are they?

— Pedro tiene catorce años
PAY-dro T'YAY-nay ka-TOR-say AHN-yohs
Peter is fourteen years old

y Jorge tiene doce.
ee HOR-hay T'YAY-nay DOH-say.
and George is twelve.

Y ésta es Dolores.
Ee ESS-ta ess Doh-LO-rays.
And this is Dolores.

Tiene casi diez y siete años.
T'YAY-nay KA-see d'yess ee S'YAY-tay AHN-yohs.
She is almost seventeen.

— ¡Qué bonita es!
¡Kay bo-NEE-ta ess!
How pretty she is!

¡Y qué ojos tan lindos!
¡Ee kay OH-hohs tahn LEEN-dohs!
And what lovely eyes!

¿A qué colegio van?
¿A kay ko-LAY-h'yo vahn?
What school do they go to?

— Los muchachos van
Lohs moo-CHA-chohs vahn
The boys go

a un colegio en Los Ángeles.
ah oon ko-LAY-h'yo en Lohs AHN-heh-lays.
to a school in Los Angeles.

Pero nuestra hija estudia
PAY-ro NWESS-tra EE-ha ess-TOO-d'ya
But our daughter studies

en una escuela de niñas
en OO-na ess-KWAY-la day NEEN-yahs
in a girls' school

en Barcelona.
en Bar-say-LO-na.
in Barcelona.

Tenemos parientes allá
Tay-NAY-mohs pa-R'YEN-tays ahl-YA
We have relatives there

Remember
padres — parents
parientes — relatives

74

y vive con ellos.
ee VEE-vay kohn EL-yohs.
and she lives with them.

— ¿De veras?
¿Day VAY-rahs?
Really?

¿Está contenta tan lejos
¿Ess-TA kohn-TEN-ta tahn LAY-hohs
Is she happy so far away

de sus padres?
day soos PA-drays?
from her parents?

— ¡Cómo no!
¡KO-mo no!
Of course!

Está muy feliz.
Ess-TA mwee fay-LEESS.
She is very happy.

— Sin duda habla español muy bien, ¿no?
Seen DOO-da AH-bla ess-pahn-YOHL mwee b'yen, ¿no?
She undoubtedly speaks Spanish very well, doesn't she?

— ¡Claro! Mejor que yo.
¡CLA-ro! Meh-HOR kay yo.
Yes indeed! Better than I.

— Pero Ud. habla el castellano perfectamente.
PAY-ro oo-STED AH-bla el kahs-tel-YA-no pair-FEK-ta-MEN-tay.
But you speak Spanish perfectly.

Castellano

Español and *castellano* both mean "Spanish."
The Spanish language evolved from the language spoken in *Castilla*, a province located in the center of Spain.

— Mil gracias.
Meel GRA-s'yahs.
A thousand thanks.

Ud. es muy amable.
Oo-STED ess mwee ah-MA-blay.
You are very kind.

Oh, aquí viene mi marido.
Oh, ah-KEE V'YAY-nay mee ma-REE-doh.
Oh, here comes my husband.

Probablemente es hora de partir.
Pro-ba-blay-MEN-tay ess OH-ra day par-TEER.
It's probably time to go.

TEST YOUR SPANISH

Translate these sentences into Spanish. Score 10 points for each correct translation. See answers below.

1. Are you (feminine) married? _____

2. Yes; that gentleman is my husband. _____

3. Do you have children? _____

4. We have four — three sons and a daughter. _____

5. What beautiful children! _____

6. How old are they? _____

7. She is almost seventeen. _____

8. I am single. (masc.) _____

9. She is very happy. _____

10. A thousand thanks. _____

Answers: 1. ¿Está Ud. casada? 2. Sí; aquel caballero es mi marido. 3. ¿Tiene Ud. hijos? 4. Tenemos cuatro — tres hijos y una hija. 5. ¡Qué niños tan hermosos! 6. ¿Cuántos años tienen? 7. Tiene casi diez y siete años. 8. Soy soltero. 9. Está muy feliz. 10. Mil gracias.

SCORE _____%

77

step 7

HOW TO READ, WRITE, SPELL AND PRONOUNCE SPANISH

Este es el alfabeto español:
ESS-tay ess el ahl-fa-BAY-toh ess-pahn-YOHL:
This is the Spanish alphabet:

A	B	C	CH	D	E		F
ah	bay	say	chay	day	ay		AY-fay
G	**H**	**I**	**J**	**K**	**L**		**LL**
hay	AH-chay	ee	HO-ta	ka	EL-lay		EL-yay
M	**N**	**Ñ**	**O**	**P**	**Q**		**R**
AY-may	AY-nay	EN-yay	oh	pay	koo		AY-ray
S	**T**	**U**	**V**	**X**	**Y**	**Z**
ES-say	tay	oo	vay	AY-kees	ee-GR'YAY-ga	SAY-ta

The missing W
While "W" is not properly a spanish letter, it is pronounced *doh-bleh* vay or *doh-bleh* oo when used in foreign words.

El alfabeto español
El ahl-fa-BAY-toh ess-pahn-YOHL
The Spanish alphabet

tiene 28 letras.
T'YAY-nay VAIN-tee OH-cho LAY-trahs.
has 28 letters.

El alfabeto inglés
El ahl-fa-BAY-toh een-GLAYs
The English alphabet

tiene 26 letras.
T'YAY-nay vain-tee-SAYSS LAY-trahs.
has 26 letters.

78

El alfabeto español
El ahl-fa-BAY-toh ess-pahn-YOHL
The Spanish alphabet

tiene más letras
T'YAY-nay mahs LAY-trahs
has more letters

que el alfabeto inglés.
kay el ahl-fa-BAY-toh een-GLAYS.
than the English alphabet.

¿Cuántas más? Dos más.
¿KWAN-tahs mahs? Dohs mahs.
How many more? Two more.

El alfabeto inglés
El ahl-fa-BAY-toh een-GLAYS
The English alphabet

tiene menos letras
T'YAY-nay MAY-nohs LAY-trahs
has fewer letters

que el alfabeto español.
kay el ahl-fa-BAY-toh ess-pahn-YOHL.
than the Spanish alphabet.

¿Cuántas menos? Dos menos.
¿KWAN-tahs MAY-nohs? Dohs MAY-nohs.
How many less? Two less.

Muchas letras son las mismas,
MOO-chahs LAY-trahs sohn lahs MEES-mahs,
Many letters are the same,

pero algunas son diferentes,
PAY-ro ahl-GOO-nahs sohn dee-fay-REN-tays,
but some are different,

como la *ch*, la *ll*, y la *ñ*,
KO-mo la *chay*, la *EL-yay*, ee la *EN-yay*,
like the *ch*, the double *l*, and the *ñ*,

Spanish Step by Step

La pronunciación de las letras
La pro-noon-s'ya-S'YOHN day lahs LAY-trahs
The pronunciation of the letters

también es diferente en español.
tahm-B'YEN ess dee-fay-REN-tay en ess-pahn-YOHL.
also is different in Spanish.

> **A choice of pronunciation**
> The time has come to speak of "South Ameri-
> can Spanish" and "Castilian." Actually they are
> the same thing, as *castellano*, the dialect of
> Castilla (Castile), became the official Spanish
> language during the Middle Ages. An im-
> pression has nevertheless grown up that "Cas-
> tilian" Spanish is different from Spanish spoken
> in the Americas. Besides certain regional differ-
> ences, this is only true in the pronunciation of
> the "z" and the "c" before "i" and "e", which
> is said with a lisp in Spain. However in Southern
> Spain, like Latin America, the "z" and the "ce"
> and "ci" are pronounced more or less like an
> "s" as we have done in phonetics. In fact, the
> reason that Latin Americans tend to speak like
> people from the south of Spain is because
> Spanish America was originally settled by peo-
> ple from Southern Spain. In general, the Span-
> ish spoken in different countries has less
> variations than there exist between British and
> U.S. English. Also, since there are many Span-
> iards living in Latin America, you will frequently
> hear the Spanish "peninsular" accent in places
> far from Spain.

Y ahora algunas preguntas:
Ee ah-OH-ra ahl-GOO-nahs pray-GOON-tahs:
And now some questions:

¿Cómo se escribe
¿KO-mo say ess-KREE-bay
How does one write

la palabra "España"?
la pa-LA-bra "Ess-PAHN-ya"?
the word "España"?

"España" se escribe
"Ess-PAHN-ya" say ess-KREE-bay
"España" is written

E S P A Ñ A.
ay, AY-say, pay, ah, EN-yay, ah.
E S P A Ñ A.

¿Dónde se pone el acento
¿DOHN-day say PO-nay el ah-SEN-toh
Where do you put the accent

en la palabra "México"?
en la pa-LA-bra "MAY-hee-ko"?
in the word "Mexico"?

Se pone el acento sobre la *e.*
Say PO-nay el ah-SEN-toh SO-bray la *ay.*
The accent is put over the *e.*

¿Dónde se pone el acento
¿DOHN-day say PO-nay el ah-SEN-toh
Where does one put the accent

en el apellido "Jiménez"?
en el ah-pel-YEE-doh "Hee-MAY-ness"?
on the last name "Jimenez"?

Se pone el acento sobre la primera *e.*
Say PO-nay el ah-SEN-toh SO-bray la pree-MAY-ra *ay.*
The accent is put over the first *e.*

How do you call yourself?
The expression *se pone,* literally "it puts itself,"
is equivalent to "one puts" or "it is put". This
se is used with the verb form corresponding to
that of *Ud., él* or *ella.*

Me llamo means "I call myself" or "I am called" (or "my name is") as *llamar* means "to call" and *llamarse* is "to be called" or "to be named."

Here are the four basic forms of the reflexive verb *llamarse:*

me llamo — I am named
se llama — you, he, she or it is named
nos llamamos — we are named
se llaman — you (plural) or they are named

Note:
What is this called in Spanish?
¿Cómo se llama esto en español?

— ¿Cómo se llama Ud.?
¿KO-mo say L'YA-ma oo-STED?
What is your name?

— Yo me llamo María Dixon.
Yo may L'YA-mo Ma-REE-yah DEEK-sohn.
My name is Mary Dixon.

— ¿Cómo se escribe su apellido?
¿KO-mo say ess-KREE-bay soo ah-pel-YEE-doh?
How is your last name written?

— Se escribe D I X O N.
Say ess-KREE-bay day, ee, AY-kees, oh, AY-nay.
It is written D I X O N.

— ¿Cómo se llaman esos señores?
¿KO-mo say L'YA-mahn es-sohs sen-YO-rays?
What is the name of those people?

The dominant masculine
Although one of the persons referred to is masculine and one is feminine the plural is *señores,* literally "gentlemen."

— Se llaman Ricardo y Pilar Martín.
Say L'YA-mahn Ree-KAR-doh ee Pee-LAR Mar-TEEN.
Their names are Richard and Pilar Martin

— ¿Sabe Ud. cómo me llamo?
¿SA-bay oo-STED KO-mo may L'YA-mo?
Do you know what my name is?

— Sí. Ud. se llama Jorge Castillo.
See. Oo-STED say L'YA-ma HOR-hay Kahs-TEEL-yo.
Yes. Your name is George Castillo.

Nosotros escribimos cartas
No-SO-trohs ess-kree-BEE-mohs KAR-tahs
We write letters

a nuestros amigos.
ah NWESS-trohs ah-MEE-gohs.
to our friends.

Escribimos el nombre y la dirección
Ess-kree-BEE-mohs el NOHM-bray ee la dee-rek-S'YOHN
We write the name and address

en el sobre,
en el SO-bray,
on the envelope,

ponemos la carta adentro
po-NAY-mohs la KAR-ta ah-DEN-tro
we put the letter inside

luego cerramos el sobre,
LWAY-go say-RRA-mohs el SO-bray,
then we close the envelope,

y ponemos estampillas.
ee poh-NAY-mohs ess-tahm-PEEL-yahs.
and we put on stamps.

> **Estampillas - sellos**
> In Spain and the Hispanic islands of the Caribbean *sellos* is the preferred word for stamps.

INSTANT CORRESPONDENCE: A THANK-YOU NOTE AND A POSTCARD

Una carta a un amigo:
OO-na KAR-ta ah oon ah-MEE-go:
A letter to a friend:

Querido Roberto,
Kay-REE-do Ro-BAIR-toh,
Dear Robert,

Muchas gracias por las flores.
MOO-chahs GRA-s'yahs por lahs FLO-rays.
Many thanks for the flowers.

¡Son bellísimas!
¡Sohn behl-YEE-see-mahs!
They are very beautiful!

Las rosas amarillas
Lahs RO-sahs ah-ma-REEL-yahs
Yellow roses

son mis flores favoritas.
sohn mees FLO-rays fa-vo-REE-tahs.
are my favorite flowers.

Ud. es muy amable.
Oo-STED ess mwee ah-MA-blay.
You are very kind.

¡Hasta muy pronto!
¡AHS-ta mwee PROHN-toh!
Until very soon!

Sinceramente, Anita
Seen-say-ra-MEN-tay, Ah-NEE-ta
Sincerely, Anita

Una tarjeta postal a una amiga:
OO-na tar-HAY-ta pos-TAHL ah OO-na ah-MEE-ga:
A post card to a friend:

Querida Isabel,
Kay-REE-da Ee-sa-BELL,
Dear Isabel,

Mis mejores saludos desde Acapulco.
Mees may-HO-rays sa-LOO-dohs DES-day Ah-ka-POOL-ko.
My best greetings from Acapulco.

Todo aquí es muy bello.
TOH-doh ah-KEE ess mwee BELL-yo.
Everything here is beautiful.

El clima es magnífico
El KLEE-ma ess mahg-NEE-fee-ko
The climate is magnificent

y la gente es muy interesante.
ee la HEN-tay ess mwee een-tay-ray-SAHN-tay.
and the people are very interesting.

> **Gente**
> *Gente*—"people" is singular in Spanish although plural in English. It is feminine in gender even when it includes males.

Pero Ud. no está aquí. . . ¡qué pena!
PAY-ro oo-STED no ess-TA ah-KEE. . . ¡kay PAY-na!
But you are not here. . . what a shame!

Cariñosamente, Ricardo
Ka-reen-yo-sa-MEN-tay, Ree-KAR-doh
Affectionately, Richard

85

TEST YOUR SPANISH

Translate these sentences into English. Score 10 points for each correct translation. See answers below.

1. Muchas gracias por las flores.   _____

2. ¡Son bellísimas!   _____

3. Las rosas amarillas son mis flores favoritas.   _____

4. Gracias otra vez.   _____

5. Hasta muy pronto.   _____

6. Mis mejores saludos desde Acapulco.   _____

7. Todo aquí es muy bello.   _____

8. El clima es magnífico.   _____

9. La gente es muy interesante.   _____

10. Ud. no está aquí   _____

SCORE _____%

step 8 BASIC VERBS RELATING TO SENSES

Aquí tenemos otros verbos muy importantes:
**Ah-KEE tay-NAY-mohs OH-trohs VAIR-bohs mwee
eem-por-TAHN-tays:**
Here we have some other very important verbs:

ver, mirar, leer, escribir, oír, escuchar,
vair, mee-RAR, lay-AIR, ess-kree-BEER, oh-EER, ess-koo-CHAR,
"to see," "to look at," "to read," "to write," "to hear," "to listen to,"

comer, beber y otros más.
ko-MAIR, bay-BAIR ee OH-trohs mahs.
"to eat," "to drink" and still others.

Con los ojos vemos.
Kohn lohs OH-hohs VAY-mohs.
We see with our eyes.

Yo le veo a Ud.
Yo lay VAY-oh ah oo-STED.
I see you.

Ud. me ve a mí.
Oo-STED may vay ah mee.
You see me.

Pronouns as direct objects
The direct object forms of the pronouns you are
familiar with are as follows:

> me — *me*
> you, him, her, it — *le* or *lo* (mas.), *la* (fem.).
> us — *nos*
> you (plural), them — *les* or *los* (mas.), *las*
> (fem.)

These object pronouns are placed before the verb except in three cases which will be explained in a later step.

The extra *a*, as in *a mí, a Ud., a él, a ella, a nosotros, a Uds., a ellos, a ellas* is often put in to make doubly sure we can see what the action is. If we were to say *Le vemos* it would not be sure if we meant "we see you" or "we see him" but the *a Ud.* or *a él* would clearly specify who is being seen.

Nosotros vemos películas.
No-SO-trohs VAY-mohs pay-LEE-koo-lahs.
We see films.

Miramos a los actores en la televisión.
Mee-RA-mohs ah lohs ahk-TOH-rays en la tay-lay-vee-S'YOHN.
We watch the actors on (the) television.

The personal "a"
A ("to") is used here because actors are people the personal a must be used when people are the direct object.

Con los ojos leemos.
Kohn lohs oh-HOHS lay-AY-mohs.
We read with our eyes.

Este hombre está leyendo un periódico.
Ess-tay OHM-bray ess-TA lay-YEN-doh oon pay-ree-YO-dee-ko.
This man is reading a newspaper.

The present participle "-ing"
The present participle corresponding to the English "-ing," ends in *-ando* for the 1st. conjugation and *-iendo* for the 2nd. and 3rd.

For the present progressive tense we use the present of *estar*.

I am looking. — *Estoy mirando.*
Is he eating? — *¿Está comiendo?*
She is writing. — *Está escribiendo.*

But remember that in Spanish the present indic-
ative tense can also be translated as the
progressive.

Leo. — I read (or) I am reading.
Estoy leyendo. — I am reading.
Ella canta. — She sings. (or)
She is singing.
Ella está cantando. — She is singing.

Esa mujer no está leyendo un periódico,
ES-sa moo-HAIR no ess-TA lay-YEN-doh oon pay-ree-YO-dee-ko,
That woman is not reading a newspaper,

sino una revista.
SEE-no OO-na ray-VEE-sta.
but a magazine.

"Pero" and "sino"
In most cases "but" is *pero*, but when a negative idea is contrasted with an affirmative (the
negative must be first), the conjunction is *sino*.

Ella no es su esposa sino su secretaria.
She is not his wife but his secretary.

Escribimos con un lápiz o una pluma.
Ess-kree-BEE-mohs kohn oon LA-pees oh OO-na PLOO-ma.
We write with a pencil or a pen.

Yo escribo cartas a mano.
Yo ess-KREE-bo KAR-tahs ah MA-no.
I write letters by hand.

La secretaria está escribiendo una carta
La say-kray-TA-r'ya ess-TA ess-kree-B'YEN-doh OO-na KAR-ta
The secretary is writing a letter

en la máquina de escribir.
en la MA-kee-na day ess-kree-BEER.
on the typewriter.

Oímos con los oídos.
Oh-EE-mohs kohn lohs oh-EE-dohs.
We hear with our ears.

89

The diphthong
Notice how the accent over *oímos* influences the pronunciation and splits the *diphthong*, which is the combination of two vowels. Without the written accent *oi* would be *oy*; with the written accent it becomes *oh-EE*.

Oímos muchos sonidos diferentes.
Oh-EE-mohs MOO-chos so-NEE-dohs dee-feh-REN-tays.
We hear many different sounds.

Escuchamos la radio.
Ess-koo-CHA-mohs la RA-d'yo.
We listen to the radio.

Oímos música, noticias y propaganda.
Oh-EE-mohs MOO-see-ka, no-TEE-s'yahs ee pro-pa-GAHN-da.
We hear music, news and advertising.

Una dama está cantando.
OO-na DA-ma ess-TA kahn-TAHN-doh.
A lady is singing.

La gente está escuchando.
La HEN-tay ess-TA ess-koo-CHAHN-doh.
The people are listening.

Cuando ella termina, todo el mundo dice:
KWAN-doh EL-ya tair-MEE-na, TOH-doh el MOON-doh
                                     DEE-say:
When she finishes, everyone says:

Muy bien, excelente; ¡qué bien canta!
Mwee b'yen, ek-say-LEN-tay; ¡kay b'yen KAHN-ta!
Very good, excellent; how well she sings!

Respiramos con la nariz.
Res-pee-RA-mohs kohn la na-REESS.
We breathe with our nose.

Con la nariz también olemos.
Kohn la na-REESS tahm-B'YEN oh-LAY-mohs.
We also smell with our nose.

Con la boca comemos y bebemos.
Kohn la BO-ka ko-MAY-mohs ee bay-BAY-mohs.
We eat and drink with our mouth.

Comemos pan, carne, verdura y fruta.
Ko-MAY-mohs pahn, KAR-nay, vair-DOO-ra ee FROO-ta.
We eat bread, meat, vegetables and fruit.

Bebemos café, té, cerveza, vino . . . y agua.
Bay-BAY-mohs ka-FAY, tay, sehr-VAY-sa, VEE-no . . . ee AH-gwa.
We drink coffee, tea, beer, wine . . . and water.

> **Beber-tomar**
> While *beber* is the word for "to drink," it is more polite, especially when tendering invitations, to use *tomar* — "to take."
>
> What will you have to drink? — *¿Qué toma Ud.?*

El Sr. López no bebe agua, sino vino.
El sen-YOR LO-pays no BAY-bay AH-gwa, SEE-no VEE-no.
Mr. Lopez doesn't drink water, but wine.

Caminamos y corremos con las piernas y los pies.
Ka-mee-NA-mohs ee ko-RRAY-mohs kohn lahs P'YAIR-nahs ee lohs p'yess.
We walk and run with the legs and feet.

Algunos chicos están corriendo en el parque.
AHL-GOO-nohs CHEE-kohs ess-TAHN ko-RR'YEN-doh en el PAR-kay.
Some boys are running in the park.

Corren detrás de una pelota.
KO-rren day-TRAHS day OO-na pay-LO-ta.
They run after a ball.

En una discoteca algunos jóvenes están bailando.
En OO-na dees-ko-TAY-ka ahl-GOO-nohs HO-veh-nays ess-TAHN by-LAHN-doh.
In a discotheque some young people are dancing.

Cuando bailan mueven todo el cuerpo.
KWAN-doh BY-lahn MWAY-ven TOH-doh el KWAIR-po.
When they dance they move the whole body.

Con el cuerpo sentimos sensaciones.
Kohn el KWAIR-po sen-TEE-mohs sen-sa-S'YO-nays.
With our body we feel sensations.

Sentimos calor y frío,
Sen-TEE-mohs ka-LOR ee FREE-yo,
We feel heat and cold,

hambre y sed, dolor y placer.
AHM-bray ee sed, doh-LOR ee pla-SAIR.
hunger and thirst, pain and pleasure.

Aquí presentamos unos ejemplos
Ah-KEE pray-sen-TA-mohs OO-nohs ay-HEM-plohs
Here we present some examples

del uso del pronombre
del OO-so del pro-NOM-bray
of the use of the pronoun

como complemento directo:
KO-mo kohm-play-MEN-toh dee-REK-toh:
as direct object:

Juan está en el campo.
Hwan ess-TA en el KAHM-po.
John is in the country.

Mira los pájaros y los árboles.
MEE-ra lohs PA-ha-rohs ee lohs AR-bo-lays.
He looks at the birds and the trees.

Los mira.
Lohs MEE-ra.
He looks at them.

Mira las flores.
MEE-ra lahs FLO-rays.
He looks at the flowers.

Las mira.
Lahs MEE-ra.
He looks at them.

Un toro está comiendo hierba.
Oon TOH-ro ess-TA ko-M'YEN-doh YAIR-ba.
A bull is eating grass.

La está comiendo.
La ess-TA ko-M'YEN-doh.
He's eating it.

Juan no ve el toro.
Hwan no vay el TOH-ro.
John doesn't see the bull.

No lo ve.
No lo vay.
He doesn't see it.

Pero el toro ve a Juan.
PAIR-ro el TOH-ro vay ah Hwan.
But the bull sees John.

Lo ve.
Lo vay.
It sees him.

Juan oye el toro.
Hwan OH-yay el TOH-ro.
John hears the bull.

Lo oye y lo ve.
Lo OH-yay ee lo vay.
He hears him and he sees him.

Juan corre a la cerca.
Hwan KO-rray ah la SAIR-ka.
John runs to the fence.

La salta.
La SAHL-ta.
He jumps (over) it.

Está salvo.
Ess-TA SAHL-vo.
He is safe.

INSTANT CONVERSATION:
AT A DISCO

PABLO:
PA-blo
PAUL:
 ¿Ve a aquella muchacha?
 ¿Vay ah ah-KEL-ya moo-CHA-cha?
 Do you see that girl?

ANTONIO:
Ahn-TOHN-yo
ANTHONY:
 ¿Cómo dice?
 ¿KO-mo DEE-say?
 What are you saying?

 No le oigo muy bien.
 No lay OY-go mwee b'yen.
 I don't hear you very well.

 Hay mucho ruido aquí.
 I MOO-cho RWEE-doh ah-KEE.
 There's a lot of noise here.

PABLO:
 Estoy diciendo:
 Ess-TOY dee-S'YEN-doh:
 I am saying:

 ¿Ve a aquella muchacha?
 ¿Vay ah ah-KEL-ya moo-CHA-cha?
 Do you see that girl?

ANTONIO:
 ¿Cuál? Veo a muchas.
 ¿Kwal? VAY-oh ah MOO-chahs.
 Which one? I see many.

Which & what
¿*Cuál?* — Which one? (of several).
¿*Qué?* — What?
¿*Qué* libro? — What book?

PABLO:

La que está cerca del micrófono.
La kay ess-TA SAIR-ka del mee-KRO-fo-no.
The one that is near the microphone.

ANTONIO:

¿La rubia que está cantando?
¿La ROO-b'ya kay ess-TA kahn-TAHN-doh?
The blonde that is singing?

¿O la otra que está tocando el piano?
¿Oh la OH-tra kay ess-TA toh-KAHN-doh el P'YA-no?
Or the other one that is playing the piano?

PABLO:

No, no, no. La chica bonita
No, no, no. La CHEE-ka bo-NEE-ta
No, no, no. The pretty girl

con el pelo negro.
kohn el PAY-lo NAY-gro.
with the black hair.

Lleva un traje rojo.
L'YAY-va oon TRA-hay RO-ho.
She's wearing a red dress.

ANTONIO:

¿La que está bailando
¿La kay ess-TA by-LAHN-doh
The one that's dancing

con el viejo?
kohn el V'YAY-ho?
with the old fellow?

PABLO:
 ¡Sí, ésa es!
 ¡See, EH-sa ess!
 Yes, that's the one!

ANTONIO:
 Es muy bella.
 Ess mwee BEL-ya.
 She's very beautiful.

 ¡Y qué bien baila!
 ¡Ee kay b'yen BY-la!
 And how well she dances!

PABLO:
 ¿La conoce?
 ¿La ko-NO-say?
 Do you know her?

Conocer and saber
Compare:
 conocer — to know (a person)
 to be familiar with something
 saber — to know (a fact)
 to know how to do something

Since you have not had *conocer* before, note its form:

 conozco, conoce, conocemos, conocen.

ANTONIO:
 No, no la conozco.
 No, no la ko-NOHS-ko.
 No, I don't know her.

PABLO:
 ¿Sabe quién es?
 ¿SA-bay k'yen ess?
 Do you know who she is?

ANTONIO:
 No, no sé quién es.
 No, no say k'yen ess.
 No, I don't know who she is.

¿Lo sabe Ud.?
¿Lo SA-bay oo-STED?
Do you know (it)?

Lo when unspecified
When "it" refers to something unspecified or an idea its object form is masculine — *lo*.

PABLO:
¡Hombre! Claro que no sé.
¡OHM-bray! KLA-ro kay no say.
Really now! Of course I don't know.

Por eso estoy preguntando.
Por EH-so ess-TOY preh-goon-TAHN-doh.
That's why I'm asking.

ANTONIO:
¡Está bien! ¡Está bien!
¡Ess-TA b'yen! ¡Ess-TA b'yen!
OK! OK!

Veo que Ud. está muy interesado.
VEH-oh kay oo-STED ess-TA mwee een-tay-reh-SA-doh.
I see you are very interested.

Vamos a ver a mi amigo Pepe.
VA-mohs ah vair ah mee ah-MEE-go PAY-pay.
Let's go see my friend Pepe.

Él conoce a todo el mundo.
El ko-NO-say ah TOH-doh el MOON-doh.
He knows everybody.

Todo el mundo
Todo el mundo — literally "all the world," but used here to mean "everybody."

TEST YOUR SPANISH

Match these phrases. Score 10 points for each correct answer. See answers below.

1. I see you.

2. You see me.

3. We listen to the radio.

4. We feel heat and cold.

5. Do you see that girl?

6. What do you say?

7. I don't hear you very well.

8. There's a lot of noise here.

9. Do you know her?

10. Do you know who she is?

_____ Sentimos el calor y el frío.

_____ ¿Ve a aquella muchacha?

_____ No le oigo muy bien.

_____ ¿Sabe quién es?

_____ ¿La conoce?

_____ Ud. me ve a mí.

_____ Hay mucho ruido aquí.

_____ ¿Cómo dice?

_____ Yo le veo a Ud.

_____ Escuchamos la radio.

Answers: 4 5 7 10 9 2 8 6 1 3

SCORE _____%

step 9 PROFESSIONS AND OCCUPATIONS

Para saber el puesto o la profesión
PA-ra sa-BAIR el PWESS-toh oh la pro-fay-S'YOHN
In order to know the position or the profession

> **Remember**
> *Para saber* is literally "for to know." *Para* is
> used with the infinitive of a verb where "to" has
> the sense of "for the purpose of" or "in order
> to".

de una persona, decimos:
day OO-na pair-SO-na, day-SEE-mohs:
of a person, we say:

"¿Dónde trabaja Ud.?"
"¿DOHN-day tra-BA-ha oo-STED?"
"Where do you work?"

o: "¿Cuál es su profesión?"
oh: "¿Kwahl ess soo pro-fay-S'YOHN?"
or: "What is your profession?"

Un hombre de negocios trabaja en una oficina.
**Oon OHM-bray day nay-GO-s'yohs tra-BA-ha en OO-na
oh-fee-SEE-na.**
A businessman works in an office.

Los obreros trabajan en las fábricas.
Lohs oh-BRAY-rohs tra-BA-hahn en lahs FA-bree-kahs.
Workers work in the factories.

Los médicos atienden a los enfermos.
Lohs MAY-dee-kohs ah-T'YEN-den ah lohs en-FAIR-mohs.
Doctors take care of the sick.

Los actores y actrices
Lohs ahk-TOH-ress ee ahk-TREE-sayss
Actors and actresses

trabajan en el teatro o en el cine.
tra-BA-hahn en el tay-AH-tro oh en el SEE-nay.
work in the theatre or in the movies.

Un artista pinta cuadros.
Oon ar-TEES-ta PEEN-ta KWA-drohs.
An artist paints pictures.

Un autor escribe libros.
Oon aw-TOR ess-KREE-bay LEE-brohs.
An author writes books.

Un músico toca el piano u otro instrumento.
Oon MOO-see-ko TOH-ka el P'YA-no oo OH-tro eens-troo-MEN-toh.
A musician plays the piano or another instrument.

> **Tocar**
> *Tocar* means "to touch" or "to play" as applied
> to a musical instrument.
>
> The word for "or" — *o* becomes *u* if the next
> word begins with an *o*.

Un mecánico hace reparaciones.
Oon meh-KA-nee-ko AH-say ray-pa-ra-S'YO-ness.
A mechanic makes repairs.

Un cartero entrega el correo.
Oon kar-TAY-ro en-TRAY-ga el ko-RRAY-oh.
A mailman delivers the mail.

Un conductor de autobús conduce el autobús.
**Oon kohn-dook-TOR day ow-toh-BOOS kohn-DOO-say el
ow-toh-BOOSS.**
A bus driver drives the bus.

Los choferes de taxi conducen taxis.
Lohs cho-FAY-rays day TAHK-see kohn-DOO-sen TAHK-sees.
Taxi drivers drive taxis.

Los bomberos apagan los incendios.
Lohs bohm-BAY-rohs ah-PA-gahn lohs een-SEN-d'yohs.
Firemen put out fires.

Los policías dirigen la circulación
Lohs po-lee-SEE-yahs dee-REE-hen la seer-koo-la-S'YOHN.
Policemen direct the traffic

Slightly irregular
Among the new verbs just presented three undergo slight modifications in the present tense: *dirigir* ("to direct"), *conducir* ("to drive"), and *atender* ("to take care of").

Here are the forms:

dirijo,	dirige,	dirigimos,	dirigen
conduzco,	conduce,	conducimos,	conducen
atiendo,	atiende,	atendemos,	atienden

y arrestan a los criminales.
ee ah-RRESS-tahn ah lohs cree-mee-NA-lays.
and arrest criminals.

INSTANT CONVERSATION:
AT A PARTY

— ¡Qué fiesta tan divertida!
¡Kay F'YES-ta tahn dee-vair-TEE-da!
What a nice party!

> **Tan**
> *Tan* means "so" or "as" but here it is used
> with *que* to make the "what a . . ." more effec-
> tive. *¡Qué día tan bello!* — What a beautiful
> day!

— Sí. Los invitados son muy interesantes.
See. Lohs een-vee-TA-dohs sohn mwee een-tay-ray-SAHN-tayss.
Yes. The guests are very interesting.

— Es verdad. La señora de Céspedes
Ess vair-DAHD. La sen-YO-ra day SESS-pay-dayss
It's true. Mrs. Cespedes

tiene una gran variedad de amistades.
T'YAY-nay OO-na grahn va-r'yay-DAHD day ah-mees-TA-dayss.
has a great variety of friends.

> **Vocabulary dividend**
> The *-ad* ending often corresponds to the *-ty*
> ending in English with the words that both En-
> glish and Spanish derive from Latin. Words end-
> ing in *-dad* or *-tad* are all feminine. Here are
> some others:
>
> *variedad* — variety
> *libertad* — liberty
> *piedad* — pity (or) piety
> *fraternidad* — fraternity
> *posibilidad* — possibility
> *probabilidad* — probability
> *cualidad* — quality

cantidad — quantity
necesidad — necessity

Amistad, another example, means "friendship" (as well as "amity") and, in the plural, is used for "friends" when speaking of them in a general way.

As you can see, your Spanish vocabulary is advancing *a grandes pasos* — "in great steps."

En aquel grupo que está
En ah-KEL GROO-po kay ess-TA
In the group that is

cerca de la ventana
SAIR-ka day la ven-TA-na
near the window

hay un abogado, un compositor,
I oon ah-bo-GA-doh, oon kohm-po-see-TOR,
there is a lawyer, a composer,

un ingeniero, un arquitecto,
oon een-hay-N'YAY-ro, oon ar-kee-TEK-toh,
an engineer, an architect,

un dentista y un torero.
oon den-TEES-ta ee oon toh-RAY-ro.
a dentist, and a bullfighter.

— Es un grupo bastante diverso.
Ess oon GROO-po bahs-TAHN-tay dee-VAIR-so.
It is quite a diverse group.

¿Qué cree Ud. que están discutiendo:
¿Kay KRAY-ay oo-STED kay ess-TAHN dees-koo-T'YEN-doh:
What do you think they are discussing:

arquitectura, música, derecho . . . ?
ar-kee-tek-TOO-ra, MOO-see-ka, day-RAY-cho . . . ?
architecture, music, law . . . ?

— Las corridas, sin duda.
Lahs ko-RREE-dahs, seen DOO-da.
The bullfights, no doubt.

— ¿Sabe quién es aquella mujer hermosa?
¿SA-bay k'yen ess ah-KEHL-ya moo-HAIR air-MO-sa?
Do you know who that beautiful woman is?

Tiene un traje lindísimo.
T'YEH-nay oon TRA-hay leen-DEE-see-mo.
She has a very lovely dress.

— Es una bailarina del Ballet Nacional.
Ess OO-na by-la-REE-na del Ba-LAY Na-s'yo-NAHL.
She's a ballerina from the National Ballet.

Se llama Beatriz Flores.
Say L'YA-ma Bay-ah-TREESS FLO-rays.
Her name is Beatrice Flores.

— Y ¿los dos caballeros
Ee ¿lohs dohs ka-bahl-YAY-rohs
And the two gentlemen

que están con ella?
kay ess-TAHN kohn EL-ya?
who are with her?

— El señor de edad
El sen-YOR day ay-DAHD
The elderly gentleman

es un director de cine,
ess oon dee-rek-TOR day SEE-nay,
is a movie director,

y el señor más joven y buen mozo
ee el sen-YOR mahs HO-ven ee bwen MO-so
and the younger and handsome gentleman

es un actor.
ess oon ahk-TOR.
is an actor.

104

— Mire quién está entrando ahora.
MEE-ray k'yen ess-TA en-TRAHN-doh ah-OH-ra.
Look who's coming in now.

Es Francisco de Alarcón,
Ess Frahn-SEES-ko day Ah-lar-KOHN,
It is Francisco de Alarcon,

el famoso explorador de la selva.
el fa-MO-so ess-plo-ra-DOR day la SELL-va.
the famous jungle explorer.

— ¿De veras? Hay un artículo sobre él
¿Day VAY-rahs? I oon ar-TEE-koo-lo SO-bray el
Really? There is an article about him

en el periódico de hoy.
en el pay-R'YO-dee-ko day oy.
in today's newspaper.

¡Qué vida de aventuras!
¡Kay VEE-da day ah-ven-TOO-rahs!
What a life of adventures!

— Es cierto. A propósito,
Ess S'YAIR-toh. Ah pro-PO-see-toh,
That's true. By the way,

yo lo conozco.
yo lo ko-NOHS-ko.
I know him.

Vamos a charlar un rato con él.
VA-mohs ah char-LAR oon RA-toh kohn el.
Let's go chat with him a while.

> **Vamos**
> *Vamos* — "we go" or "we are going" is extremely useful for it can also mean "let's" when followed by a plus the infinitive of another verb.

105

TEST YOUR SPANISH

Match these people to the work they do. Score 10 points for each correct answer. See answers below.

1.	Un hombre de negocios	A	conduce el autobús.
2.	Los médicos	B	apagan los incendios.
3.	Un artista	C	entrega el correo.
4.	Los obreros	D	arrestan a los criminales.
5.	Un músico	E	pinta cuadros.
6.	Un cartero	F	toca el piano.
7.	Los bomberos	G	trabajan en el cine.
8.	Un conductor de autobús	H	trabaja en una oficina
9.	Los policías	I	trabajan en las fábricas.
10.	Los actores y actrices	J	atienden a los enfermos.

Answers: 1-H; 2-J; 3-E; 4-I; 5-F; 6-C; 7-B; 8-A; 9-D; 10-G.

SCORE _____%

106

step 10 HOW TO ASK AND GIVE DIRECTIONS: CAR TRAVEL

Aquí hay unos ejemplos
Ah-KEE I OO-nohs ay-HEM-plohs
Here are some examples

de cómo dar una orden
day KO-mo dar OO-na OR-den
of how to give an order

y también del uso de los pronombres
ee tahm-B'YEN del OO-so day lohs pro-NOHM-bress
and also of the use of the pronouns

con las órdenes.
kohn lahs OR-day-nays.
with the commands.

Un hombre en un automóvil
Oon OHM-bray en oon ow-toh-MO-veel
A man in an automobile

habla con un peatón.
AH-bla kohn oon pay-ah-TOHN.
speaks to a pedestrian.

Le pregunta: "¿Es éste el camino
Lay pray-GOON-ta: ¿Ess ESS-tay el ka-MEE-no
He asks him: "Is this the road

para Ciudad Victoria?"
PA-ra s'yoo-DAHD Veek-TOR-ya?
for Victoria City?"

El peatón le contesta:
El pay-ah-TOHN lay kohn-TESS-ta:
The pedestrian answers:

107

Pronouns as indirect objects

"*Le* ("him" or "to him") is an indirect object pronoun. Here are the others for the pronouns you already know:

> me (or) to me — *me*
> to you, to him, to her — *le*
> to us — *nos*
> to you (plural), to them — *les*

The additions *a mí, a él, a ella, a Ud.*, etc., are sometimes added to show clearly what the action is.

"No, señor. Éste no es.
"No, sen-YOR. ESS-tay no ess.
"No, sir. This is not it.

Siga derecho dos calles más.
SEE-ga day-RAY-cho dohs KAHL-yays mahs.
Continue straight two more streets

Commands

You have just seen another way to give commands. (The first one you learned was to use *sírvase* followed by an infinitive).

In this simple and shorter way to express the imperative, simply change the -*a* ending (3rd person, present tense) of the 1st. conjugation to -*e:*

> *habla* — you speak
> *¡Hable!* — Speak!

and for the 2nd. and 3rd. conjugations, change the -*e* ending of the present for the *Ud.* form to -*a*

> *Ud. aprende* — you learn
> *¡Aprenda!* — Learn!
> *Ud. escribe* — you write
> *¡Escriba!* — Write!

However, when a verb ends in -*go* for the *yo* form it keeps the -*g* and any other spelling change in the imperative, as is the case with *siga*. Therefore the imperatives for *salir* ("to leave"), *venir* ("to come"), *decir* ("to say"), *traer* ("to bring"), etc. are:

¡salga! ¡venga! ¡diga! ¡traiga!

The only other important exceptions are for *ser* ("to be") and *ir* ("to go"), the imperative forms of which are ¡*sea!* and ¡*vaya!*

Tome a la izquierda.
TOH-may ah la ees-K'YAIR-da.
Turn left.

Siga hasta el semáforo.
SEE-ga AHS-ta el say-MA-fo-ro.
Continue until the traffic light.

Luego tome a la derecha.
LWAY-go TOH-may ah la day-RAY-cha.
Then turn right.

Tomar = virar
Tomar, as we have seen, means "to take" or "to drink". It also can mean "to turn", as in

¡*Tome a la derecha!* — "Turn to the right!"

Still another word for "turn" is *virar*.

Ésa es la carretera.
EH-sa ess la ka-rray-TEH-ra.
That is the road.

Pero tenga cuidado.
PAY-ro TEN-ga kwee-DA-do.
But be careful.

Hay límite de velocidad."
I LEE-mee-tay day vay-lo-see-DAHD."
There is a speed limit."

Le da las gracias
Lay da lahs GRA-s'yahs
He thanks him

y continúa dos calles más.
ee kohn-tee-NOO-ah dohs KAHL-yays mahs.
and continues two streets more.

Luego toma a la izquierda
LWAY-go TOH-ma ah la ees-K'YAIR-da
Then he turns left

y sigue hasta la luz
ee SEE-gay AHS-ta la looss
and continues until the light

y luego toma a la derecha.
ee LWAY-go TOH-ma ah la day-RAY-cha.
and then he turns right.

Pero un policía en motocicleta
PAY-ro oon po-lee-SEE-yah en mo-toh-see-KLAY-ta
But a policeman on a motorcycle

lo sigue. Lo para.
lo SEE-gay. Lo PA-ra.
follows him. He stops him.

El policía le dice:
El po-lee-SEE-ah lay DEE-say:
The policeman says to him:

"¿Por qué tanta prisa?
"¿Por kay TAHN-ta PREE-sa?
"Why such a hurry?

Muéstreme su permiso."
MWESS-tray-may soo pair-MEE-so."
Show me your license."

Position of pronoun objects
Pronoun objects generally come in front of the verb *except* in the *affirmative* imperative when they must follow and are *attached* to it. As far

110

as the negative imperative is concerned, they precede the verb as usual.

Do it! — ¡Hágalo!
Don't do it! — ¡No lo haga!

El señor le muestra el permiso.
El sen-YOR lay MWESS-tra el pair-MEE-so.
The gentleman shows him the license.

Luego le dice:
LWAY-go lay DEE-say:
Then he says to him:

"Déme la patente también."
"DAY-may la pa-TEN-tay tahm-B'YEN."
"Give me the registration also."

El señor se la da.
El sen-YOR say la da.
The gentleman gives it to him.

El policía escribe una citación
El po-lee-SEE-ah ess-KREE-bay OO-na see-ta-S'YOHN
The policeman writes a summons

y se la da al señor.
ee say la da ahl sen-YOR.
and gives it to the gentleman.

Euphony
Although we told you that *le* is "him" or "to him" you have no doubt noticed *se* in *se la da* when logically it should be written *le la da*. However, because Spanish has a tendency to make things as musical as possible, when there are two pronouns beginning with *l*, the first is changed to *s* for the purpose of euphony.

Le da también el permiso
Lay da tahm-B'YEN el pair-MEE-so
He also gives him the license

y la patente.
ee la pa-TEN-tay.
and the registration.

"¡Tómelos!", le dice,
"¡TOH-may-lohs!", lay DEE-say,
"Take them!" he says to him,

"¡Y tenga cuidado en el futuro!"
"¡Ee TEN-ga kwee-DA-doh en el foo-TOO-ro!"
"And be careful in the future!"

INSTANT CONVERSATION: GIVING ORDERS

UNA SEÑORA:
OO-na sen-YO-ra:
A LADY:
   María, tráigame una taza de café, por favor.
   Ma-REE-ya, TRY-ga-may OO-na TA-sa day ka-FAY, por fa-VOR.
   María, bring me a cup of coffee, please.

UNA CRIADA:
OO-na kree-AH-da:
A MAID:
   Aquí tiene, señora.
   Ah-KEE T'YAY-nay, sen-YO-ra.
   Here you are, madam.

LA SEÑORA:
   Gracias. Oiga, alguien llama
   GRA-s'yahs. OY-ga, AHL-gh'yen LYA-ma
   Thank you. Listen, someone is knocking

   a la puerta.
   ah la PWAIR-ta.
   at the door.

   Ábrala, por favor.
   AH-bra-la, por fa-VOR.
   Open it, please.

LA SEÑORA:
   ¿Quién es?
   ¿K'yen ess?
   Who is it?

LA CRIADA:

Es el muchacho del mercado
Ess el moo-CHA-cho del mair-KA-doh
It's the boy from the market

con los comestibles.
kohn lohs ko-mays-TEE-blays.
with the groceries.

LA SEÑORA:

Bien. Ponga la carne, la leche,
B'yen. PON-ga la KAR-nay, la LAY-chay,
Good. Put the meat, milk,

y la mantequilla en la nevera
ee la mahn-tay-KEEL-ya en la nay-VAY-ra
and butter in the refrigerator

y lo demás en la
ee lo day-MAHS en la
and the rest in the

despensa de la cocina.
des-PEN-sa day la ko-SEE-na.
kitchen cabinet.

¿Dónde está la factura?
¿DOHN-day ess-TA la fahk-TOO-ra?
Where is the bill?

LA CRIADA:

Él la tiene, señora.
El la T'YAY-nay, sen-YO-ra.
He has it, madam.

LA SEÑORA:

Déjela en la mesa, por favor.
DAY-hay-la en la MAY-sa, por fa-VOR.
Leave it on the table, please.

Y aquí está la lista para mañana.
Ee ah-KEE ess-TA la LEES-ta PA-ra mahn-YA-na.
And here is the list for tomorrow.

Tómela y désela al muchacho.
TOH-may-la ee DAY-say-la ahl moo-CHA-cho.
Take it and give it to the boy.

LA CRIADA:
Enseguida, señora.
En-say-GHEE-da, sen-YO-ra.
Right away, madam.

LA SEÑORA:
Mire, María, ahora voy
MEE-ray, Ma-REE-yah, ah-OH-ra voy
Look, María, now I'm going

al salón de belleza.
ahl sa-LOHN day bel-YAY-sa.
to the beauty parlor.

> **En el salón de belleza**
> The following will be useful for ladies when they
> go to the "beauty parlor" — *el salón de belleza:*
>
> > wash and set — *lavar y peinar*
> > too hot — *demasiado caliente*
> > a rinse — *un tinte*
> > lighter — *más claro*
> > darker — *más obscuro*
> > a manicure — *una manicura*
> > a wig — *una peluca*
>
> and for men when they visit "the barber" — *el
> barbero* (A barber shop is called *una peluquería*
> or *barbería*):
>
> > a haircut — *un corte de pelo*
> > not too short — *no demasiado corto*
> > a shave — *una afeitada*
> > a massage — *un masaje*

LA SEÑORA:
Si alguien llama
See AHL-gh'yen L'YA-ma
If anyone calls

115

tome el recado
TOH-may el ray-KA-doh
take the message

y escríbalo en este papel.
ee ess-KREE-ba-lo en ESS-tay pa-PEL.
and write it on this paper.

Mientras estoy fuera,
M'YEN-trahs ess-TOY FWAY-ra,
While I am out,

limpie la casa y prepare la cena; por favor.
LEEM-p'yay la KA-sa ee pray-PA-ray la SAY-na; por fa-VOR.
clean the house and prepare the dinner; please.

LA CRIADA:
¿Eso es todo, señora?
¿AY-so ess TOH-doh, sen-YO-ra?
Is that all, madam?

LA SEÑORA:
Una cosa más.
OO-na KO-sa mahs.
One thing more.

Tome estos dos vestidos
TOH-may ESS-tohs dohs vess-TEE-dohs
Take these two dresses

y llévelos a la tintorería.
ee L'YAY-vay-lohs ah la teen-toh-ray-REE-ya.
and carry (take) them to the cleaners.

LA CRIADA:
Está bien, señora.
Ess-TA b'yen, sen-YO-ra.
Very well, madam.

LA SEÑORA:
Ahora, ¿dónde están mis llaves?
Ah-OH-ra, ¿DOHN-day ess-TAHN mees L'YA-vays?
Now, where are my keys?

LA CRIADA:
Allí están, en el escritorio.
Ahl-YEE ess-TAHN, en el ess-kree-TOR-yo.
There they are, on the desk.

LA SEÑORA:
Démelas, por favor.
DAY-may-lahs, por fa-VOR.
Give them to me, please.

Y ¿mis anteojos? Oh, está bien.
Ee ¿mees ahn-tay-OH-hohs? Oh, ess-TA b'yen.
And my glasses? Oh, it's all right.

Aquí los tengo, en mi cartera.
Ah-KEE lohs TEN-go, en mee kar-TAY-ra.
I have them here, in my handbag.

LA SEÑORA:
Y ahora, ¿qué? El teléfono...
Ee ah-OH-ra, ¿kay? El tay-LAY-fo-no...
And now what? The telephone...

Contéstelo, por favor.
Kohn-TESS-tay-lo, por fa-VOR.
Answer it, please.

¿Quién es?
¿K'yen ess?
Who is it?

LA CRIADA:
Es mi amigo José.
Ess mee ah-MEE-go Ho-SAY.
It's my friend José.

Me invita esta noche a un baile.
May een-VEE-ta ESS-ta NO-chay ah oon BY-lay.
He is inviting me to a dance tonight.

LA SEÑORA:

Pero tenemos invitados esta noche.
PAY-ro tay-NAY-mohs een-vee-TA-dohs ESS-ta NO-chay.
But we have guests tonight.

Pues, bien. Sirva la comida primero
Pwess, b'yen. SEER-va la ko-MEE-da pree-MAY-ro
Well, alright. Serve the meal first

> **Pues, así**
> *Pues* and *así* are two words that constantly
> occur in Spanish conversation. *Pues* means
> "well," "then," "indeed," or "let me see," and
> can be used as an expression of hesitation
> while considering a reply. *Así* means "like this,"
> "like that," "this way," "that way" (as used
> here), "so" or "thus."

y después, vaya al baile, si desea.
ee dess-PWESS, VA-ya ahl BY-lay, see day-SAY-ah.
and then, go to the dance, if you wish.

TEST YOUR SPANISH

Translate these orders into Spanish, using the imperative. Where pronouns are used, gender is indicated. Score 5 points for each correct answer. See answers on the following page.

1. Come! ⎯⎯⎯⎯⎯⎯⎯⎯⎯⎯⎯⎯⎯⎯⎯⎯⎯⎯⎯⎯

2. Go! ⎯⎯⎯⎯⎯⎯⎯⎯⎯⎯⎯⎯⎯⎯⎯⎯⎯⎯⎯⎯⎯

3. Leave! ⎯⎯⎯⎯⎯⎯⎯⎯⎯⎯⎯⎯⎯⎯⎯⎯⎯⎯⎯

4. Be careful! ⎯⎯⎯⎯⎯⎯⎯⎯⎯⎯⎯⎯⎯⎯⎯⎯⎯

5. Wait! ⎯⎯⎯⎯⎯⎯⎯⎯⎯⎯⎯⎯⎯⎯⎯⎯⎯⎯⎯

6. Look! ⎯⎯⎯⎯⎯⎯⎯⎯⎯⎯⎯⎯⎯⎯⎯⎯⎯⎯⎯

7. Be quiet! ⎯⎯⎯⎯⎯⎯⎯⎯⎯⎯⎯⎯⎯⎯⎯⎯⎯

8. Listen to me! ⎯⎯⎯⎯⎯⎯⎯⎯⎯⎯⎯⎯⎯⎯⎯

9. Tell me! ⎯⎯⎯⎯⎯⎯⎯⎯⎯⎯⎯⎯⎯⎯⎯⎯⎯

10. Show me! ⎯⎯⎯⎯⎯⎯⎯⎯⎯⎯⎯⎯⎯⎯⎯⎯

11. Bring it! (use masculine for "it".) ⎯⎯⎯⎯⎯⎯⎯

12. Take it! (fem.) ⎯⎯⎯⎯⎯⎯⎯⎯⎯⎯⎯⎯⎯⎯

13. Write it! (fem.) ⎯⎯⎯⎯⎯⎯⎯⎯⎯⎯⎯⎯⎯

14. Do it! (masc.) ⎯⎯⎯⎯⎯⎯⎯⎯⎯⎯⎯⎯⎯⎯

15. Don't do it! (masc.) ⎯⎯⎯⎯⎯⎯⎯⎯⎯⎯⎯

16. Open it! (fem.) ⎯⎯⎯⎯⎯⎯⎯⎯⎯⎯⎯⎯⎯

17. Give them to me! (masc.) ⎯⎯⎯⎯⎯⎯⎯⎯⎯

18. Leave it there! (masc.) _____

19. Close it! (fem.) _____

20. Don't give it to him! (fem.) _____

SCORE _____%

HOW TO SAY "WANT," "CAN," "MAY," "MUST," AND "WOULD LIKE TO"

Mi auto no puede caminar.
Mee OW-toh no PWAY-day ka-mee-NAR.
My car cannot go.

¿Por qué no puede caminar?
¿Por kay no PWAY-day ka-mee-NAR?
Why can't it go?

Porque no hay gasolina en el tanque.
POR-kay no I ga-so-LEE-na en el TAHN-kay.
Because there's no gas in the tank.

El motor no puede funcionar sin gasolina.
El mo-TOR no PWAY-day foon-s'yo-NAR seen ga-so-LEE-na.
The motor can't work without gas.

"Can" + "must"

Poder — "to be able" or "can," necesitar — "to need," and deber — "must" or "to be obliged to" either stand alone or are followed by another verb in the infinitive. Necesitar and deber are regular, (see Step 5), but poder in the present tense undergoes a change in its base:

puedo, puede, podemos, pueden.

When a pronoun is used as object with an infinitive it is frequently attached to the infinitive.

I can see it. — Puedo verlo, or Lo puedo ver.
He must do it. — Debe hacerlo, or Lo debe
hacer.
Can you see it? — ¿Puede verlo? or ¿Lo
puede ver?

121

Debemos poner gasolina en el tanque.
Day-BAY-mohs po-NAIR ga-so-LEE-na en el TAHN-kay.
We must put gas in the tank.

Necesitamos gasolina.
Nay-say-see-TA-mohs ga-so-LEE-na.
We need gas.

¿Dónde podemos comprar gasolina?
¿DOHN-day po-DAY-mohs kohm-PRAR ga-so-LEE-na?
Where can we buy gas?

Podemos comprarla
Po-DAY-mohs kohm-PRAR-la
We can buy it

en un puesto de gasolina.
en oon PWESS-toh day ga-so-LEE-na.
in a gas station.

En el puesto de gasolina
While on the subject of service stations, note the following key expressions:

Fill it! — ¡Llénelo!
Check the oil. — Fíjese en el aceite.
Look at the air in the tires. — Vea el aire en las llantas.
Look at the water in the battery. — Vea el agua en la batería.
This isn't working well. — Esto no funciona bien.
Can you fix it? — ¿Puede repararlo?
This tire must be changed. — Esta llanta debe cambiarse.
How long must we wait? — ¿Cuánto tiempo hay que esperar?

Jorge quiere ver
HOR-hay K'YAY-ray vair
George wants to see

la corrida de toros,
la ko-RREE-da day TOH-rohs,
the bullfight,

122

pero no puede entrar a la Plaza.
PAY-ro no PWAY-day en-TRAR ah la PLA-sa.
but he can't go into the Arena.

¿Por qué no puede entrar?
¿Por kay no PWAY-day en-TRAR?
Why can't he go in?

No puede porque no tiene entrada.
No PWAY-day POR-kay no T'YAY-nay en-TRA-da.
He can't because he doesn't have a ticket.

Remember
¿Por qué? — Why?
Porque. — Because.

¿Por qué no compra una entrada?
¿Por kay no KOHM-pra OO-na en-TRA-da?
Why doesn't he buy a ticket?

No puede comprar una entrada
No PWAY-day kohm-PRAR OO-na en-TRA-da
He can't buy a ticket

porque no tiene suficiente dinero.
POR-kay no T'YAY-nay soo-fee-S'YEN-tay dee-NAY-ro.
because he hasn't enough money.

No se puede comprar una entrada
No say PWAY-day kohm-PRAR OO-na en-TRA-da
One can't buy a ticket

sin dinero.
seen dee-NAY-ro.
without money.

Si quiere ver la corrida
See K'YAY-ray vehr la ko-RREE-da
If he wants to see the bullfight

To wish — to mean
Querer — "to want" or "to wish" is conjugated *quiero, quiere, queremos, quieren*. *Querer* when combined with *decir* is equivalent to "to mean."

¿Qué quiere decir? — What do you mean? (or) What does it mean?

debe comprar una.
DAY-bay kohm-PRAR OO-na.
he must buy one.

Pero aquí hay un amigo suyo.
PAY-ro ah-KEE I oon ah-MEE-go SOO-yo.
But here is a friend of his.

"Oiga," le dice, "¿puede prestarme unos pesos
**"OY-ga," lay DEE-say, "¿PWAY-day prays-TAR-me OO-nohs
PAY-sohs**
"Listen," he says to him, "can you lend me some pesos

para ir a ver la corrida?"
PA-ra eer ah vair la ko-RREE-da?"
to go to see the bullfight?"

"Tal vez. ¿Cuándo puede devolvérmelos?"
"Tahl vehss. ¿KWAN-doh PWAY-day day-vol-VAIR-may-lohs?"
"Maybe. When can you give them back to me?"

Pronouns with the infinitive
Devolvérmelos shows two pronouns *me* ("to me") and *los* ("them"), both added on to the infinitive, *devolver* ("to give back"). This construction could also be expressed as, *¿Cuándo me los puede devolver?* But be sure not to place the pronoun between the two verb forms.

"Mañana, sin falta."
"Mahn-YA-na, seen FAHL-ta."
"Tomorrow, without fail."

Dos muchachas tienen una llanta pinchada.
Dohs moo-CHA-chahs T'YAY-nen OO-na L'YAHN-ta peen-CHA-da.
Two girls have a flat tire.

No pueden cambiarla ellas mismas
No PWAY-den kahm-B'YAR-la EL-yahs MEES-mahs
They can't change it themselves

porque les falta un gato.
por-kay lays FAHL-ta oon GA-toh.
because they need a jack.

> **To need**
> "To need" is expressed by the word *faltar* —
> "to lack," used with the indirect object. In other
> words, when you need something it is lacking to
> you.
>
> > *Me falta una toalla* — I need a towel
> > *Les faltau dinero* — They need (or lack)
> > money

Allí viene un joven
Ahl-YEE V'YAY-neh oon HO-ven
There comes a young man

en un carro deportivo.
en oon KA-rro deh-por-TEE-vo.
in a sports car.

Les dice: "¿Puedo ayudarlas?"
Lays DEE-say: "¿PWAY-doh ah-yoo-DAR-lahs?"
He says to them: "May I help you?"

"¡Cómo no!
"¡KO-mo no!
"Of course!

¿Puede prestarnos su gato?"
¿PWAY-day prays-TAR-nohs soo GA-toh?"
Can you lend us your jack?"

> **For flat tires — Llantas pinchadas**
> The most frequent meaning for *gato* is "cat." It
> is also used for the automobile jack.

125

"Puedo hacer aun más," dice él.

"PWAY-doh ah-SEHR ah-OON mahs," DEE-say el.

"I can do even more," he says.

"Puedo cambiar la rueda yo mismo."

"PWAY-doh kham-B'YAR la RWAY-da yo MEES-mo."

"I can change the tire myself."

INSTANT CONVERSATION: A TV PROGRAM

RAÚL:
Ra-OOL:
Raul:

¡Qué lástima!
¡Kay LAHS-tee-ma!
What a shame!

"Qué" as an exclamation

Certain exclamations such as this one, *¡Qué lástima!* are so frequently used that you should learn them by heart. Others include:

¡Qué pena! — What a shame!
¡Qué chistoso! — How funny!
¡Qué raro! — How unusual!
¡Qué bien! — How fine!
¡Qué interesante! — How interesting!
¡Que amable! — How kind!
¡Qué sabroso! — How good! (Especially for food).
¡Qué barbaridad! — How awful!
¡Qué bonito! — How pretty!

Remember to change the *o* endings to *a* when referring to a feminine object, especially the final exclamation. . . .

Van a dar un buen programa
Vahn ah dar oon bwen pro-GRA-ma
They are going to give a good program

esta noche en la televisión
ESS-ta NO-chay en la tay-lay-vee-S'YOHN
tonight on television

pero no puedo verlo.
PAY-ro no PWAY-doh VAIR-lo.
but I can't see it.

JOSÉ:
Ho-SAY:
JOSEPH:
¿Por qué no?
¿Por kay no?
Why not?

RAÚL:
Porque mi televisión está rota.
POR-kay mee tay-lay-vee-S'YOHN ess-TA RRO-ta.
Because my television is broken.

Debo llamar al servicio de televisión
DAY-bo l'ya-MAR ahl sair-VEE-s'yo day tay-lay-vee-S'YOHN
I must call the television service

para repararla.
PA-ra ray-pa-RAR-la.
to repair it.

JOSÉ:
Mire, si quiere ver el programa,
MEE-ray, see K'YAY-ray vair el pro-GRA-ma,
Look, if you want to look at the program,

venga a mi casa.
VEN-ga ah mee KA-sa.
come to my house.

Puede verlo allá.
PWAY-day VAIR-lo ahl-YA.
You can see it there.

RAÚL:
Es Ud. muy amable.
Ess oo-STED mwee ah-MA-blay.
You are very kind.

128

Freedom in word order
Raúl says: *Es Ud. muy amable,* instead of *Ud. es muy amable,* in order to give a more polite twist to the phrase. Spanish, being essentially a poetic language, allows considerable latitude in word order.

Pero no quiero molestarlo.
PAIR-ro no K'YAY-ro mo-less-TAR-lo.
But I don't want to bother you.

JOSÉ:

¡Hombre! No es molestia.
¡OHM-bray! No ess mo-LESS-t'ya.
Really now! It's no bother.

Si es un buen programa
See ess oon bwen pro-GRA-ma
If it's a good program

yo quiero verlo también.
yo K'YAY-ro VAIR-lo tahm-B'YEN.
I want to see it too.

Podemos verlo juntos.
Po-DAY-mohs VAIR-lo HOON-tohs.
We can see it together.

¿Qué programa es?
¿Kay pro-GRA-ma ess?
What program is it?

RAÚL:

Es un programa de bailes flamencos
Ess oon pro-GRA-ma day BY-less fla-MEN-kohs
It's a program of flamenco dances

directo de Granada.
dee-REK-toh day Gra-NA-da.
directly from Granada.

JOSÉ:
¿Verdad? Quiero ver eso.
¿Vair-DAHD? K'YAY-ro vair AY-so.
Really? I want to see that.

¿A qué hora empieza?
¿Ah kay OH-ra emp-YAY-sa?
At what time does it start?

RAÚL:
A las diez en punto.
Ah lahs d'yess en POON-toh.
At ten sharp.

JOSÉ:
Entonces tenemos tiempo
En-TOHN-says tay-NAY-mohs T'YEM-po
Then we have time

para comer primero.
PA-ra ko-MAIR pree-MAY-ro.
to eat first.

¿No quiere comer conmigo?
¿No K'YAY-ray ko-MAIR kohn-MEE-go?
Don't you want to eat with me?

> **Conmigo**
> *Conmigo* ("with me") has the *-go* ending for eu-
> phonic reasons. *Consigo* is the corresponding
> form for *con él, con ella,* or *con Ud.*, but it must
> concern the action of the same person to whom
> it refers:
>
> *Lleve esto consigo* — Take this with you.
> but:
> *Voy con Ud.* — I'm going with you.

RAUL:
¡Magnífico! Pero yo quiero invitarle a Ud.
¡Mahg-NEE-fee-ko! PAY-ro yo K'YAY-ro een-vee-TAR-lay ah
⠀⠀⠀⠀⠀⠀⠀⠀⠀⠀⠀⠀⠀⠀⠀⠀⠀⠀⠀⠀⠀⠀**oo-STED.**
Magnificent (Great)! But I want to invite you.

JOSÉ:

¡Hombre! Eso no puede ser.
¡OHM-bray! AY-so no PWAY-day sair.
Man! That can't be.

Ud. tiene que ser mi invitado.
Oo-STED T'YAY-nay kay sair mee een-vee-TA-doh.
You must be my guest.

> **To have to**
> *Tener que,* which means "must" or "to have to," is followed by the infinitive of the verb referred to:
>
> I have to work. — *Tengo que trabajar.*
> You must see it. — *Tiene que verlo.*

Podemos comer en un pequeño restaurante
Po-DAY-mohs ko-MAIR en oon pay-KEN-yo rest-ow-RAHN-tay
We can eat at a little restaurant

que conozco.
kay ko-NOHS-ko.
that I know.

Está cerca de mi departamento.
Ess-TA SAIR-ka day mee day-par-ta-MEN-toh.
It's near my apartment.

Vamos. Debemos comer rápidamente
VA-mohs. Day-BAY-mohs ko-MAIR RA-pee-da-MEN-tay
Let's go. We must eat quickly

si no queremos perder el programa.
see no kay-RAY-mohs pair-DAIR el pro-GRA-ma.
if we don't wish to miss the program.

TEST YOUR SPANISH

Match these exclamations and phrases. Score 5 points for each correct match. See answers on following page.

1.	¡Qué lástima!	_____ How pretty!
2.	¡Qué pena!	_____ How funny!
3.	¡Qué chistoso!	_____ What a pity!
4.	¡Qué raro!	_____ How awful!
5.	¡Qué bien!	_____ How interesting!
6.	¡Qué bonito!	_____ How good!
7.	¡Qué interesante!	_____ How fine!
8.	¡Qué barbaridad!	_____ What a life!
9.	¡Qué bueno!	_____ What a shame!
10.	¡Qué vida!	_____ How unusual!
11.	¿Debe ir?	_____ Can you give it back to me?
12.	Debo trabajar.	_____ They can't come.
13.	Necesitamos dinero.	_____ I must work.
14.	¿Puede prestármelo?	_____ Can you lend it to me?
15.	¿Por qué no?	_____ We need money.
16.	¡Oigame!	_____ I want to see it.
17.	No pueden venir.	_____ I must call her.

18. Debo llamarla. _____ Listen to me!

19. Quiero verlo. _____ Must you go?

20. ¿Puede devolvérmelo? _____ Why not?

Answers: 6 3 1 8 7 9 5 10 2 4 20 17 12 14 13 19 18 16 11 15

SCORE _____%

step 12   HOW TO USE REFLEXIVE VERBS

El señor Herrera se levanta temprano.
El sen-YOR Eh-RRAY-ra say lay-VAHN-ta tem-PRA-no.
Mr. Herrera gets up early.

Se lava, se afeita,
Say LA-va, say ah-FAY-ta,
He washes (himself), he shaves (himself),

se cepilla los dientes
say say-PEEL-ya lohs D'YEN-tays
he brushes his teeth

y se peina.
ee say PAY-na.
and he combs (his hair).

Entonces se viste.
En-TOHN-says say VEES-tay.
Then he dresses (himself).

Reflexive verbs

This step deals principally with reflexive verbs. A reflexive verb means that it has a reflexive action on the subject. It shows what one does or is doing to oneself, like shaving, bathing, getting dressed, getting undressed, have a somewhat different meaning when used reflexively. *Levantar* means "to lift," but *levantarse* -"to lift oneself" means "to get up."

Reflexive verbs can be recognized when you see them in the dictionary by the *-se* attached to the infinitive. Here are the four forms you are familiar with for *levantarse:*

(*yo*) *me levanto*
(*Ud.*, *él*, *ella*) *se levanta*
(*nosotros*) *nos levantamos*
(*Uds.*, *ellos*, *ellas*) *se levantan*

Unlike the subject pronouns (in parenthesis) the reflexive pronouns cannot be dropped.

Un poco más tarde sus hijos se levantan.
Oon PO-ko mahs TAR-day soos EE-hohs say lay-VAHN-tahn.
A little later his children get up.

Se lavan, se peinan y se visten.
Say LA-vahn, say PAY-nahn ee say VEES-ten.
They wash themselves, they comb (their hair) and they dress themselves.

Entonces todos se sientan a la mesa
En-TOHN-say TOH-dohs say S'YEN-tahn ah la MAY-sa
Then they all sit down at the table

para desayunarse.
PA-ra des-ah-yoo-NAR-say.
to have breakfast.

Reflexive for emphasis
Other verbs, in themselves not reflexive, sometimes are given additional emphasis by being put in the reflexive.

ir — to go
irse — to go off
llevar — to carry
llevarse — to carry off

Se desayunan con jugo de naranja,
Say day-sa-YOO-nahn kohn HOO-go day na-RAHN-ha,
They have breakfast with orange juice,

panecillos y café con leche.
pa-nay-SEEL-yohs ee ka-FAY kohn LAY-chay.
rolls and coffee with milk.

El señor Herrera se pone la chaqueta
El sen-YOR Eh-RRAY-ra say PO-nay la cha-KAY-ta
Mr. Herrera puts on his jacket

y el sombrero
ee el sohm-BRAY-ro
and his hat

y se va a la oficina.
ee say va ah la oh-fee-SEE-na.
and goes off to the office.

Los niños se ponen las gorras,
Lohs NEEN-yohs say PO-nen lahs GO-rrahs,
The children put on their caps,

toman sus maletines
TOH-mahn soos ma-lay-TEE-nays
take their bookbags

y se van a la escuela.
ee say vahn ah la ess-KWAY-la.
and go off to school.

Ahora la señora Herrera
Ah-OH-ra la sen-YO-ra Eh-RRAY-ra
Now Mrs. Herrera

se siente cansada.
say S'YEN-tay kahn-SA-da.
feels tired.

Se acuesta otra vez para descansar
Say ah-KWES-ta OH-tra vess PA-ra des-kahn-SAR
She goes to bed again to rest

y pronto se duerme.
ee PROHN-toh say DWEHR-may.
and soon falls asleep.

En España y en Latinoamérica
En Ess-PAHN-ya ee en La-tee-no-ah-MAY-ree-ka
In Spain and in Latin America

se almuerza más tarde
say ahl-MWAIR-sa mahs TAR-day
one has lunch later

> **The impersonal se**
> Although *se almuerza* resembles a reflexive
> construction, this form is really the impersonal
> *se* for "one," as in the expression:
> *Aquí se habla español.* — Here one speaks
> Spanish.

que en los Estados Unidos,
kay en lohs Ess-TA-dohs Oo-NEE-dohs,
than in the United States,

usualmente a las dos y pico
oo-swahl-MEN-tay ah lahs dohs ee PEE-ko
usually a little after two

o más tarde aún.
oh mahs TAR-day ah-OON.
or even later.

Después del almuerzo muchas personas
Des-PWESS del ahl-MWAIR-so MOO-chahs pair-SO-nahs
After lunch many people

se acuestan y descansan.
say ah-KWESS-tahn ee des-KAHN-sahn.
lie down and rest.

Esto se llama la siesta.
ESS-toh say L'YA-ma la S'YESS-ta.
This is called the siesta.

Después de la siesta vuelven a trabajar.
Des-PWESS day la S'YES-ta VWEL-ven ah tra-ba-HAR.
After the siesta they go back to work.

Las oficinas y tiendas
Lahs oh-fee-SEE-nahs ee T'YEN-dahs
Offices and stores

están abiertas despúes de las cinco—
ess-TAHN ah-B'YEHR-tahs des-PWESS day lahs SEEN-ko—
are open after five—

hasta las siete u ocho.
AHS-ta lahs S'YEH-teh oo OH-cho.
until seven or eight.

Entonces la gente vuelve a casa para cenar
En-TOHN-sehs la HEN-tay VWEL-vay ah KA-sa PA-ra say-NAR
Then people return home to have dinner

o va a los restaurantes.
oh va ah lohs rest-ow-RAHN-tays.
or go to the restaurants.

— Señor Marín, ¿dónde piensa Ud.
Sen-YOR Mar-EEN, ¿DOHN-day P'YEN-sa oo-STED
Mr. Marin, where do you think

que es mejor vivir,
kay ess meh-HOR vee-VEER,
(that) it is better to live,

> **Retain the "que"**
> Que for "that" as a conjunction is not dropped
> as it tends to be in English.
>
> Do you think (that) he is coming?
> *¿Piensa Ud. que viene?*
> I think (that) she is very nice.
> *Pienso que ella es muy simpática.*

en los Estados Unidos
en lohs Ess-TA-dohs Oo-NEE-dohs
in the United States

o en los países latinos?
oh en lohs pa-EE-says la-TEE-nohs?
or in the Latin countries?

— Pienso que es mejor vivir en España
P'YEN-so kay ess meh-HOR vee-VEER en Ess-PAHN-ya
I think that it is better to live in Spain

o en Latinoamérica.
oh en La-tee-no-ah-MAY-ree-ka.
or in Latin America.

Nationalities of the Spanish world

Note the different nouns and adjectives for sections of Spanish-speaking America:

Latinoamérica — *latinoamericano*
Sud América — *sudamericano*
Sur América — *suramericano*
Hispanoamérica — *hispanoamericano*
Centroamérica — *centroamericano*

As Spanish is the chief language of more individual countries than any other tongue, you should know the adjectives corresponding to the Spanish speaking nationalities. These are given in the masculine form. If applied to a woman the adjective ends with an *a*.

Argentina — *argentino*
Bolivia — *boliviano*
Chile — *chileno*
Colombia — *colombiano*
Costa Rica — *costarricense* (masc. & fem.)
Cuba — *cubano*
Ecuador — *ecuatoriano*
España — *español*
Guatemala — *guatemalteco*
Honduras — *hondureño*
México — *mexicano*
Panamá — *panameño*
Paraguay — *paraguayo*
Perú — *peruano*
Puerto Rico — *puertorriqueño*
República Dominicana — *dominicano*
Salvador — *salvadoreño*
Uruguay — *uruguayo*
Venezuela — *venezolano*

— ¿Por qué?
¿Por kay?
Why?

— Porque allí se duerme la siesta
POR-kay ahl-YEE say DWAIR-may la S'YES'ta
Because there one sleeps the siesta

y hay más tiempo para descansar.
ee I mahs T'YEM-po PA-ra dess-kahn-SAR.
and there is more time to rest.

INSTANT CONVERSATION: GOING TO A BUSINESS MEETING

— ¡Apúrese! Vamos a llegar tarde a la reunión.
¡Ah-POO-reh-say! VA-mohs ah l'yeh-GAR TAR-day ah la ray-oo-N'YOHN.
Hurry up! We're going to be late for the meeting.

— ¡Cálmese! Tenemos tiempo todavía.
¡KAHL-may-say! Teh-NAY-mohs T'YEM-po toh-da-VEE-yah.
Calm down! We still have time.

> **Commands, positive & negative**
> When a reflexive verb is used as an affirmative command the reflexive pronoun follows and is attached. But when the command is negative, it goes in front and separate:
>
> Hurry up! — *¡Apúrese!*
> Don't hurry! — *¡No se apure!*

— Vamos a ver. ¿Qué más necesitamos?
VA-mohs ah vair. ¿Kay mahs nay-say-see-TA-mohs?
Let's see. What more do we need?

— No se olvide de llevarse los informes.
No say ol-VEE-day day l'yay-VAR-say lohs een-FOR-mays.
Don't forget to take the reports.

Y debemos llevarnos también
Ee day-BAY-mohs l'yeh-VAR-nohs tahm-B'YEN
And we should also take along

la correspondencia sobre el contrato.
la ko-rres-pon-DEN-s'ya SO-bray el kohn-TRA-toh.
the correspondence on the contract.

— ¡Ya! Todo está listo.
¡Ya! TOH-doh ess-TA LEESS-toh.
There! Everything is ready.

> **Ya**
> Ya is an all important word for "Now!",
> "There!" "already", "still", "ready", "finally",
> etc., depending on how it is used.

¿Quién va a buscar el automóvil?
¿K'yen va ah boos-KAR el ow-toh-MO-veel?
Who is going to get the car?

— Yo voy. Quédese aquí.
Yo voy. KAY-day-say ah-KEE.
I'll go. Stay here.

No se vaya. Vuelvo en seguida.
No say VA-ya. VWEL-vo en say-GHEE-da.
Don't go away. I'll be right back.

> **Present tense for the future**
> The present tense is frequently used for the future tense:
>
> > Vuelvo can mean: I'm coming back.
> > I come back.
> > or, I'll be back.
>
> The regular future tense will be discussed in step 17.

— ¡Espérese! Lo más importante de todo —
¡Ess-PAY-ray-say! Lo mahs eem-por-TAHN-tay day TOH-doh —
Wait! The most important thing of all —

el contrato. ¿Dónde está?
el kohn-TRA-toh. ¿DOHN-day ess-TA?
the contract. Where is it?

> **"Lo" with a adjectives**
> Lo and an adjective can best be translated as
> though they are followed by "thing" or
> "aspect."
>
> > Lo importante — The important thing

Lo chistoso — The funny thing
Lo raro — The unusual thing

Lo más chistoso — The funniest (thing)
Lo más raro — The most unusual (thing)

Lo más raro del caso — The most unusual
aspect of the affair

— ¡Hombre! No se preocupe.
¡OHM-bray! No say pray-oh-KOO-pay.
Now really! Don't worry.

Aquí lo tengo.
Ah-KEE lo TEN-go.
I have it here.

Cálmese y, sobre todo,
KAHL-may-say ee, SO-bray TOH-doh,
Calm yourself and, above all,

no se ponga nervioso durante la reunión.
no se POHN-ga nair-v'YO-so doo-RAHN-tay la ray-oon-YOHN.
don't get nervous during the meeting.

143

TEST YOUR SPANISH

Translate these phrases into Spanish using reflexive verbs. Score 10 points for each correct translation. See answers below.

1. He gets up.

2. He washes himself.

3. He shaves himself.

4. They dress themselves.

5. They sit down.

6. He puts on his hat.

7. I have breakfast.

8. She goes to bed.

9. Don't forget.

10. Don't worry.

SCORE ____%

144

Es un día de verano en la playa.
Ess oon DEE-ya day vay-RA-no en la PLA-ya.
It is a summer's day at the beach.

El cielo es azul claro
El S'YAY-lo ess ah-SOOL KLA-ro
The sky is light blue

con nubes blancas.
kohn NOO-bays BLAHN-kahs.
with white clouds.

El mar es azul oscuro.
El mar ess ah-SOOL ohs-KOO-ro.
The sea is dark blue.

Tres muchachas están sentadas en la playa.
Trayss moo-CHA-chahs ess-TAHN sen-TA-dahs en la PLA-ya.
Three girls are seated on the beach.

No quieren nadar.
No K'YAY-ren na-DAR.
They don't want to swim.

El agua está fría,
El AH-gwa ess-TA FREE-yah,
The water is cold,

A matter of euphony
Although *agua* is feminine and should take *la* as a singular article, it uses *el* so that two "a's" do not come together.

el agua — the water   *las aguas* — the waters

Other words of this type include (*el*) *alma* — "soul", and (*el*) *arte* — "art".

pero el sol está caliente.
PAIR-ro el sol ess-TA ka-L'YEN-tay.
but the sun is hot.

Les gusta tomar el sol.
Lays GOOS-ta toh-MAR el sol.
They like to take the sun.

It pleases you
Gustar ("to like") is a verb used with the indirect object. Whatever is liked becomes the subject. Instead of literally saying "I like", in Spanish we say "it pleases me".

I like — *me gusta*
you like, he or she likes — *le gusta*
we like — *nos gusta*
you (plural) or they like — *les gusta*

However, if what you like is plural, then *gusta* becomes *gustan*.

Do you like American movies?
¿Le gustan las películas americanas?

Gustar means "to prefer" or "to like more" when *más* is used with it.

Which do you prefer? — *¿Cuál le gusta más?*

Una de ellas tiene
OO-na day EHL-yahs T'YAY-nay
One of them has

un traje de baño rojo y blanco.
oon TRA-hay day BAHN-yo RO-ho ee BLAHN-ko.
a red and white bathing suit.

El traje de la otra es verde.
El TRA-hay day la OH-tra ess VAIR-day.
The other's suit is green.

La tercera lleva un bikini negro.
La tair-SAY-ra l'YAY'va oon bee-KEE-nee NAY-gro.
The third one is wearing a black bikini.

Delante de las muchachas
Day-LAHN-tay day lahs moo-CHA-chahs
In front of the girls

unos jóvenes están tocando guitarra
OO-nohs HO-vay-nays ess-TAHN toh-KAHN-doh ghee-TA-rra
some young men are playing the guitar

y cantando canciones.
ee kahn-TAHN-doh kahn-S'YO-nays.
and singing songs.

Las chicas están escuchando la música.
Lahs CHEE-kahs ess-TAHN ess-koo-CHAHN-doh la MOO-see-ka.
The girls are listening to the music.

A ellas les gusta oír la música.
Ah EL-yahs lays GOOS-ta oh-EER la MOO-see-ka.
They like to hear the music.

A los muchachos les gusta tocar.
Ah lohs moo-CHA-chohs lays GOOS-ta toh-KAR.
The boys like to play.

La muchacha rubia le dice
La moo-CHA-cha ROO-b'ya lay DEE-say
The blonde girl says

> **A double indirect object**
> Le dice means "says to her" and the expression a la trigueña means "to the brunette," so the sentence has two indirect objects. This use of double indirect objects is a frequent occurrence.

a la trigueña:
a la tree-GHEN-ya:
to the brunette:

"Qué bien cantan, ¿verdad?"
"Kay b'yen KAHN-tahn, ¿vair-DAHD?"
"How well they sing, don't they?"

"Es cierto," responde ella.
"Ess S'YAIR-toh," res-POHN-day EL-ya.
"It's true," she answers.

"Todos cantan bien,
"TOH-dohs KAHN-tahn b'yen,
"They all sing well,

pero el de la izquierda canta mejor que los otros."
**PAIR-ro el day la ees-k'YAIR-da KAHN-ta meh-HOR kay lohs
OH-trohs."**
but the one on the left sings better than the others."

"Se equivoca," dice la rubia.
"Say ay-kee-VO-ka," DEE-say la ROO-b'ya.
"You are wrong," says the blond.

"El que está a la derecha canta el mejor de todos."
**"El kay ess-TA ah la day-RAY-cha KAHN-ta el may-HOR day
toh-dohs."**
"The one who is on the right sings the best of all."

Comparison of adverbs
Note the following comparisons of adverbs. Adverbs are compared regularly like this:

>slowly, more slowly, the most slowly (of all)
>*despacio, más despacio, el (la, etc.) más
>despacio*

and the exceptions:

>well, better, the best
>*bien, mejor, el mejor*
>badly, worse, the worst
>*mal, peor, el peor*

Después de un rato los chicos dejan de cantar.
**Des-PWES day oon RA-toh lohs CHEE-kohs DAY-hahn day
kahn-TAR.**
After a while, the boys stop singing.

Uno dice al otro
OO-no DEE-say ahl OH-tro
One says to the other

"Son bonitas esas chicas, ¿no?"
"Sohn bo-NEE-tahs ES-sahs CHEE-kahs, ¿no?"
"They are pretty, those girls, aren't they?"

"A mí me gusta más la trigueña."
"Ah mee may GOOS-ta mahs la tree-GAYN-ya."
"I prefer the dark one."

"¡Qué va!" dice el otro,
"¡Kay va!" DEE-say el OH-tro,
"Don't be silly," says the other,

"la rubia es más bonita que ella."
"la ROO-b'ya ess mahs bo-NEE-ta kay EL-ya."
"the blonde is prettier than she."

El tercero dice, "Mentira — la pelirroja es la más bonita de todas."
El tair-SAIR-ro DEE-say, "Men-TEE-ra — la pay-lee-RRO-ha ess la mahs bo-NEE-ta day TOH-dahs."
The third one says, "Not true — the redhead is the prettiest of all."

Comparison of adjectives
Adjectives are compared by prefixing *más* for
the comparative and *el* (or *la* or their plurals)
followed by *más* for the superlative.

> big, bigger, biggest
> *grande, más grande, el más grande*
> small, smaller, smallest
> *pequeño, más pequeño, el más pequeño*

and the irregular:

> good, better, best
> *bueno, mejor, el mejor*
> bad, worse, the worst
> *malo, peor, el peor*

INSTANT CONVERSATION: SHOPPING

UNA SEÑORA:
OO-na sen-YO-ra
A LADY:
> Tenemos que comprar unos regalos
> **Tay-NAY-mohs kay kohm-PRAR OO-nohs ray-GA-lohs**
> We have to buy some gifts
>
> para los amigos y la familia.
> **PA-ra lohs ah-MEE-gohs ee la fa-MEEL-ya.**
> for our friends and family.
>
> Aquí hay una tienda buena. ¿Entramos?
> **Ah-KEE I OO-na T'YEN-da BWAY-na. ¿En-TRA-mohs?**
> Here is a nice store. Shall we go in?

UNA EMPLEADA:
OO-na em-pleh-YA-da
AN EMPLOYEE:
> ¿Ud. desea, señora?
> **¿Oo-STED deh-SAY-ah, sen-YO-ra?**
> You wish, madam?

LA SEÑORA:
> Por favor, muéstrenos
> **Por fa-VOR, MWESS-tray-nohs**
> Please, show us
>
> algunos pañuelos de seda.
> **ahl-GOO-nohs pahn-WAY-lohs day SAY-da.**
> some silk scarves.

> **Pañuelo**
> *Pañuelo* means "handkerchief" as well as
> "small scarf."

LA EMPLEADA:
Aquí tiene dos, señora,
Ah-KEE T'YAY-nay dohs, sen-YO-ra,
Here are two, madam,

Verde y azul
VAIR-day ee ah-ZOOL
Green and blue

o negro y blanco.
oh NAY-gro ee BLAHN-ko.
or black and white.

Not all adjectives change
Not all adjectives change for masculine and feminine. If an adjective ends in an -e like *verde,* or a consonant like *azul,* it stays the way it is. However, when the noun is plural, an -s is added (if the adjective ends in a vowel) or -es if necessary to make a vowel sound.

> *la vela azul* — the blue sail
> *las velas azules* — the blue sails

¿Le gustan?
¿Lay GOOS-tahn?
Do you like them?

LA SEÑORA:
Me gusta éste.
May GOOS-ta ESS-tay.
I like this one.

Los colores son más alegres,
Lohs ko-LO-rays sohn mahs ah-LAY-grays,
The colors are more cheerful,

y el diseño es más bonito.
ee el dee-SEN-yo ess mahs bo-NEE-toh.
and the design is prettier.

LA SEÑORA:

¿Cuánto cuesta?

¿KWAN-toh KWESS-ta?

How much is it?

LA EMPLEADA:

Doscientos diez pesos, señora.

Dohs-S'YEN-tohs d'yess PAY-sohs, sen-YO-ra.

Two hundred and ten pesos, madam.

LA SEÑORA:

¡Caramba! Es un poco caro.

¡Ka-RAHM-ba! Ess oon PO-ko KA-ro.

Oh! It's a little expensive.

> **¡Caramba!**
> *¡Caramba!* is really untranslatable. It means:
> "Well, now," "You don't say," "Heavens!" etc.
> depending on the speaker.

LA SEÑORA:

¿Tiene algo un poco más económico?

¿T'YAY-nay AHL-go oon PO-ko mahs ay-ko-NO-mee-ko?

Have you something a little cheaper?

LA EMPLEADA:

Sí, señora. Pero no es de seda pura.

See, sen-YO-ra. PAY-ro no ess day SAY-da POO-ra.

Yes, madam. But it is not pure silk.

¿Cómo encuentra estos?

¿KO-mo en-KWEN-tra ESS-tohs?

How do you find these?

Vienen en amarillo, rosa,

V'YAY-nen en ah-ma-REEL-yo, RO-sa,

They come in yellow, pink,

violeta y otros colores.

v'yo-LAY-ta ee OH-trohs ko-LO-rays.

violet and other colors.

Además, son menos caros.
Ah-day-MAHS, sohn MAY-nohs KA-rohs.
Besides, they are less expensive.

Setenta y cinco pesos.
Seh-TAYN-ta ee SEEN-ko PAY-sohs.
Seventy-five pesos.

LA SEÑORA:
No son tan bonitos como los otros.
No sohn tahn bo-NEE-tohs KO-mo lohs OH-trohs.
They are not so pretty as the others.

> **Tan**
> *Tan* meaning "so" is used in negative comparisons:
>
> > not so expensive — *no tan caro*
> > not so good — *no tan bueno*

Sin embargo, vamos a comprar
Seen em-BAR-go, VA-mohs ah kohm-PRAR
However, let's buy

éste de color violeta
ESS-tay day ko-LOR v'yo-LAY-ta
this violet one

para tía Isabel.
PA-ra TEE-ya Ee-sa-BEL.
for aunt Isabel.

EL MARIDO DE LA SEÑORA:
El ma-REE-doh day la sen-YO-ra
The lady's husband
De acuerdo. Y ahora,
Day ah-KWAIR-doh. Ee ah-OH-ra,
All right, and now,

> **In accord**
> *De acuerdo*, literally "in accord" is another way of saying "all right" or "agreed."
>
> > Are you in agreement? — *¿Está de acuerdo?*

¿qué compramos para mamá?
¿kay kohm-PRA-mohs PA-ra ma-MA?
what shall we buy for mother?

LA EMPLEADA:
Mire este bonito collar, señor.
MEE-ray ESS-tay bo-NEE-toh kohl-YAR, sen-YOR.
Look at this pretty necklace, sir.

> **Not the same**
> Sometimes Spanish words resemble English
> ones, but have different meanings. *Collar* is
> "necklace"; the English "collar" is rendered by
> *cuello*, which also means "neck."

Cuesta sólo trescientos treinta pesos.
KWES-ta SO-lo trayss-S'YEN-tohs TRAIN-ta PAY-sohs.
It costs only three hundred and thirty pesos.

Es muy hermoso, ¿no le parece?
Ess mwee air-MO-so, ¿no lay pa-REH-say?
It's very beautiful, don't you think so?

EL MARIDO:
Sí, es verdad.
See, ess vair-DAHD.
Yes, that's true.

LA SEÑORA:
¿Lo compramos, querido?
¿Lo kohm-PRA-mohs, kay-REE-doh?
Shall we buy it, dear?

EL MARIDO:
Sí, ¿por qué no? Lo tomamos.
See, ¿por kay no? Lo toh-MA-mohs.
Yes, why not? We'll take it.

Y ahora, quisiera comprar
Ee ah-OH-ra, kee-S'YAY-ra kohm-PRAR
And now, I'd like to buy

"Want" or "would like"
Quisiera ("would like") is a special form of
querer — the imperfect subjunctive. This tense
will be introduced in a later step, but it is useful
to learn this one form here which can be used
for *yo, Ud., él,* and *ella* because it is so common in everyday speech. In Spanish as in English, it is more polite to say "I would like" than
"I want."

What do you want? — *¿Qué quiere?*
What would you like? — *¿Qué quisiera?*

In the latter case, adding Ud. at the end would
make the construction even more polite.

algo para mi secretaria.
AHL-go PA-ra mee say-kray-TA-r'ya.
something for my secretary.

Aquellos aretes grandes —
Ah-KEL-yohs ah-RAY-tays GRAHN-days —
Those big earrings —

¿quiere mostrármelos?
¿K'YAY-ray mohs-TRAR-may-lohs?
will you show them to me?

LA EMPLEADA:
Ciertamente, señor.
S'yair-ta-MEN-tay, sen-YOR.
Certainly, sir.

Son de oro,
Sohn day OH-ro,
They are (made) of gold,

y son muy bonitos.
ee sohn mwee bo-NEE-tohs.
and are very pretty.

LA SEÑORA:
Alfredo, ¡por Dios!
Ahl-FRAY-doh, ¡por D'yohs!
Alfredo, really!

155

No podemos gastar tanto dinero
No po-DAY-mohs gahs-TAR TAHN-toh dee-NAY-ro
We cannot spend so much money

en regalos.
en ray-GA-lohs.
on presents.

En todo caso,
En TOH-doh KA-so,
In any case,

esos aretes no se pueden llevar
ES-sohs ah-RAY-tays no say PWAY-den l'yay-VAR
those earrings cannot be worn

Reflexive and passive
The reflexive and passive have the same form, literally translated *no se pueden llevar* is "not able to wear themselves."

en la oficina.
en la oh-fee-SEE-na.
in the office.

¿Por qué no comprar
¿Por kay no kohm-PRAR
Why not buy

aquel prendedor de plata
ah-KEL pren-day-DOR day PLA-ta
that silver pin over there

en forma de paloma?
en FOR-ma day pa-LO-ma?
shaped like a dove?

Es un bonito recuerdo —
Ess oon bo-NEE-toh rray-KWEHR-doh —
It's a pretty souvenir —

y práctico.
ee PRAHK-tee-ko.
and practical.

EL MARIDO:
Pues, bien.
Pwess, b'yen.
Then, all right.

Tomo el prendedor.
TOH-mo el pren-day-DOR.
I'll take the pin.

LA EMPLEADA:
Señora, ¿no quiere Ud. ver los aretes?
Sen-YO-ra, ¿no K'YAY-ray oo-STED vair lohs ah-RAY-tays?
Madam, don't you want to see the earrings?

Son lindos, ¿no?
Sohn LEEN-dohs, ¿no?
They are lovely, aren't they?

LA SEÑORA:
Sí, ¡son exquisitos!
See, ¡sohn ess-kee-SEE-tohs!
Yes, they are exquisite!

Pero supongo que son muy caros.
PAIR-ro soo-POHN-go kay sohn mwee KA-rohs.
But I suppose they are very expensive.

> **The added prefix**
> *Supongo* is from *suponer,* and is therefore con-
> jugated the same as *poner.* Such verbs are
> usually easy to recognize as only the prefix is
> different.

LA EMPLEADA:
Bastante, pero son de los mejores.
Bahs-TAHN-tay, PAY-ro sohn day lohs may-HO-rays.
Quite, but they are of the best.

Valen doscientos cuarenta pesos.
VA-len dohs-S'YEN-tohs kwa-REN-ta PAY-sohs.
They are worth two hundred and forty pesos.

Spanish Step by Step

EL MARIDO:
No importa.
No eem-POR-ta.
It doesn't matter.

Los compro para mi mujer.
Lohs KOHM-pro PA-ra mee moo-HAIR.
I'll buy them for my wife.

LA SEÑORA:
¡Ay! ¡Qué amable!
¡I! ¡Kay ah-MA-blay!
Oh! How nice!

Un millón de gracias, querido mío.
Oon meel-YOHN day GRA-s'yahs, kay-REE-doh MEE-yo.
A million thanks, my dear.

Possessives after the noun
When the possessive adjective is used after the noun *mi* becomes *mío* and *su* becomes *suyo*. It has the same meaning as if it were before the noun, but is a bit more intensive, as used here.

TEST YOUR SPANISH

Fill in the verb forms. Score 10 points for each correct answer. See answers below.

1. Shall we go in?
   ¿ _____?

2. You wish, madam?
   ¿Ud. _____, señora?

3. Do you like them?
   ¿Le _____?

4. I like this one.
   Me _____ éste,

5. Shall we buy it?
   ¿Lo _____?

6. We'll take it.
   Lo _____.

7. Will you show them to me?
   ¿Quiere _____?

8. Which do you prefer?
   ¿Cuál le _____más?

9. What do you want?
   ¿Qué _____?

10. What would you like to buy?
    ¿Qué _____comprar?

Answers: 1. ¿Entramos? 2. desea 3. gustan 4. gusta. 5. compramos 6. tomamos 7. mostrármelos 8. gusta 9. quiere 10. quisiera

SCORE _____%

159

MARKETING AND
NAMES OF FOODS

Una señora va al mercado.
OO-na sen-YO-ra va ahl mair-KA-doh.
A lady goes to the market.

Va primero a la carnicería.
Va pree-MAY-ro ah la kar-nee-say-REE-ya.
She goes first to the butcher's.

Ella le pregunta al carnicero:
EL-ya lay pray-GOON-ta ahl kar-nee-SAY-ro:
She asks the butcher:

The -ero suffix
When a noun ends in -ero it often indicates the
person who performs an action or sells something. The first part of the word gives you the
key to what it is.

cartero — mail carrier
verdulero — vegetable seller
cochero — driver
tendero — shopkeeper
carnicero — butcher
panadero — baker
ranchero — rancher, farmer
zapatero — shoemaker
camarero — waiter
basurero — garbage man
marinero — sailor
pistolero — gunman

"¿Cuánto vale esta carne por kilo?"
"¿KWAN-toh VA-lay ESS-ta KAR-nay por KEE-lo?"
"How much is this meat per kilo?"

Compra filete de bistek,
KOHM-pra fee-LAY-tay day bees-TEK,
She buys steak,

un pollo, cerdo, jamón,
oon POHL-yo, SAIR-doh, ha-MOHN,
a chicken, pork, ham,

y chuletas de cordero.
ee choo-LAY-tahs day kor-DAY-ro.
and lamb chops.

Después va a la verdulería.
Des-PWESS va ah la vair-doo-lay-REE-ya.
Afterwards she goes to the vegetable stand.

> **The -ía suffix**
> When a noun ends in *ía* it frequently indicates a place where something is sold:
>
> *carnicería* — butcher shop
> *librería* — book store
> *florería* — flower shop
> *peluquería* — barber shop
> *panadería* — bakery
> *pastelería* — pastry shop
> *lechería* — dairy
> *zapatería* — shoe shop
> *sastrería* — (the) tailor's
> *tintorería* — (the) dry cleaner's
>
> and not to forget *cafetería*, which is already a part of English.

Compra verduras, judías verdes, hongos,
KOHM-pra vair-DOO-rahs, hoo-DEE-yahs VAIR-days, OHN-gohs,
She buys vegetables, green beans, mushrooms,

cebollas, tomates, lechuga, frijoles, y ajo.
say-BOHL-yahs, toh-MA-tays, lay-CHOO-ga, free-HO-lays, ee AH-ho.
onions, tomatoes, lettuce, beans, and garlic.

Consulta su lista otra vez
Kohn-SOOL-ta soo LEE-sta OH-tra vess
She consults her list again.

"A ver, ¿falta algo?
"Ah vair, ¿FAHL-ta AHL-go?
"Let's see, is anything missing?

Ah, sí . . . Debo comprar algunas frutas . . .
Ah, see . . . DAY-bo kohm-PRAR ahl-GOO-nahs FROO-tahs . . .
Oh, yes . . . I must buy some fruit . . .

naranjas, limones, piñas,
na-RAHN-hahs, lee-MO-nays, PEEN-yahs,
oranges, lemons, pineapples,

plátanos, manzanas, uvas y duraznos."
PLA-ta-nohs, mahn-SA-nahs, OO-vahs ee doo-RAHS-nohs."
bananas, apples, grapes and peaches."

Entonces en la tienda de comestibles
En-TOHN-says en la T'YEN-da day ko-may-STEE-blays
Then in the grocery store

compra arroz, café, azúcar, sal,
KOHM-pra ah-RROHS, ka-FAY, ah-SOO-kar, sahl,
she buys rice, coffee, sugar, salt,

pimienta, aceite de oliva, y salsa picante.
**pee-M'YEN-ta, ah-SAY-tay day oh-LEE-va, ee SAHL-sa
pee-KAHN-tay.**
pepper, olive oil and hot sauce.

Luego va a la panadería.
LWAY-go va ah la pa-na-day-REE-ya.
Then she goes to the bakery.

Allí compra pan, panecillos,
Ahl-YEE KOHM-pra pahn, pa-nay-SEEL-yohs,
There she buys bread, rolls,

galletas y una torta.
gahl-YAY-tahs ee OO-na TOR-ta.
cookies and a cake.

162

En la lechería compra leche, crema,
En la lay-chay-REE-ya KOHM-pra LAY-chay, KRAY-ma,
At the dairy she buys milk, cream,

mantequilla y una docena de huevos.
mahn-tay-KEEL-ya ee OO-na doh-SAY-na day WAY-vohs.
butter and a dozen eggs.

En la pescadería compra un pescado,
En la pess-ka-day-REE-ya KOHM-pra oon pess-KA-doh,
At the fish market she buys a fish,

dos kilos de camarones y una langosta.
dohs KEE-lohs day ka-ma-RO-nays ee OO-na lahn-GOHS-ta.
two kilos of shrimps and a lobster.

Pregunta: "¿Está todo esto fresco?"
Preh-GOON-ta: "¿Ess-TA TOH-doh ESS-toh FRES-ko?"
She asks: "Is this all fresh?"

El tendero contesta:
El ten-DAY-ro kohn-TESS-ta:
The shopkeeper replies:

"Desde luego, señora. ¡Está fresquísimo!"
"DES-day LWAY-go, sen-YO-ra. ¡Ess-TA fres-KEE-see-mo!"
"Of course, madam. It is very fresh!"

Luego vuelve a casa con su auto cargado de paquetes.
**L'WAY-go VWEL-vay ah KA-sa kohn soo OW-toh car-GA-doh day
pa-KAY-tays.**
Then she returns home with her car loaded with packages.

Tiene bastante comida para una semana.
T'YAY-nay bahs-TAHN-tay ko-MEE-da PA-ra OO-na say-MA-na.
She has enough food for a week.

163

INSTANT CONVERSATION: IN A RESTAURANT

UN CLIENTE:
Oon klee-YEN-tay:
A CUSTOMER:
> ¿Está libre esta mesa?
> **¿Ess-TA LEE-bray ESS-ta MAY-sa?**
> Is this table free?

UN CAMARERO:
Oon ka-ma-RAY-ro:
A WAITER:
> Cómo no, señor.
> **KO-mo no, sen-YOR.**
> Certainly, sir.

> **¡Cómo no!**
> *¡Cómo no!* literally "how not!" is a good way to say "Certainly!". Other frequent idiomatic expressions for saying "yes" include:
>
> > *Desde luego.* — Of course.
> > *Claro.* — Certainly. Of course.
> > *Seguro or Seguramente.* — Surely.

> Siéntese, por favor.
> **S'YEN-tay-say, por fa-VOR.**
> Sit down, please.

> Aquí tiene la lista de platos.
> **Ah-KEE T'YAY-nay la LEES-ta day PLA-tohs.**
> Here is the menu.

EL CLIENTE:
> Gracias. Para empezar,
> **GRA-s'yahs. PA-ra em-pay-SAR,**
> Thank you. To start,

164

un coctel de camarones.
oon kohk-TEL day ka-ma-RO-nays.
a shrimp cocktail.

EL CAMARERO:
Y ¿de sopa?
Ee ¿day SO-pa?
And for soup?

Tenemos un gazpacho frío muy bueno.
Tay-NAY-mohs oon gahs-PA-cho FREE-yo mwee BWAY-no.
We have a very good cold gazpacho.

EL CLIENTE:
No quiero sopa, gracias.
No K'YAY-ro SO-pa, GRA-s'yahs.
I don't want soup, thank you.

EL CAMARERO:
Bien, señor.
B'yen, sen-YOR.
Very well, sir.

Y como plato principal
Ee KO-mo PLA-toh preen-see-PAHL
And as a main course

tenemos arroz con pollo,
tay-NAY-mohs ah-RROHS kohn POHL-yo,
we have chicken with rice,

lechón asado,
lay-CHOHN ah-SA-do,
roast pork,

ropa vieja,
RO-pa V'YAY-ha,
braised beef,

y el picadillo está muy bueno.
ee el pee-ka-DEEL-yo ess-TA mwee BWAY-no.
and the spiced chopped beef is very good.

EL CLIENTE:

Yo prefiero un filete.

Yo pray-F'YAY-ro oon fee-LAY-tay.

I prefer a steak.

EL CAMARERO:

Perfectamente, señor.

Pair-fek-ta-MEN-tay, sen-YOR.

Very well, sir.

¿Cómo le gusta el filete —

¿KO-mo lay GOOS-ta el fee-LAY-tay —

How do you like the steak —

poco cocido, término medio, bien cocido?

PO-ko ko-SEE-do, TAIR-mee-no MAY-d'yo, b'yen ko-SEE-doh?

rare, medium, well done?

EL CLIENTE:

A mí me gusta poco cocido.

Ah mee may GOOS-ta PO-ko ko-SEE-do.

I like it rare.

EL CAMARERO:

Y, ¿qué verduras quiere?

Ee, ¿kay vehr-DOO-rahs K'YAY-ray?

And what vegetables do you wish?

EL CLIENTE:

Guisantes, papas fritas,

Ghee-SAHN-tays, PA-pahs FREE-tahs,

Peas, fried potatoes,

y una ensalada con aceite y vinagre.

ee OO-na en-sa-LA-da kohn ah-SAY-tay ee vee-NA-gray.

and a salad with oil and vinegar.

Y, con el filete,

Ee, kohn el fee-LAY-tay,

And, with the steak,

una botella de vino tinto.

OO-na bo-TEL-ya day VEE-no TEEN-toh.

a bottle of red wine.

Marqués de Riscal, si lo tiene.
Mar-KAYS day Rees-KAHL, see lo T'YAY-nay.
Marqués de Riscal, if you have it.

EL CAMARERO:
En seguida, señor.
En say-GEE-da, sen-YOR.
Right away, sir.

EL CAMARERO:
¿El señor desea postre?
¿El sen-YOR day-SAY-ah POHS-tray?
Does the gentleman wish dessert?

¿Flan, un pastel?
¿Flahn, oon pahs-TEL?
Custard, a piece of pastry?

EL CLIENTE:
Vamos a ver.
VA-mohs ah vair.
Let's see.

Tráigame, pues, queso con guayaba
TRY-ga-may, pwess, KAY-so kohn gwa-YA-ba
Well, bring me cheese with guava

y luego café.
ee LWAY-go ka-FAY.
and then coffee.

EL CLIENTE:
La cuenta, por favor.
La KWEN-ta, por fa-VOR.
The bill, please.

EL CAMARERO:
Aquí la tiene, caballero.
Ah-KEE la T'YAY-nay, ka-bahl-YAY-ro.
Here you are, sir.

EL CLIENTE:

Dígame — ¿Está el servicio incluído
DEE-ga-may — ¿Ess-TA el sehr-VEE-s'yo een-kloo-EE-doh
Tell me — Is the service included

> **¿Servicio incluído?**
> In many places, bills in restaurants and hotels are increased by a ten to fifteen percent charge for what, in Spain, is called *servicio*. The "service charge" is, in effect, a mandatory tip.

en la cuenta?
en la KWEN-ta?
in the bill?

EL CAMARERO:

No, señor. No está incluído.
No, sen-YOR. No ess-TA een-kloo-EE-doh.
No, sir. It is not included.

¿Está satisfecho con su almuerzo?
¿Ess-TA sa-tees-FAY-cho kohn soo ahl-MWAIR-so?
Are you satisfied with your lunch?

EL CLIENTE:

¡Cómo no! La comida aquí es excelente.
¡KO-mo no! La ko-MEE-da ah-KEE ess ek-say-LEN-tay.
Yes, indeed! The food here is excellent.

Tenga.
TEN-ga.
Here you are.

EL CAMARERO:

Gracias, señor.
GRA-s'yahs, sen-YOR.
Thank you, sir.

Vuelvo enseguida con el cambio.
VWEL-vo en-say-GHEE-da kohn el KAHM-b'yo.
I'll be right back with the change.

168

EL CLIENTE:
No se moleste. Guárdelo.
No say mo-LAYS-tay. GWAHR-day-lo.
Don't bother. Keep it.

> **No es molestia**
> "To bother (oneself)" or "to take the trouble"
> is expressed by the reflexive verb *molestarse.*
> Sometimes you will hear the noun *molestia*
> used:
>
> > *No se moleste.* — Don't bother (yourself).
> > *Al contrario, no es molestia* — On the con-
> > trary, it's no bother.

EL CAMARERO:
Mil gracias, caballero.
Meel GRA-s'yahs, ka-bahl-YAY-ro.
A thousand thanks, sir.

Vuelva otra vez.
VWEL-va OH-tra vess.
Come back again.

TEST YOUR SPANISH

Write the Spanish equivalents for these occupations and shops. Score 10 points for each correct answer. See answers below.

1. butcher _____

2. shopkeeper _____

3. mailman _____

4. baker _____

5. rancher _____

6. gunman _____

7. flower shop _____

8. butcher shop _____

9. dairy _____

10. cafeteria _____

Answers: 1. carnicero 2. tendero 3. cartero 4. panadero 5. ranchero 6. pistolero 7. florería 8. carnicería 9. lechería 10. cafetería

SCORE _____%

HOW AND WHEN
TO USE THE
FAMILIAR FORM

Estos son unos ejemplos
ESS-tohs sohn OO-nohs ay-HEM-plohs
These are some examples.

del uso de *tú*.
del OO-so day *too*.
of the use of (the familiar) *you*.

Tú se usa entre miembros de una familia.
***Too* say OO-sa EN-tray M'YEM-brohs day OO-na fa-MEEL-ya.**
Tú is used between members of a family.

"Tú" the familiar "you"

Tú, the familiar form for "you", is the pronoun used in informal speech, and implies a certain degree of intimacy. The present tense of the verb used with *tú* is formed by adding -*s* to the form for *Ud., él, and ella*. The affirmative imperative or command form for *tú* is generally the same as the regular form for *Ud.:*

Study! — *¡Estudia!*
Learn! — *¡Aprende!*
Write! — *¡Escribe!*

The object form of *tú* is *te*, and the possessive is *tu*, without an accent to avoid confusion with the subject *tú*.

Following a preposition the familiar form is *ti*, and, when combined with *con*, it becomes *contigo*.

UNA MADRE:
OO-na MA-dray:
A MOTHER:

171

¡Óyeme! ¡Termina tu comida!
¡OH-yay-may! ¡Tair-MEE-na too ko-MEE-da!
Listen to me! Finish your meal!

SU HIJA:
Soo EE-ha:
HER DAUGHTER:
No tengo hambre, mamá.
No TEN-go AHM-bray, ma-MA.
I'm not hungry, mother.

LA MADRE:
¡Tómate la leche también!
¡TOH-ma-tay la LAY-chay tahm-B'YEN!
Drink up the milk too!

LA HIJA:
No tengo sed tampoco.
No TEN-go sed tahm-PO-ko.
I'm not thirsty either.

LA MADRE:
Si no terminas todo,
See no tair-MEE-nahs TOH-doh,
If you don't finish everything,

se lo voy a decir a tu padre.
say lo voy ah day-SEER ah too PA-dray.
I am going to tell your father.

LA HIJA:
Pero mamá, ¿por qué
PAIR-ro ma-MA, ¿por kay
But mother, why

tú me haces comer tanto?
too may AH-says ko-MAIR TAHN-toh?
do you make me eat so much?

Yo no quiero ser gorda.
Yo no K'YAY-ro sehr GOR-da.
I don't want to be fat.

Tú se usa entre buenos amigos.
Too say OO-sa EN-tray BWAY-nohs ah-MEE-gohs.
Tú is used between good friends.

— Hola, Pepe. ¿Cómo estás?
OH-la, PAY-pay. ¿KO-mo ess-TAHS?
Hi, Joe. How are you?

— Regular, Julio. ¿Y tú?
Reh-goo-LAR, HOO-l'yo. ¿Ee too?
All right, Julio. And you?

— Así, así. Mira, ¿sabes que hay una fiesta
Ah-SEE, ah-SEE. MEE-ra, ¿SA-bays kay I OO-na F'YESS-ta
So-so. Look, do you know that there's a party

en casa de Tito esta noche?
en KA-sa day TEE-toh ESS-ta NO-chay?
at Tito's house tonight?

¿No vas a ir?
¿No vahs ah eer?
Aren't you going?

— No estoy invitado.
No ess-TOY een-vee-TA-doh.
I'm not invited.

— Pero no importa.
PAIR-ro no eem-POR-ta.
But it doesn't matter.

Todo el mundo está invitado.
TOH-doh el MOON-doh ess-TA een-vee-TA-doh.
Everyone's invited.

Hombre, ¡tienes que venir!
OHM-bray, ¡T'YAY-nays kay vay-NEER!
Man, you have to come!

Tú se usa entre enamorados.
Too say OO-sa EN-tray ay-na-mo-RA-dohs.
Tú is used between people in love.

ELLA:
EL-ya:
SHE:

Dime, ¿me quieres?
DEE-may, ¿may K'YAY-rays?
Tell me, do you love me?

> **"To love" or "to want"**
> *Querer*, which literally means "to want" also
> means "to love". There is another word for "to
> love" — *amar*; but *querer* is the form most gen-
> erally used.

ÉL:
El:
HE:

Sí. Te quiero mucho.
See. Tay K'YAY-ro MOO-cho.
Yes. I love you very much.

ELLA:
¿Me vas a querer siempre?
¿May vahs ah kay-RAIR S'YEM-pray?
Are you going to love me always?

ÉL:
¿Quién sabe?
¿K'yen SA-bay?
Who knows?

ELLA:
¿Por qué dices "Quién sabe"?
¿Por kay DEE-says "K'yen SA-bay"?
Why do you say "Who knows"?

Eres un bruto. Te odio.
AY-rays oon BROO-toh. Tay OH-d'yo.
You are a brute. I hate you.

Tú se usa cuando se habla con niños.
Too say OO-sa KWAN-doh say AH-bla kohn NEEN-yohs.
Tú is used when speaking to children.

174

UNA DAMA:
Oo-na DA-ma:
A LADY:

Oye, preciosa. ¿Cómo te llamas?
OH-yay, pray-S'YO-sa. ¿KO-mo tay L'YA-mahs?
Listen, precious. What's your name?

UNA CHIQUILLA:
Oo-na chee-KEEL-ya:
A LITTLE GIRL:

Me llamo Josefina.
May L'YA-mo Ho-say-FEE-na.
My name is Josephine.

LA DAMA:

Y este niñito, ¿es tu hermano?
Ee ESS-tay neen-YEE-toh, ¿ess too air-MA-no?
And this little boy, is he your brother?

LA CHIQUILLA:

Sí. Es muy chiquito todavía.
See. Ess mwee chee-KEE-toh toh-da-VEE-ya.
Yes. He's still very small.

Diminutives
Adding -ito, -cito, or -illo to a noun (changing
the o to a when the noun is feminine) makes it a
diminutive.

gato — cat	gatito — kitten
casa — house	casita — little house
amor — love	amorcito — little love
guerra — war	guerrilla — little war

No sabe hablar.
No SA-bay ah-BLAR.
He doesn't know how to talk.

LA DAMA:

Pero tú sabes hablar bien, ¿verdad?
PAY-ro too SA-bays ah-BLAR b'yen, ¿vair-DAHD?
But you know how to speak well, don't you?

Aquí tienes un bombón para tí
Ah-KEE T'YAY-nays oon bohm-BOHN PA-ra tee
Here's a candy for you

y otro para tu hermanito.
ee OH-tro PA-ra too air-ma-NEE-toh.
and another one for your little brother.

Sonríe, quiero sacarte una foto.
Sohn-REE-ay, k'YAY-ro sa-KAR-tay OO-na FO-toh.
Smile, I want to take a picture of you.

Tú se usa cuando se habla a animales.
Too **say OO-sa KWAN-doh say AH-bla ah ah-nee-MA-lays.**
Tú is used when speaking to animals.

— ¡Tú!, !Lobito! ¡Bájate del sofá!
¡Too¡ ¡Lo-BEE-toh! ¡BA-ha-tay del so-FA!
You! Lobito (little wolf)! Get off the sofa!

¡No molestes al gato!
¡No mo-LAYS-tays al GA-toh!
Don't bother the cat!

> **The personal "a"**
> We have noted that *a* is necessary when a person is used as an object; this is often done also with "personalized" animals such as dogs, cats, horses, bulls, etc.

Deja al gato tranquilo.
DAY-ha al GA-toh trahn-KEE-lo.
Leave the cat alone.

¡Cállate! ¡No hagas tanto ruido!
¡KAHL-ya-tay! ¡No AH-gahs TAHN-toh RWEE-doh!
Keep quiet! Don't make so much noise!

"Tu" — with negative command

A negative command for *tú* does not use the imperative form which you saw in the first note to Step 15, but switches back to the regular formal command, while adding an -s for *tú*.

No comas. Don't eat.

¡Sal de aquí, perro malo!
¡Sahl day ah-KEE, pair-rro MA-lo!
Get out of here, bad dog!

"Tú" with animals

While it is true that animals would scarcely notice the informal form of address, onlookers would certainly find it strange if you used the pronoun *Usted* for "you" to an animal. *Usted* is a shortened form of *su merced*, meaning "your grace."

INSTANT CONVERSATION: AT A SIDEWALK CAFÉ

ÉL:
El:
HE:

>Tengo sed.
>**TEN-go sed.**
>I'm thirsty.

>¿Quieres tomar una copa aquí?
>**¿K'YAY-rays toh-MAR OO-na KO-pa ah-KEE?**
>Do you want to have a drink here?

ELLA:
El-ya:
SHE:

>¡Qué buena idea! Vamos.
>**¡Kay BWAY-na ee-DAY-ah! VA-mohs.**
>What a good idea! Let's go.

ÉL:

>Aquí hay una mesa libre.
>**Ah-KEE I OO-na MAY-sa LEE-bray.**
>Here is a free table.

>¡Camarera!
>**¡Ka-ma-RAY-ra!**
>Waitress!

CAMARERA:
Ka-ma-RAY-ra:
WAITRESS:

>Buenas tardes. ¿Qué desean?
>**BWAY-nahs TAR-days. ¿KAY day-SAY-ahn?**
>Good afternoon. What do you wish?

ÉL:

¿Qué tomas, querida?
¿Kay TOH-mahs, kay-REE-da?
What will you have, darling?

ELLA:

No sé. . . . una limonada, quizás.
No say. . . . OO-na lee-mo-NA-da, kee-SAHS.
I don't know . . . a lemonade, perhaps.

ÉL:

Bien. Tráiganos una limonada
B'yen. TRY-ga-nohs OO-na lee-mo-NA-da
Good. Bring us a lemonade

y para mí un coñac con soda,
ee PA-ra mee oon kohn-YAHK kohn SO-da,
and for me a brandy and soda,

y póngale hielo, por favor.
ee POHN-ga-lay YAY-lo, por fa-VOR.
and put ice in, please.

ELLA:

Mira, querido, ¿quieres cambiar la orden?
MEE-ra, kay-REE-doh, ¿K'YAY-rays kahm-B'YAR la OR-den?
Look, darling, do you want to change the order?

Quiero probar el vino de Jerez,
K'YAY-ro pro-BAR el VEE-no day hay-RAYS,
I want to try the sherry,

en lugar de la limonada.
en loo-GAR day la lee-mo-NA-da.
instead of the lemonade.

ÉL:

Está bien. Así son las mujeres.
Ess-TA b'yen. Ah-SEE sohn lahs moo-HAY-rays.
That's o.k. That's how women are.

Siempre cambian de parecer.
S'YEM-pray KAHM-b'yahn day pa-ray-SAIR.
They always change their minds.

¡Camarera! Cambie la orden, por favor.
¡Ka-ma-RAY-ra! KAHM-b'yay la OR-den, por fa-VOR.
Waitress! Change the order, please.

Una copita de Jerez para la señora.
OO-na ko-PEE-ta day hay-RAYSS PA-ra la sen-YO-ra.
A small glass of sherry for the lady.

ELLA:
¿No estás enojado conmigo?
¿No ess-TAHS ay-no-HA-doh kohn-MEE-go?
You're not angry with me?

ÉL:
Sabes que nunca estoy enojado contigo, mi vida.
**Sa-bays kay NOON-ka ess-TOY ay-no-HA-doh kohn-TEE-go, mee
VEE-da.**
You know I'm never angry with you, my life.

> Besides *mi amor* and *mi vida* other phrases of
> endearment in this poetic and imaginative lan-
> guage include:
>
> *querido* — beloved (to a man)
> *querida* — beloved (to a woman)
> *mi tesoro* — my treasure
> *mi cielo* — my heaven
> *mi alma* — my soul
> *mi corazón* — my heart
> *mi amor* — my love

Aquí vienen las bebidas. ¡Salud!
Ah-KEE V'YAY-nen lahs bay-BEE-dahs. ¡Sa-LOOD!
Here come the drinks. Health!

ELLA:
¡Salud y pesetas!
¡Sa-LOOD ee pay-SAY-tahs!
Health and money!

ÉL:

O, como también se dice:
Oh, KO-mo tahm-B'YEN say DEE-say:
Or, as they say also:

¡Salud, pesetas y amor!
¡Sa-LOOD, pay-SAY-tahs ee ah-MOR!
Health, money and love!

ELLA:

¡Y muchos años para disfrutarlos!
¡Ee MOO-chohs AHN-yohs PA-ra dees-froo-TAR-lohs!
And many years to enjoy them!

TEST YOUR SPANISH

Translate these phrases into Spanish, using the familiar (tú) form. Score 10 points for each correct answer. See answers below.

1. What's your name? _____

2. How are you? _____

3. Aren't you going? _____

4. You have to come! _____

5. Do you love me? _____

6. I love you very much. _____

7. You are a brute. _____

8. I hate you. _____

9. Listen to me! _____

10. Keep quiet! _____

Answers: 1. ¿Cómo te llamas? 2. ¿Cómo estás? 3. ¿No vas a ir? 4. ¡Tienes que venir! 5. ¿Me quieres? 6. Te quiero mucho. 7. Eres un bruto. 8. Te odio. 9. ¡Óyeme! 10. ¡Cállate!

SCORE ____%

step 16

DAYS, MONTHS, DATES, SEASONS, THE WEATHER

Los días de la semana son:
Lohs DEE-yahs day la say-MA-na sohn:
The days of the week are:

lunes, martes, miércoles,
LOO-nays, MAR-tays, M'YAIR-ko-lays,
Monday, Tuesday, Wednesday,

jueves, viernes, sábado y domingo.
HWAY-vays, V'YAIR-nays, SA-ba-doh ee doh-MEEN-go.
Thursday, Friday, Saturday and Sunday.

Los meses se llaman:
Lohs MAY-says say L'YA-mahn:
The months are called:

enero, febrero, marzo, abril,
ay-NAY-ro, fay-BRĄY-ro, MAR-so, ah-BREEL,
January, February, March, April,

mayo, junio, julio, agosto,
MA-yo, HOON-yo, HOOL-yo, ah-GO-sto,
May, June, July, August,

septiembre, octubre, noviembre y diciembre.
sep-T'YEM-bray, ok-TOO-bray, nohv-YEM-bray ee dee-S'YEM-bray.
September, October, November and December.

Enero es el primer mes del año.
Ay-NAY-ro ess el pree-MAIR mays del AHN-yo.
January is the first month of the year.

El primero de enero es el día de año nuevo.
El pree-MAY-ro day ay-NAY-ro ess el DEE-ya del AHN-yo NWAY-vo.
The first of January is New Years Day.

Entonces les decimos a nuestros amigos:
En-TOHN-says lays day-SEE-mohs ah NWAYS-trohs ah-MEE-gohs:
Then we say to our friends:

"¡Feliz Año Nuevo!"
"¡Feh-LEES AHN-yo NWAY-vo!"
"Happy New Year!"

El veinticinco de diciembre
El vain-tee-SEEN-ko day dee-S'YEM-bray
The twenty-fifth of December

es el día de Pascuas de Navidad.
ess el DEE-ya day PAHS-kwahs day Na-vee-DAHD.
Is Christmas Day.

La gente se dice: "¡Felices Pascuas!"
La HEN-tay say DEE-say: "¡Feh-LEE-says PAHS-kwahs!"
People say to each other: "Merry Christmas!"

> **Pascuas**
> Both Christmas and Easter are called Pascuas.
> For purpose of differentiation the former is
> called *Pascuas de Navidad* ("Nativity") and the
> latter *Pascuas Floridas* ("Flowery"). (The State
> of Florida gets its name because of its discov-
> ery on Easter Day.)

La fecha del día de independencia
La FAY-cha del DEE-ya day een-day-pen-DENS-ya
The date of Independence Day

varía según el país.
va-REE-ya say-GOON el pa-EES.
varies according to the country.

En México, por ejemplo,
En MAY-hee-ko, por ay-HEM-plo,
In Mexico, for example,

es el quince de septiembre.
ess el KEEN-say day sep-T'YEM-bray.
it is the fifteenth of September.

Entonces todo el mundo dice: "¡Viva México!"
En-TOHN-says TOH-doh el MOON-doh DEE-say "¡VEE-va MAY-hee-ko!"
Then everyone says: "(Long) Live Mexico!"

El año se divide en cuatro estaciones —
El AHN-yo say dee-VEE-day en KWA-tro ess-ta-S'YO-nays —
The year is divided into four seasons —

> **Dividirse**
> Note that se *divide,* literally "divides itself", is used as a passive construction — "is divided."

primavera, verano, otoño e invierno.
pree-ma-VAY-ra, vay-RA-no, oh-TOHN-yo ay een-V'YAIR-no.
spring, summer, autumn and winter.

En invierno hace mucho frío,
En een-V'YAIR-no AH-say MOO-cho FREE-yo,
In winter it is very cold,

y en el verano hace calor.
ee en el vay-RA-no AH-say ka-LOHR.
and in summer it is hot.

En la primavera y en el otoño
En la pree-ma-VAY-ra ee en el oh-TOHN-yo
In spring and in autumn

generalmente hace buen tiempo.
heh-neh-rahl-MEN-tay AH-say bwen T'YEM-po.
it is generally good weather.

> **Hace frío — hace calor**
> The 3rd. person form of *hacer* ("to make") is used to describe some aspects of the weather and temperature:
>
> | *hace calor* | *hace frío* | *hace sol* | *hace viento* |
> |---|---|---|---|
> | it's hot | it's cold | it's sunny | it's windy |
>
> Remember that when a person is hot, cold, hungry or thirsty, *tener* is used instead of *hacer.*

El clima de España
El KLEE-ma day Ess-PAHN-ya
The climate of Spain

es un poco parecido al clima de Norte América.
ess oon PO-ko pa-ray-SEE-doh ahl KLEE-ma day NOR-tay
Ah-MAY-ree-ka.
is a little like the climate of North America.

Hay cambio de estaciones.
I KAHM-b'yo day ess-ta-S'YO-nays.
There is a change of seasons.

Pero en Centro América
Pair-ro en SEN-tro Ah-MAY-ree-ka
But in Central America

y la parte norte de Suramérica,
ee la PAR-tay NOR-teh day soor-Ah-MAY-ree-ka,
and the northern part of South America,

como Venezuela, Colombia, y Ecuador,
KO-mo Veh-neh-SWAY-la, Ko-LOHM-B'ya, ee Eh-kwa-DOR,
like Venezuela, Colombia, and Equador,

> *Ecuador* means "equator," which is exactly
> where the country is. Some other Spanish
> countries, as well as some states and cities in
> the U.S. have names that mean something in
> Spanish.
>
> *Puerto Rico* — Rich Port
> *Costa Rica* — Rich Coast
> *Montaña* — Mountain
> *Nevada* — Snowfall
> *El Salvador* — The Savior
> *Honduras* — Depths
> *Los Angeles* — The Angels
> *Colorado* — Red

el clima es diferente.
el KLEE-ma ess dee-fay-REN-tay.
the climate is different.

Hace siempre calor en la costa
AH-say S'YEM-pray ka-LOR en la KOS-ta
It's always hot on the coast

y frío en las montañas.
ee FREE-yo en lahs mohn-TAHN-yahs.
and cold on the mountains.

Hay solamente dos estaciones —
I so-la-MEN-tay dohs ess-ta-S'YO-nays —
There are only two seasons —

la temporada seca
la tem-po-RA-da SAY-ka
the dry season

que corresponde a los meses de
kay ko-rray-SPOHN-day ah los MAY-says day
which corresponds to the months of

otoño e invierno, cuando no llueve nunca,
oh-TOHN-yo eh een-V'YAIR-no, KWAN-doh no L'WAY-vay
                                        NOON-ka,
autumn and winter, when it never rains,

y la temporada de las lluvias,
ee la tem-po-RA-da day lahs L'YOO-v'yahs,
and the rainy season,

que incluye los meses de primavera y verano,
kay een-KLOO-yay lohs MAY-says day pree-ma-VAY-ra ee vay-RA-no,
which includes the months of spring and summer,

cuando llueve muy frecuentemente.
KWAN-doh L'WAY-vay mwee fray-kwen-tay-MEN-tay.
when it rains very frequently.

En los países al sur del ecuador,
En lohs pa-EE-says ahl soor del eh-kwa-DOR,
In the countries south of the equator,

las temporadas son opuestas a las del norte del ecuador.
**lahs tem-po-RA-dahs sohn oh-PWESS-tahs ah lahs del NOR-tay del
eh-kwa-DOR.**
the seasons are opposite to those north of the equator.

Por ejemplo, en Chile, Argentina y Uruguay,
Por eh-HEM-plo, en CHEE-lay, Ar-hen-TEE-na ee Oo-roo-G'WHY,
For example, in Chile, Argentina and Uruguay,

hace frío en julio y agosto
AH-say FREE-yo en HOO-l'yo ee ah-GOHS-toh
it is cold in July and August

y calor en enero y febrero.
ee ka-LOR en eh-NAY-ro ee fay-BRAY-ro.
and hot in January and February.

INSTANT CONVERSATION:
TALKING ABOUT THE WEATHER

Todo el mundo hace comentarios sobre el tiempo.
TOH-doh el MOON-doh AH-say ko-men-TA-r'yohs SO-bray el
T'YEM-po.
Everyone makes comments about the weather.

En la primavera, cuando el sol brilla
En la pree-ma-VAY-ra, KWAN-doh el sol BREEL-ya
In spring, when the sun shines

y sopla una brisa agradable
ee SO-pla OO-na BREE-sa ah-gra-DA-blay
and a pleasant breeze blows

y el aire huele a flores, se dice:
ee el I-ray WAY-lay ah FLO-rays, say DEE-say:
and the air smells of flowers, one says:

"¡Qué día tan bello!"
"¡Kay DEE-ya tahn BEL-yo!"
"What a beautiful day!"

Y, cuando la noche está clara
Ee, KWAN-doh la NO-chay ess-TA KLA-ra
And, when the night is clear

y vemos la luna
ee VAY-mohs la LOO-na
and we see the moon

y las estrellas brillantes, decimos:
ee lahs ess-TREL-yahs breel-YAHN-tays, day-SEE-mohs:
and the bright stars, we say:

"¡Qué noche tan linda!"
"¡Kay NO-chay tahn LEEN-da!"
"What a lovely night!"

189

En el verano cuando el sol es muy fuerte decimos:
En el vay-RA-no KWAN-doh el sol ess mwee FWEHR-tay day-SEE-mohs:
In summer when the sun is very strong we say:

"Hace un calor terrible, ¿no?"
"AH-say oon ka-LOR teh-RREE-blay, ¿no?"
"It's terribly hot, isn't it?"

Cuando llueve se dice frecuentemente:
KWAN-doh l'WAY-vay say DEE-say fray-kwen-tay-MEN-tay:
When it rains one frequently says:

"Hace mal tiempo hoy.
"AH-say mahl T'YEM-po oy.
"The weather is bad today.

Está lloviendo otra vez."
Ess-TA l'yo-V'YEN-doh OH-tra vess."
It's raining again."

En el otoño cuando empieza el frío se dice:
En el oh-TOHN-yo KWAN-doh em-P'YAY-sa el FREE-yo say DEE-say:
In the autumn when the cold weather starts one says:

"Hace bastante fresco, ¿verdad?"
"AH-say bahs-TAHN-tay FRESS-ko, ¿vair-DAHD?
"It's quite cool, isn't it?"

En el invierno cuando nieva a menudo se dice:
En el een-V'YAIR-no KWAN-doh N'YAY-va ah may-NOO-doh say
DEE-say:
In winter when it snows we often say:

"Está nevando mucho.
"Ess-TA neh-VAHN-doh MOO-cho.
"It's snowing a lot.

¡Qué frío hace!
¡Kay FREE-yoh AH-say!
How cold it is!

Los caminos deben estar malísimos,
Lohs ka-MEE-nohs DAY-ben ess-TAR ma-LEE-see-mohs,
The roads must be very bad,

190

con tanto hielo y nieve."
kohn TAHN-toh YAY-lo ee N'YAY-vay."
with so much ice and snow."

Cuando hace mucho viento con truenos y relámpagos,
KWAN-doh AH-say MOO-cho V'YEN-toh kohn TR'WAY-nohs ee
ray-LAHM-pa-gohs,
When it's very windy with thunder and lightning,

y mucha lluvia, se dice:
ee MOO-cha L'YOO-v'ya, say DEE-say:
and much rain, one says:

"¡Vaya una tormenta!"
"¡VA-ya OO-na tor-MEN-ta!"
"What a storm!"

Y cuando hay mucha neblina
Ee KWAN-doh I MOO-cha nay-BLEE-na
And when there is much fog

a veces decimos:
ah VAY-says day-SEE-mohs:
sometimes we say:

"¡Qué neblina!
"¡Kay nay-BLEE-na!"
"What a fog!

Casi no se puede ver nada.
KA-see no say PWAY-day vair NA-da.
One can hardly see anything.

Es muy peligroso guiar.
Ess mwee peh-lee-GRO-so ghee-YAR.
It's very dangerous to drive.

Es mejor quedarse en casa."
Ess meh-HOR kay-DAR-say en KA-sa."
It's better to stay at home."

> **"Quedar" and "quedarse"**
> *Quedarse* is a reflexive verb meaning "to re-
> main" or "to stay." In its non-reflexive form
> *quedar* is used for "to be" and can substitute
> for either *ser* or *estar* when referring to location.

191

TEST YOUR SPANISH

Translate these comments on the weather into English. Score 10 points for each correct answer. See answers below.

1. ¡Qué día tan bello!   _____

2. ¡Qué noche tan linda!   _____

3. Hace un calor terrible, ¿no?   _____

4. Hace mal tiempo hoy.   _____

5. Está lloviendo otra vez.   _____

6. Hace bastante fresco, ¿no?   _____

7. Está nevando mucho.   _____

8. ¡Qué frío hace!   _____

9. ¡Vaya una tormenta!   _____

10. ¡Qué neblina!   _____

Answers: 1. What a beautiful day! 2. What a lovely night! 3. It's terribly hot, isn't it? 4. The weather is bad today. 5. It's raining again. 6. It's quite cool, isn't it? 7. It's snowing a lot. 8. How cold it is! 9. What a storm! 10. What a fog!

SCORE _____%

step 17
HOW TO FORM THE FUTURE TENSE

El tiempo futuro es muy fácil.
El T'YEM-po foo-TOO-ro ess mwee FA-seel.
The future tense is very easy.

Para la forma *yo* se añade una *é* al infinitivo.
PA-ra la FOR-ma *yo* say ahn-YA-day OO-na é ahl een-fee-nee-TEE-vo.
For the form "I" one adds an é to the infinitive.

Mañana por la mañana me levantaré muy temprano.
Mahn-YA-na por la mahn-YA-na may lay-vahn-ta-RAY mwee tem-PRA-no.
Tomorrow morning I will get up very early.

Iré al médico.
Ee-RAY ahl MAY-dee-ko.
I'll go to the doctor.

¿Dónde hay un médico?
When visiting or being visited by a doctor, note the following constructions for indicating where you feel discomfort:

I have a headache. — *Tengo dolor de cabeza.*
I have a sore throat. — *Tengo dolor de garganta.*
I have a stomach-ache. — *Tengo dolor de estómago.*
I'm dizzy. — *Tengo vértigo.*
It hurts here. — *Me duele aquí.*

The doctor might give you a prescription (*una receta*) and he may say:

You must stay in bed. — *Debe guardar cama.*
Take this three times a day. — *Tome esto tres veces al día.*

You will feel better. — *Ud. se sentirá mejor.*
Come back in two days. — *Vuelva en dos días.*

Le pediré algo para mi tos.
Lay peh-dee-RAY AHL-go PA-ra mee tohs.
I shall ask him for something for my cough.

Le llamaré desde su despacho,
Leh l'ya-ma-RAY DEHS-day soo dehs-PA-cho,
I'll call you from his office,

y le diré a que hora estaré de vuelta.
ee lay dee-RAY ah kay OH-ra ess-ta-RAY day VWEL-ta.
and I'll tell you what time I'll be back.

To form the future
Most verbs form their future by adding the future endings you are now learning to the infinitive of the verb. Therefore you can look up almost any verb in the dictionary and know how to form the future tense. Some verbs slightly change their base in the future and you should learn some of these special future stems by heart. Here are the most important in their infinitive form, followed, in parenthesis, by the *yo* or "first person" form.

venir (vendré), tener (tendré), salir (saldré), poner (pondré) hacer (haré), saber (sabré), poder (podré), decir (diré), querer (querré), valer (valdré), haber (habrá). The last form is given in the third person because this is the form most used in the sense of "there will be."

There are no words for "shall," "will," "won't" or "will not," as the endings of the verb indicate the future.

Para la forma de *Ud., él, ella* se añade *á* al infinitivo.
PA-ra la FOR-ma day *oo-STED, el, EL-ya* say ahn-YA-day *á* ahl een-fee-nee-TEE-vo.
For the forms "you," "he," "she" one adds an *á* to the infinitive.

¿Cuándo llegará Ramón?
¿KWAN-doh I'yay-ga-RA Ra-MOHN?
When will Ramon arrive?

Vendrá mañana.
Ven-DRA mahn-YA-na.
He'll come tomorrow.

¿Será posible hablarle sobre el contrato?
¿Seh-RA po-SEE-blay ah-BLAR-lay SO-bray el kohn-TRA-toh?
Will it be possible to speak to him about the contract?

Creo que no podrá. Saldrá a las dos.
KRAY-oh kay no po-DRA. Sahl-DRA ah lahs dohs.
I think that you won't be able to. He'll leave at two.

Volará a Venezuela, donde visitará
Vo-la-RA ah Veh-neh-SWAY-la, DOHN-day vee-see-ta-RA
He will fly to Venezuela, where he'll visit

los nuevos campos de petróleo.
lohs N'WAY-vohs KAHM-pohs day pay-TRO-lay-oh.
the new oil fields.

¿No vendrá al aeropuerto?
¿No ven-DRA ahl ah-eh-ro-PWAIR-toh?
Won't you come to the airport?

Así tendrá tiempo para hablarle.
Ah-SEE ten-DRA T'YEM-po PA-ra ah-BLAR-lay.
In this way you'll have time to speak to him.

Para la forma *tú* se añade *-ás* al infinitivo.
PA-ra la FOR-ma *too* say ahn-YA-day *-ás* ahl een-fee-nee-TEE-vo.
For the form "you" (familiar), one adds -ás to the infinitive.

ELLA:
¿Me llamarás mañana?
¿May I'ya-ma-RAHS mahn-YA-na?
Will you call me tomorrow?

ÉL:
Claro. Pero no estarás en casa.
KLA-ro. PAIR-ro no ess-ta-RAHS en KA-sa.
Of course. But you won't be home.

195

Saldrás temprano, ¿no? ¿Cuándo volverás?
Sahl-DRAHS tem-PRA-no, ¿no? ¿KWAHN-doh vol-veh-RAHS?
You will go out early, won't you? When will you be back?

ELLA:
A las cinco de la tarde.
Ah lahs SEEN-ko day la TAR-day.
At five in the afternoon.

Podrás llamarme después de las cinco.
Po-DRAHS l'ya-MAR-may des-PWESS day lahs SEEN-ko.
You'll be able to call me after five.

> **Verb form of "Ud." + s = form for tú**
> As we introduced the familiar form for "you" —
> *tú* in Step 15 we will now include it in our expla-
> nations of new tenses. Actually it is quite easy
> to use as it generally consists of simply adding
> an s to the verb form used for *Ud.*

Para la forma de *nosotros* (*nosotras*) se añade -*emos* al infinitivo.
**PA-ra la FOR-ma day *no-SO-trohs (no-SO-trahs)* say ahn-YA-day
-emos ahl een-fee-nee-TEE-vo.**
For the form "we" (masculine and feminine) one adds -*emos* to the
infinitive.

El próximo sábado todos iremos al campo.
**El PROHK-see-mo SA-ba-doh TOH-dohs ee-RAY-mohs ahl
KAHM-po.**
Next Saturday we shall all go to the country.

Tomaremos el tren y bajaremos en Vereda Nueva.
**Toh-ma-RAY-mohs el trayn ee ba-ha-RAY-mohs en Vay-RAY-da
NWAY-va.**
We will take the train and get off at Vereda Nueva (New Lane).

Luego iremos en auto a la finca de don Antonio.
**LWAY-go ee-RAY-mohs en OW-toh ah la FEEN-ka day dohn
An-TOHN-yo.**
Then we'll go by car to Don Antonio's farm.

Allí montaremos a caballo, veremos los alrededores
Ahl-YEE mohn-ta-RAY-mohs ah ka-BAHL-yo, vay-RAY-mohs los
ahl-ray-day-DOH-rays
There we'll ride horseback, we'll see the surroundings

y después nadaremos en la piscina.
ee des-PWESS na-da-RAY-mohs en la pee-SEE-na.
and afterwards we'll swim in the pool.

Por la noche cenaremos al aire libre.
Por la NO-chay seh-na-RAY-mohs ahl I-ray LEE-bray.
In the evening we'll have dinner outdoors.

Oiremos canciones y música típica.
Oy-RAY-mohs kahn-S'YO-nays ee MOO-see-ka TEE-pee-ka.
We'll hear songs and typical music.

Creo que nos divertiremos mucho.
KRAY-oh kay nohs dee-vair-tee-RAY-mohs MOO-cho.
I believe we will have a very good time.

> **¡Que se divierta!**
> The reflexive verb *divertirse* means "to amuse
> oneself" or "to have a good time." When you
> wish someone a good time say: *¡Que se di-*
> *vierta!* or, if there are several persons: *¡Que se*
> *diviertan!*

Para la forma de *Uds., ellos, ellas* se añade *-án* al infinitivo.
PA-ra la FOR-ma day *oo-STAY-dehs, EL-yohs, EL-yahs* say ahn-YA-day
"-án" ahl een-fee-nee-TEE-vo.
For the form "you" (plural) and "they" (m. and f.) one adds *-án* to the
infinitive.

UN JOVEN:
Oon HO-ven:
A YOUNG MAN:

¿Vivirán los hombres en la luna algún día?
¿Vee-vee-RAHN los OHM-brays en la LOO-na ahl-GOON
DEE-ya?
Will men live on the moon some day?

UN VIEJO:
Oon V'YAY-ho:
AN OLD ONE:

Desde luego. Pronto habrá bases allí,
DESS-day L'WAY-go. PROHN-toh ah-BRA BA-says ahl-YEE,
Of course. There will soon be bases there,

y, sin duda, servicio de vuelos diarios.
ee, seen DOO-da, sehr-VEE-s'yo day VWAY-lohs dee-AR-yos.
and, doubtlessly, daily flight service.

EL JOVEN:
¿Cree que irán a los planetas también?
¿Kray kay ee-RAHN ah los pla-NAY-tahs tahm-B'YEN?
Do you think they'll go to the planets also?

EL VIEJO:
Seguramente. Una vez en la luna
Say-goo-ra-MEN-tay. OO-na vess en la LOO-na
Certainly. Once on the moon

los viajes futuros serán más fáciles
los V'YA-hays foo-TOO-rohs seh-RAHN mahs FA-see-lays
future trips will be easier

y seguirán hasta los planetas.
ee say-ghee-RAHN AHS-ta los pla-NAY-tahs.
and they will continue to the planets.

Pero creo que los astronautas no llegarán
PAY-ro KRAY-oh kay los ahs-tro-NOW-tahs no l'yay-ga-RAHN
But I think the astronauts will not get

a las estrellas en el futuro cercano.
ah lahs ess-TREL-yahs en el foo-TOO-ro sair-KA-no.
to the stars in the near future.

Tal vez Uds. los jóvenes lo verán.
Tahl vess oo-STAY-days los HO-vay-nays lo vair-RAHN.
Maybe you young people will see it.

INSTANT CONVERSATION: PLANNING A TRIP TO MEXICO

ÉL:

Uds. irán a México la semana que viene, ¿no?
Oo-STAY-days ee-RAHN ah MAY-hee-ko la say-MA-na kay V'YAY-nay, ¿no?
You'll (pl.) go to Mexico next week, won't you?

ELLA:

Sí. Pero no partiremos juntos.
See. PAIR-ro no par-tee-RAY-mohs HOON-tohs.
Yes. But we won't leave together.

Julio irá primero
HOO-l'yo ee-RA pree-MAY-ro
Julio will go first

porque tendrá que atender unos negocios.
POR-kay ten-DRA kay ah-ten-DAIR OO-nohs nay-GO-s'yohs.
because he'll have to attend to some business.

Yo seguiré tres días más tarde.
Yo say-ghee-RAY trays DEE-yahs mahs TAR-day.
I'll follow three days later.

Nos encontraremos en México
Nohs en-kohn-tra-RAY-mohs en MAY-hee-ko
We'll meet each other in Mexico

el viernes próximo.
el V'YAIR-nays PROHK-see-mo.
next Friday.

Él:

¿Qué harán durante su visita?
¿Kay ah-RAHN doo-RAHN-tay soo vee-SEE-ta?
What will you do during your visit?

ELLA:

Tenemos todo planeado.
Tay-NAY-mohs TOH-doh pla-nay-AH-doh.
We have everything planned.

Haremos una gira por la ciudad
Ah-RAY-mohs OO-na HEE-ra por la s'yoo-DAHD
We'll take a tour of the city

y las afueras.
ee lahs ah-FWAIR-rahs.
and the outskirts.

Visitaremos los museos
Vee-see-ta-RAY-mohs lohs moo-SAY-ohs
We shall visit the museums

y los mercados.
ee lohs mair-KA-dohs.
and the markets.

Iremos a las pirámides,
Ee-RAY-mohs ah lahs pee-RA-mee-days,
We will go to the pyramids,

veremos los festivales
vair-RAY-mohs lohs fess-tee-VA-lays
we'll see the festivals

de baile y de música.
day BY-lay ee day MOO-see-ka.
of dance and of music.

Y, ¿qué más? Ah, sí . . .
Ee, ¿kay mahs? Ah, see . . .
And, what else? Oh, yes . . .

asistiremos a una corrida.
ah-sees-tee-RAY-mohs ah OO-na ko-RREE-da.
we shall go to a bullfight.

ÉL:

¿Cree que le gustará?
¿KRAY kay lay goos-ta-RA?
Do you think you'll like it?

ELLA:

¡Ya lo creo! Fíjese —
¡Ya lo KRAY-oh! FEE-heh-say-
I should say so! Just think —

¡el Cordobés será
¡el Kor-doh-BAYSS seh-RA
(The) Cordobés will be

> "El Cordobés" means "The man from Córdoba."

uno de los matadores!
OO-no day lohs ma-ta-DOH-rays
one of the bullfighters!

ÉL:

¡Qué suerte! Yo sólo lo veré
¡Kay SWAIR-tay! Yo SO-lo lo vair-RAY
What luck! I'll only see it

en la televisión.
en la tay-lay-vee-S'YOHN.
on television.

Y, ¿a qué otras ciudades irán?
Ee, ¿ah kay OH-trahs s'yoo-DA-days ee-RAHN?
And, to what other cities will you go?

ELLA:

Unos amigos nos estarán esperando
OO-nohs ah-MEE-gohs nohs ess-ta-RAHN ess-peh-RAHN-doh
Some friends will be waiting for us

en México y nos llevarán
en MAY-hee-ko ee nohs l'yay-va-RAHN
in Mexico (City) and they will take us

a Cuernavaca en su auto.
ah Kwair-na-VA-ka en soo OW-toh.
to Cuernavaca in their car.

Después de estar dos días allí
Dess-PWESS day ess-TAR dohs DEE-yahs ahl-YEE
After being there two days

Verbs following *de*
Verbs following *de* are in the infinitive and are translated by the present participle.

después de salir — after leaving
antes de salir — before leaving

Julio irá a Guadalajara
HOO-l'yo ee-RA ah Gwa-da-la-HA-ra
Julio will go to Guadalajara

donde verá a unos clientes
DOHN-day vair-RA ah OO-nohs klee-EN-tays
where he'll see some clients

mientras yo pasaré
M'YEN-trahs yo pa-sa-RAY
while I'll spend

unos días en Taxco.
OO-nohs DEE-yahs en TAHS-ko.
a few days in Taxco.

ÉL:
Seguramente le gustará mucho.
Say-goo-ra-MEN-tay lay goos-ta-RA MOO-cho.
You'll certainly like it very much.

Encontrará todo muy pintoresco allí.
En-kohn-tra-RA TOH-doh mwee peen-to-RESS-ko ahl-YEE.
You'll find everything very picturesque there.

Encontrar
Encontrar ("to find") and *conocer* ("to know") both mean "to meet." *Encontrar* also means "to meet" in the sense of meeting someone one already knows while *conocer* means "to meet" in the sense of being introduced.

ELLA:

Después saldré para la capital
Dess-PWESS sahl-DRAY PA-ra la ka-pee-TAHL
Afterwards I'll leave for the capital

donde Julio me estará esperando
DOHN-day HOO-l'yo may ess-ta-RA ess-peh-RAHN-doh
where Julio will be waiting for me

y juntos tomaremos
ee HOON-tohs toh-ma-RAY-mohs
and together we shall take

el avión para Acapulco.
el ah-V'YOHN PA-ra Ah-ka-POOL-ko.
the plane to Acapulco.

Allí pasaremos todo el día
Ahl-YEE pa-sa-RAY-mohs TOH-doh el DEE-ya
There we'll spend all day

en la playa y descansaremos.
en la PLA-ya ee dess-kahn-sa-RAY-mohs.
on the beach and we'll rest.

ÉL:

Creo que no descansarán mucho de noche.
KRAY-oh kay no dess-kahn-sa-RAHN MOO-cho day NO-chay.
I don't think you'll rest very much at night.

Acapulco es muy alegre.
Ah-ka-POOL-ko ess mwee ah-LAY-gray.
Acapulco is very lively.

Querrán ver los cabarets, sin duda,
Kay-RRAHN vehr lohs ka-ba-RATES, seen DOO-da,
You'll want to see the cabarets, undoubtedly,

y serán invitados a muchas fiestas.
ee say-RAHN een-vee-TA-dohs ah MOO-chahs F'YESS-tahs.
and you will be invited to many parties.

No habrá mucho tiempo para descansar.
No ah-BRA MOO-cho T'YEM-po PA-ra des-kahn-SAR.
There won't be much time to rest.

TEST YOUR SPANISH

Match these sentences: Score 10 points for each correct answer. See answers below.

1. No iremos a la fiesta mañana.

    _____ You'll like it a lot.

2. Nos quedaremos por dos días.

    _____ Will you be home?

3. Le gustará mucho.

    _____ I'll rest tonight.

4. Te llamaré el martes.

    _____ We won't go to the party tomorrow.

5. ¿Estarás en casa?

    _____ I'll have to get up early.

6. El se divertirá mucho.

    _____ We'll stay for two days.

7. ¿Estudiarán Uds. juntos?

    _____ He'll enjoy himself very much.

8. Veremos muchas cosas interesantes.

    _____ We'll see many interesting things.

9. Tendré que levantarme temprano.

    _____ I'll call you Tuesday.

10. Descansaré esta noche.

    _____ Will you study together?

Answers: 3, 5, 10, 1, 9, 2, 6, 8, 4, 7

SCORE _____%

El tiempo pasado.
El T'YEM-po pa-SA-doh.
The past tense.

Para los verbos que terminan en -*ar*
PA-ra lohs VAIR-bohs kay tair-MEE-nahn en -*ar*
For the verbs that end in -ar

el pasado se forma quitando la -*ar*
el pa-SA-doh say FOR-ma kee-TAHN-doh la -*ar*
the past is formed by removing the -ar

y añadiendo las terminaciones
ee ahn-ya-D'YEN-doh lahs tair-mee-na-S'YO-nays
and adding the endings

-*é, -aste, -ó, -amos, -aron.*

Éste es el pasado de *tomar:*
ESS-tay ess el pa-SA-doh day *toh-MAR:*
This is the past of "to take":

(yo) — Tomé mi desayuno temprano.
      Toh-MAY mee day-sa-YOO-no tem-PRA-no.
      I had my breakfast early.

(tú) — ¿Tomaste tu medicina ayer?
      ¿Toh-MAHS-tay too meh-dee-SEE-na ah-YAIR?
      Did you take your medicine yesterday?

(Ud., él, ella) — Tomó el tren a Madrid.
      Toh-MO el trayn ah Ma-DREED.
      (You, he, she) took the train to Madrid.

(nosotros, -as) — Tomamos café esta mañana.
      Toh-MA-mohs ka-FAY ESS-ta mahn-YA-na.
      We had coffee this morning.

205

(Uds., ellos, ellas) — ¿Qué tomaron de postre?
¿Kay toh-MA-rohn day POHS-tray?
What did you (they) have for dessert?

Aquí hay un diálogo usando ejemplos
Ah-KEE I oon D'YA-lo-go oo-SAHN-doh ay-HEM-plohs
Here is a dialogue using examples

del pasado de los verbos terminados en *-ar:*
del pa-SA-doh day lohs VAIR-bohs tehr-mee-NA-dohs en *-ar:*
of the past of the verbs ending in -ar:

— ¿Sabe lo que pasó anoche?
¿SA-bay lo kay pa-SO ah-NO-chay?
Do you know what happened last night?

— No. ¿Qué pasó?
No. ¿Kay pa-SO?
No. What happened?

— Un ladrón entró en nuestra casa.
Oon la-DROHN en-TRO en NWESS-tra KA-sa.
A thief came into our house.

— ¿Verdad? ¿Robó algo?
¿Vehr-DAHD? ¿Ro-BO AHL-go?
Really? Did he steal anything?

— ¡Claro que sí! Se llevó
¡KLA-ro kay see! Say l'yeh-VO
Of course! He took

la vajilla de plata,
la va-HEEL-ya day PLA-ta,
the silverware,

dinero y una radio.
dee-NAIR-ro ee OO-na RA-d'yo.
money and a radio.

También tomó algunas joyas.
Tahm-B'YEN toh-MO ahl-GOO-nahs HOY-yahs.
He also took some jewelry.

— Y, ¿se escapó?
Ee, ¿say ess-ka-PO?
And he escaped?

— No. Una vecina notó algo raro
No. OO-na vay-SEE-na no-TOH AHL-go RA-ro
No. A neighbor noticed something strange

y llamó a la policía.
ee l'ya-MO ah la po-lee-SEE-ya.
and called the police.

Los policías llegaron casi en seguida.
Lohs po-lee-SEE-yahs l'yeh-GA-rohn KA-see en seh-GHEE-da.
The policemen arrived almost at once.

Encontraron al ladrón en la calle.
En-kohn-TRA-rohn ahl la-DROHN en la KAHL-yay.
They found the thief in the street.

— ¿Lo pararon?
¿Lo pa-RA-rohn?
Did they stop him?

— Seguro. El protestó,
Say-GOO-ro. El pro-tehs-TOH,
Certainly. He protested,

pero cuando lo examinaron,
PAIR-ro KWAHN-doh lo ek-sa-mee-NA-rohn,
but when they examined him,

encontraron las joyas.
en-kohn-TRA-rohn las HOY-yahs.
they found the jewelry.

Entonces lo llevaron a la cárcel.
En-TOHN-says lo l'yeh-VA-rohn ah la KAR-sell.
Then they took him to jail.

Cuando yo llegué a casa
KWAN-doh yo l'yeh-GAY ah KA-sa
When I arrived home

llamé a la policía
l'ya-MAY ah la po-lee-SEE-ya
I called the police

y ellos me lo explicaron todo.
ee EL-yohs may lo ess-plee-KA-rohn TOH-doh.
and they explained it all to me.

The past tense: first conjugation
Once you learn the forms for the 1st. conjugation in the past, you have learned the past of the majority of all verbs.

However, within the -ar group there are certain verbs that change their base to preserve the sound of the verb. For example, the past ending of *llegar* (for *yo*) would be -é but this would not preserve the hard g sound and for that reason the u is inserted in *llegué*.

This is true for the past of all verbs whose infinitives end in -gar. Those ending in -car make the change to -qué.

Los verbos que terminan en *-er* o en *-ir*,
Lohs VAIR-bohs kay tair-MEE-nahn en *-er* oh en *ir*,
The verbs that end in -er or in -ir,

y también el verbo *dar*,
ee tahm-B'YEN el VAIR-bo *dar*,
and also the verb "to give,"

The past tense-conjugation: 2 and 3
The 2nd. (-er) and 3rd. (-ir) conjugations form the past in the same way. *Dar*, however, which is legally a 1st. conjugation verb, joins the 2nd. and 3rd. group for the past tense.

forman el pasado
FOR-mahn el pa-SA-doh
form the past

añadiendo las terminaciones
ahn-ya-D'YEN-doh lahs tair-mee-na-S'YO-nays
by adding the endings

208

-í, -iste, -ió, -imos, -ieron,

a la base del verbo. Así:
ah la BA-seh del VAIR-bo. Ah-SEE:
to the root of the verb. Like this:

(yo) — Viví muchos años en México.
    Vee-VEE MOO-chohs AHN-yohs en MAY-hee-ko.
    I lived many years in Mexico.

(tú) — ¿Viviste alguna vez en el campo?
    ¿Vee-VEES-tay ahl-GOO-na vess en el KAHM-po?
    Did you ever live in the country?

(Ud., él, ella) — ¿En qué siglo vivió Colón?
    ¿En kay SEE-glo vee-V'YO Ko-LOHN?
    In what century did Columbus live?

(nosotros, -as) — Vivimos seis meses en aquel departamento.
    Vee-VEE-mohs, sayss MAY-sehs en ah-
        KELL deh-par-ta-MEN-toh.
    We lived six months in that apartment.

(Uds., ellos, ellas) — Cortés y Pizarro vivieron en el siglo dieciséis.
    Kor-TAYSS ee Pee-SA-rro vee-V'YAY-rohn en el
        SEE-glo d'yess-ee-SAYSS.
    Cortes and Pizarro lived in the XVI century.

Aquí hay un ejemplo con el pasado
Ah-KEE I oon eh-HEM-plo kohn el pa-SA-doh
Here is an example with the past

de esta clase de verbos.
day ESS-ta KLA-say day VAIR-bohs.
of this class of verbs.

    Anoche leí algo
    Ah-NO-chay leh-EE AHL-go
    Last night I read something

    sobre la vida de Cristóbal Colón.
    SO-bray la VEE-da day Krees-TOH-bal Ko-LOHN.
    about the life of Christopher Columbus.

Spelling variations but the same sound
Several of the 3rd. conjugation verbs in this example have slight spelling variations in their base, such as *morir, creer, seguir, oír, leer*, but do not change their endings.

For your convenience here are the five forms of each:

leer	oír	seguir
leí	*oí*	*seguí*
leíste	*oíste*	*seguiste*
leyó	*oyó*	*siguió*
leímos	*oímos*	*seguimos*
leyeron	*oyeron*	*siguieron*

morir	creer
morí	*creí*
moriste	*creíste*
murió	*creyó*
morimos	*creímos*
murieron	*creyeron*

Note that *yó* is sometimes used instead of *-ió*. This is only a spelling change; the sound remains the same. In fact the spelling change is to keep the sound constant

Nació en Génova
Na-S'YO en HAY-no-va
He was born in Genoa

Vivió en Portugal y España.
Vee-V'YO en Por-too-GAHL ee Ess-PAHN-ya.
He lived in Portugal and Spain.

Leyó muchos libros sobre viajes
Leh-YO MOO-chohs LEE-brohs SO-bray V'YA-hays
He read many books about voyages

y oyó varios cuentos de marineros
ee oh-YO VA-r'yohs KWEN-tohs day ma-ree-NAY-rohs
and he heard several stories from sailors

que le convencieron
kay lay kohn-ven-S'YAY-rohn
that convinced him

de la redondez de la tierra.
day la ray-dohn-DESS day la T'YAY-rra.
of the roundness of the earth.

Escribió a los reyes de España
Ess-kree-B'YO ah lohs RAY-yays day Ess-PAHN-ya
He wrote to the king and queen of Spain

y ofreció descubrir una nueva ruta
ee oh-freh-S'YO dess-koo-BREER OO-na NWAY-va ROO-ta
and he offered to discover a new route

a la India por el oeste.
ah la EEN-d'ya por el oh-ESS-tay.
to India through the west.

Ellos se convencieron también,
EL-yos say kohn-ven-S'YAY-ron tahm-b'YEN,
They were convinced also,

y la reina Isabel hasta ofreció vender sus joyas
**ee la RAY-na Ee-sa-BELL AH-sta oh-fray-S'YO ven-DAIR soos
HOY-yahs**
and Queen Isabella even offered to sell her jewels

para ayudar a Colón.
PA-ra ah-yoo-DAR ah Ko-LOHN.
to help Columbus.

Finalmente se reunió dinero
Fee-nahl-MEN-tay say reh-oo-N'YO dee-NAY-ro
Finally money was collected

para los gastos de la expedición.
PA-ra los GAHS-tohs day la ess-peh-dee-S'YOHN.
for the expenses of the expedition.

Colón y sus hombres
Ko-LOHN ee soos OHM-brays
Columbus and his men

salieron de Palos en tres naves;
sa-L'YAY-rohn day PA-lohs en trayss NA-vays;
departed from Palos in three ships;

y emprendieron su viaje
ee em-pren-D'YAY-ron soo V'YA-hay
and undertook their trip

a través del Atlántico.
ah tra-VAYSS del Aht-LAHN-tee-ko.
across the Atlantic.

Después de tres meses vieron tierra
Dess-PWESS day trayss MAY-says V'YAY-rohn T'YAY-rra
After three months they saw land

y así descubrieron el Nuevo Mundo,
ee ah-SEE des-koo-bree-YAY-rohn el NWAY-vo MOON-doh,
and thus discovered the New World,

aunque se creyeron estar en la India.
OW'N-kay say kreh-YAY-rohn ess-TAR en la EEN-d'ya.
although they believed themselves to be in India.

Colón murió en Valladolid.
Ko-LOHN moo-R'YO en Vahl-ya-doh-LEED.
Columbus died in Valladolid.

En su tumba escribieron:
En soo TOOM-ba ess-kree-B'YAY-rohn:
On his tomb they wrote:

"A Castilla y a León
"Ah Kahs-TEEL-ya ee ah Leh-OHN
"To Castile and to Leon

Nuevo mundo dió Colón."
NWAY-vo MOON-doh d'yo Ko-LOHN."
Columbus gave a new world."

Aquí hay algo fácil.
Ah-KEE I AHL-go FA-seel.
Here is something easy.

El pasado de *ir* y *ser* es el mismo.
El pa-SA-doh day *eer* ee *sair* ess el MEES-mo.
The past of "to go" and "to be" is the same.

> **"Went" or "was"**
> It is interesting to note that "went" and "was"
> or "were" are translated by the same words.
> However the meaning is usually clear from the
> context.
>
> fui — I was (or) went
> fuiste — you were (or) went
> fue — he, she, it was (or) went
> fuimos— we were (or) went
> fueron— you, they were (or) went

Además, hay más de una docena
Ah-deh-MAHS, I mahs day OO-na doh-SAY-na
Furthermore, there are more than a dozen

de verbos importantes que forman el pasado
day VAIR-bohs eem-por-TAHN-tehs kay FOR-mahn el pa-SA-doh
important verbs that form the past

con las terminaciones
kohn lahs tehr-mee-na-S'YO-nehs
with the endings

-e, -iste, -o, -imos, -ieron (-eron).

Incluyen *andar, conducir, decir,*
Een-KLOO-yen *ahn-DAR, kohn-doo-SEER, day-SEER,*
They include "to walk," "to drive," "to say,"

estar, hacer, haber, poder,
ess-TAR, ah-SAIR, ah-BAIR, po-DAIR,
"to be," "to do," "to have," "to be able,"

poner, querer, saber,
po-NAIR, keh-RAIR, sa-BAIR,
"to put," "to like," "to know,"

tener, traer, venir
teh-NAIR, tra-AIR, veh-NEER
"to have," "to bring," "to come"

y sus combinaciones.
ee soos kohm-bee-na-S'YO-nays.
and their combinations.

Base-changing verbs

This last group of verbs with special endings change their base, as well as their endings, when they form the past. Here are the infinitives, followed by the first form of the past — that for *yo* in each case.

andar (*anduve*), *conducir* (*conduje*), *estar* (*estuve*), *decir* (*dije*) *hacer* (*hice*), *haber* (*hube*), *poder* (*pude*), *poner* (*puse*), *querer* (*quise*), *saber* (*supe*), *tener* (*tuve*), *venir* (*vine*), *traer* (*traje*)

Three verbs in this group undergo another slight change in that the ending for *Uds.* is *-eron* instead of *-ieron*. They are *conducir, decir* and *traer.*

Once you learn a basic verb such as *poner* you can be sure that all of its compounds are conjugated in the same way. Take *poner* — *componer* (''to compose''), *suponer* (''to suppose''), *exponer* (''to expose''), *are just a few of its compounds.*

Ejemplos:
Ay-HEM-plohs:
Examples:

— ¿Vino alguien?
¿VEE-no AHL-gh'yen?
Did someone come?

— No vino nadie.
No VEE-no NA-d'yay.
No one came.

— ¿Hubo llamadas?
¿OO-bo l'ya-MA-dahs?
Were there any calls?

—Sí, hubo una.
See, OO-bo OO-na.
Yes, there was one.

—¿Quién llamó?
¿K'yen l'ya-MO?
Who called?

—Llamó el Sr. Herrera.
L'ya-MO el sen-YOR Air-RRAY-ra.
Mr. Herrera called.

—¿Qué dijo?
¿Kay DEE-ho?
What did he say?

—Que no pudo venir ayer.
Kay no POO-doh vay-NEER ah-YAIR.
That he couldn't come yesterday.

—¿Por qué?
¿Por kay?
Why?

—Porque estuvo ocupado.
POR-kay ess-TOO-vo oh-koo-PA-doh.
Because he was busy.

Vino un amigo inesperadamente.
VEE-no oon ah-MEE-go een-ess-peh-ra-da-MEN-tay.
A friend came unexpectedly.

Tuvo que ir a otro lugar con él
TOO-vo kay eer ah OH-tro loo-GAR kohn el
He had to go somewhere else with him

y así le fue imposible venir.
ee ah-SEE lay f'way eem-po-SEE-blay vay-NEER.
and thus it was impossible for him to come.

INSTANT CONVERSATION:
WHAT HAPPENED AT THE PARTY

JORGE:
HOR-hay:
GEORGE:
¿Qué tal? ¿Qué hiciste anoche?
¿Kay tahl? ¿Kay ee-SEES-tay ah-NO-chay?
Hi! What did you do last night?

JAIME:
HY-may:
JAMES:
Pues anoche salí con Lolita.
Pwess ah-NO-chay sa-LEE kohn Lo-LEE-ta.
Well last night I went out with Lolita.

JORGE:
Y ¿qué pasó?
Ee ¿kay pa-SO?
And what happened?

Pareces bastante preocupado.
Pa-RAY-says bahs-TAHN-tay pray-oh-koo-PA-doh.
You seem quite worried.

JAIME:
Tuve una pelea con ella.
TOO-vay OO-na peh-LAY-ah kohn EL-ya.
I had a quarrel with her.

JORGE:
¿Se pelearon? ¿Por qué?
¿Say pay-lay-AH-rohn? ¿Por kay?
You quarreled? Why?

¿Qué sucedió?
¿Kay soo-say-D'YO?
What happened?

JAIME:

Fuimos a una fiesta
FWEE-mohs ah OO-na F'YESS-ta
We went to a party

en casa de Julio.
en KA-sa day HOO-l'yo.
at Julio's house.

Bailamos, cantamos
By-LA-mohs, kahn-TA-mohs
We danced, we sang

y nos divertimos mucho.
ee nohs dee-vair-TEE-mohs MOO-cho.
and we had a wonderful time.

No pasó nada inesperado.
No pa-SO NA-da een-ess-pay-RA-doh.
Nothing unexpected happened.

hasta que vino Estela.
AHS-ta kay VEE-no Es-TAY-la.
until Estela came.

Yo bailé unas piezas con ella
Yo by-LAY OO-nahs P'YAY-sahs kohn EL-ya
I danced a few dances with her

y conversamos un poco.
ee kohn-vair-SA-mohs oon PO-ko.
and we talked a bit.

Lola se puso brava.
LO-la say POO-so BRA-va.
Lola became angry.

Quiso regresar a casa en seguida.
KEE-so ray-gray-SAR ah KA-sa en say-GHEE-da.
She wanted to return home right away.

Cuando la dejé en casa
KWAN-doh la day-HAY en KA-sa
When I left her at home

no me dijo ni siquiera
no may DEE-ho nee see-K'YAY-ra
she didn't even say

buenas noches.
BWAY-nahs NO-chays.
good night to me.

JORGE:

Y esta mañana
ee ESS-ta mahn-YA-na
And this morning

¿no la llamaste por teléfono?
¿no la l'ya-MAHS-tay por tay-LAY-fo-no?
didn't you call her on the phone?

JAIME:

Desde luego. Hoy la llamé,
DES-day LWAY-go. Oy l'ya-MAY,
Of course. I called her today,

pero no pude decir nada.
PAY-ro no POO-day deh-SEER NA-da.
but I couldn't say anything.

Cuando oyó mi voz,
KWAHN-doh oh-YO mee vohs,
When she heard my voice,

colgó el teléfono.
kohl-GO el teh-LAY-fo-no.
she hung up the phone.

> **¡No cuelge! - Don't hang up!**
> *Colgar*, literally "to hang," changes the spelling
> of its 1st. person form in the past — *yo colgué*.

No me dio tiempo ni para decir una palabra.
No may d'yo T'YEM-po nee PA-ra deh-SEER OO-na pa-LA-bra.
She didn't give me time to say even one word.

JORGE:

¡Hombre! ¿Por qué no
¡OHM-bray! ¿Por kay no
Man! Why didn't you

le mandaste flores
lay mahn-DAHS-tay FLO-rays
send her flowers

con una notita?
kohn OO-na no-TEE-ta?
with a little note?

¡Vaya! ¡Qué problema!
¡VA-ya! ¡Kay pro-BLAY-ma!
Really! What a problem!

Pero fue culpa tuya,
PAIR-ro fway KOOL-pa TOO-ya,
But it was your fault,

¿no te das cuenta de eso?
¿no tay dahs KWEN-ta day ES-so?
don't you realize that?

> **Darse cuenta**
> *Darse cuenta de* — "to realize" is a frequently
> used idiom.
>
> Do you realize what time it is?
> *¿Se da Ud. cuenta de la hora que es?*

Ella siempre fue muy celosa.
EL-ya S'YEM-pray fway mwee say-LO-sa.
She was always very jealous.

JAIME:

¡Quizá! Pero, ¿qué otra cosa pude hacer?
¡Kee-SA! PAIR-ro, ¿kay OH-tra KO-sa POO-day ah-SAIR?
Perhaps! But what else could I do?

Tuve que ser amable con Estela, ¿no?
TOO-vay kay sair ah-MA-blay kohn Ess-TAY-la, ¿no?
I had to be nice to Estela, didn't I?

TEST YOUR SPANISH

Translate these sentences into Spanish. Score 10 points for each correct answer. See answers below.

1. Do they know what happened yesterday? _____

2. At what time did he arrive? _____

3. We found the money in the street. _____

4. I took it to the police. _____

5. Who explained it to you? _____

6. Did you ever live in Mexico? _____

7. I was born in San Juan. _____

8. He read many interesting books. _____

9. We went to the movies last week. _____

10. What did he say when he called? _____

SCORE _____%

220

step 19

HOW TO USE THE CONDITIONAL FOR REQUESTS, INVITATIONS, AND REPORTED SPEECH

Cuando ofrecemos algo a alguien
KWAN-doh oh-fray-SAY-mohs AHL-go ah AHL-gh'yen
When we offer something to someone

frecuentemente usamos el modo condicional:
fray-kwen-tay-MEN-tay oo-SA-mohs el MO-doh kohn-dee-s'yo-NAHL:
we frequently use the conditional mood:

¿Le gustaría un cigarrillo?
¿Lay goos-ta-REE-ya oon see-ga-RREEL-yo?
Would you like a cigarette?

¿No le gustaría una copa?
¿No lay goos-ta-REE-ya OO-na KO-pa?
Wouldn't you like a drink?

¿Querría un chocolate?
¿Kay-RREE-ya oon cho-ko-LA-tay?
Would you like a chocolate?

The conditional (would)
The conditional is not a tense but a mood, and corresponds to several uses of the English "would." As you have seen in previous Steps, Spanish does not use short words to influence the meanings of verbs, but changes the endings, and the proper use of the conditional is an important step to speaking not only correct but polite Spanish. It is more polite, for example, to say "Would you like a cigarette?" rather than "Do you want a cigarette?"

The conditional endings are -*ía, ías, íamos, -ían*. The reason that we give only 4 is that the form for yo, Ud., él and ella is the same. For example, the conditional of hablar ("to speak") is:

(*yo, Ud., él, ella*) *hablaría*
(*tú*) *hablarías*
(*nosotros, nosotras*) *hablaríamos*
(*Uds., ellos, ellas*) *hablarían*

These conditional endings are added directly to the infinitive, except for a few examples of the irregular future which we took up in Step 17, and which become, instead of *haré, diré, podré, vendré; haría* ("I would do"), *diría* ("I would say"), *podría* ("I would be able"), *vendría* ("I would come"), etc.

Para formar el modo condicional
PA-ra for-MAR el MO-do kohn-dee-s'yo-NAHL
To form the conditional mood

deben acordarse
DAY-ben ah-kor-DAR-say
you must remember

de la combinación -*ía*
day la kohm-bee-na-S'YOHN -*ía*
the combination -*ía*

que se pone directamente
kay say PO-nay dee-rek-ta-MEN-tay
which is put directly

al infinitivo
ahl een-fee-nee-TEE-vo
on to the infinitive

o a la base del futuro.
oh ah la BA-say del foo-TOO-ro.
or on to the base of the future.

El condicional se puede usar
El kohn-dee-s'yo-NAHL say PWAY-day oo-SAR
The conditional can be used

para pedir permiso:
PA-ra pay-DEER pair-MEE-so:
to ask permission:

> ¿Me permitiría sacar una foto de Ud.?
> **¿May pair-mee-tee-REE-ya sa-KAR OO-na FO-toh day oo-STED?**
> Would you permit me to take a picture of you?
>
> ¿Y me sacaría una a mí?
> **¿Ee may sa-ka-REE-ya OO-na a mee?**
> And would you take one of me?

El condicional también se usa
El kohn-dee-s'yo-NAHL tahm-B'YEN say OO-sa
The conditional is also used

para hacer y, a veces,
PA-ra ah-SAIR ee, ah VAY-says,
to make and, sometimes,

rehusar invitaciones:
ray-oo-SAR een-vee-ta-S'YO-nays:
to refuse invitations:

ÉL:
> ¿Le gustaría dar una vuelta
> **¿Lay goos-ta-REE-ya dar OO-na VWEL-ta**
> Would you like to take a ride
>
> en el auto?
> **en el OW-toh?**
> in the car?
>
> Podríamos ir a La Zaragozana
> **Po-DREE-ya-mohs eer ah La Sa-ra-go-SA-na**
> We could go to La Zaragozana
>
> para almorzar.
> **PA-ra ahl-mor-SAR.**
> to have lunch.
>
> Estoy seguro que le agradaría.
> **Ess-TOY seh-GOO-ro kay lay ah-gra-da-REE-ya.**
> I'm sure you would like it.

Agradar-gustar
Agradar, used impersonally like *gustar*, is another word for "to like." Remember that *gustar* and *agradar* are used with the indirect object. In Spanish when you like something you say "it pleases you."

ELLA:
Me gustaría aceptar su invitación
May goos-ta-REE-ya ah-sep-TAR soo een-vee-ta-S'YOHN
I would like to accept your invitation

pero hoy no podría.
PAIR-ro oy no po-DREE-ya.
but I couldn't today.

ÉL:
Entonces, ¿no sería posible mañana?
En-TOHN-says, ¿no say-REE-ya po-SEE-blay mahn-YA-na?
Then, wouldn't it be possible tomorrow?

ELLA:
Sí, creo que mañana podría.
See, KRAY-oh kay mahn-YA-na po-DREE-ya.
Yes, I believe tomorrow I might be able to.

"could" & "might"
Just as the present tense of *poder* means "can" or "may," the conditional means "could" or "might." There is no special word for "might."

Para pedir algo cortesmente:
PA-ra peh-DEER AHL-go kor-tays-MEN-tay:
To ask for something politely:

— ¿Me haría el favor
¿May ah-REE-ya el fa-VOR
Would you do me the favor

de prestarme veinte bolívares?
day press-TAR-may VAIN-tay bo-LEE-va-rays?
of lending me twenty bolivars?

Se los devolvería
Say lohs day-vol-VAIR-REE-ya
I would give them back to you

dentro de una semana.
DEN-tro day OO-na say-MA-na.
within a week.

— Lo haría con gusto
Lo ah-REE-ya kohn GOOS-toh
I would do so with pleasure

pero hoy no tengo.
PAIR-ro oy no TEN-go.
but I don't have (any) today.

— ¡Caramba! ¿No tendría siquiera diez?
¡Ka-RAHM-ba! ¿No ten-DREE-ya see-K'YAIR-ra d'yess?
Now really! Wouldn't you have even ten?

Para arreglar precios o tarifas:
PA-ra ah-rray-GLAR PRAY-s'yohs oh ta-REE-fahs:
To arrange prices or fares:

— ¿Cuánto cobraría hasta el aeropuerto?
¿KWAN-toh ko-bra-REE-ya AHS-ta el ah-ay-ro-PWAIR-toh?
How much would you charge as far as the airport?

— Le saldría como por 20 pesos.
Lay sahl-DREE-ya KO-mo por VAIN-tay PAY-sohs.
It would come out to about 20 pesos for you.

— ¡Hombre! ¿No podría hacerme
¡OHM-bray! ¿No po-DREE-ya ah-SAIR-may
Man! Couldn't you make me

un precio un poco mejor?
oon PRAY-s'yo oon PO-ko may-HOR?
a little better price?

¿Tomaría quince pesos?
¿Toh-ma-REE-ya KEEN-say PAY-sohs?
Would you take fifteen pesos?

Para indicar lo que se ha dicho
PA-ra een-dee-KAR lo kay say ah DEE-cho
To indicate what has been said

sobre propósitos futuros:
SO-bray pro-PO-see-tohs fu-TOO-rohs:
about future plans:

— ¡Hola! ¿Podría hablar con la Srta. López?
¡OH-la! ¿Po-DREE-ya ah-BLAR kohn la sen-yo-REE-ta LO-pays?
Hello! Could I speak to Miss Lopez?

— No está, señor. Salió. Está en la calle.
No ess-TA, sen-YOR. Sa-L'YO. Ess-TA en la KAHL-yay.
She's not in, sir. She went out. She's in the street.

> **En la calle**
> *Está en la calle* literally means "She is in the street," and is a coloquial way of saying someone is not home.

— Qué raro. Me dijo que
Kay RA-ro. May DEE-ho kay
How strange. She told me that

estaría en casa a esta hora.
ess-ta-REE-ya en KA-sa ah ESS-ta OH-ra.
she would be home at this hour.

¿No dijo cuándo volvería?
¿No DEE-ho KWAN-doh vol-vair-REE-ya?
She didn't say when she would return?

— Dijo que tardaría bastante;
DEE-ho kay tar-da-REE-ya bahs-TAHN-tay;
She said that she would take a long time;

que iría primero a hacer unas compras
kay ee-REE-ya pree-MAY-ro ah ah-SAIR OO-nahs KOHM-prahs
that she would first go to do some shopping

y después tomaría el té con una amiga,
ee dess-PWESS toh-ma-REE-ya el tay kohn OO-na ah-MEE-ga,
and afterwards she would have tea with a friend,

pero que debería regresar a casa
PAIR-ro kay de-be-REE-ya ray-gray-SAR ah KA-sa
but that she should return home

a eso de las ocho.
ah ES-so day lahs OH-cho.
at about eight.

¿Tendría la bondad
¿Ten-DREE-ya la bohn-DAHD
Would you be kind enough

de llamar más tarde?
day l'ya-MAR mahs TAR-day?
to call later?

— Bien. Pero ¿me haría el favor
B'yen. PAIR-ro ¿may ah-REE-ya el fa-VOR
Fine. But would you do me the favor

de decirle que llamó el Sr. Blanco?
day day-SEER-lay kay l'ya-MO el sen-YOR BLAHN-ko?
of telling her that Mr. Blanco called?

INSTANT CONVERSATION:
INVITATION TO A FOOTBALL GAME

— ¿Le gustaría ver
¿Lay goos-ta-REE-ya vair
Would you like to see

el partido de fútbol mañana?
el par-TEE-doh day FOOT-bohl man-YA-na?
the football game tomorrow?

Los deportes (sports)
Fútbol is the Spanish word for "soccer." Other sports are sometimes the same in both Spanish and English: *tenis, golf, béisbol* and are masculine gender. "Horseraces" are *carreras de caballo,* "boxing" is *boxeo,* and "wrestling" is *lucha libre.*

The following expressions will be useful when you see sporting events in Spanish countries:

Who is winning? — *¿Quién está ganando?*
Great! — *¡Olé!*
Kill the umpire! — *¡Que maten al árbitro!*
Give us our money back! — *¡Que nos devuelvan el dinero!*

— Sí, pero no sé si tendría tiempo.
See, PAIR-ro no say see ten-DREE-ya T'YEM-po.
Yes, but I don't know if I would have time.

Tengo trabajo que debería terminar
TEN-go tra-BA-ho kay day-bay-REE-ya tair-mee-NAR
I have work that I should finish

"Ought" and "should"
You will remember from Step 11 that *deber*
means "must", but in its conditional form it
means "ought" or "should" in the sense of
obligation:

You should see that movie.
Debería ver esa película.
I really ought to go now.
De veras debería irme ahora.

antes del lunes.
AHN-tays del LOO-nays.
before Monday.

— Pero podría dejar el trabajo
PAIR-ro po-DREE-ya day-HAR el tra-BA-ho
But you could leave the work

hasta la noche.
AHS-ta la NO-chay.
until the evening.

El partido sólo tomaría unas horas.
El par-TEE-doh SO-lo toh-ma-REE-ya OO-nahs OH-rahs.
The game would only take a few hours.

Además, Juan dijo que vendría a buscarnos
Ah-day-MAHS, Hwan DEE-ho kay ven-DREE-ya ah boos-KAR-nohs
Besides, John said that he would come to get us

en su coche.
en soo KO-chay.
in his car.

También dijo que no deberíamos dejar de ir
Tahm-B'YEN DEE-ho kay no day-bay-REE-ya-mohs day-HAR day eer
He also said that we shouldn't miss going

a este partido
ah ESS-tay par-TEE-doh
to this match

que sería el más emocionante
kay say-REE-ya el mahs eh-mo-s'yo-NAHN-tay
which should be the most exciting one

de la temporada, ya que el campeonato
day la tem-po-RA-da, ya kay el kahm-pay-oh-NA-toh
of the season, since the championship

dependería del resultado.
day-pen-day-REE-ya del ray-sool-TA-doh.
would depend on the outcome.

TEST YOUR SPANISH

Fill in these verbs in the conditional mood. Score 10 points for each correct answer. See answers below.

1. Would you like a cigarette?
   ¿Le _____ un cigarrillo?

2. Would you do me a favor?
   ¿Me _____ un favor?

3. Would you permit me to smoke?
   ¿Me _____ fumar?

4. Could you take a ride with me tomorrow?
   ¿_____ Ud. dar una vuelta conmigo mañana?

5. I would accept but I can't go tomorrow.
   _____ pero no puedo ir mañana.

6. Would you lend me ten dollars?
   ¿Me _____ Ud. diez dólares?

7. Would you have time to do it?
   ¿ _____ Ud. tiempo de hacerlo?

8. Could I call you later?
   ¿_____ llamarlo más tarde?

9. He told me he would return soon.
   Me dijo que _____ pronto.

10. I ought to go now.
    _____ irme ahora.

SCORE _____%

HOW TO FORM THE PAST PARTICIPLE AND THE PERFECT TENSE

Caminando por una ciudad
Ka-mee-NAHN-doh por OO-na s'yoo-DAHD
Walking through a city

> **The present participle**
> *Caminando* is an example of how the present participle is used without a preposition to form a phrase. *Caminando* here could be translated as "while walking", "when walking", "by walking" etc. according to the context.

vemos diferentes letreros.
VAY-mohs dee-fay-REN-tays lay-TRAY-rohs.
we see different signs.

Algunos dicen cosas como
Ahl-GOO-nohs DEE-sen KO-sahs KO-mo
Some say things like

PROHIBIDO ESTACIONAR o
Proee-BEE-doh ess-ta-s'yo-NAR oh
NO PARKING or

ABIERTO HASTA LAS 5 o
Ah-B'YAIR-toh AHS-ta lahs SEEN-ko oh
OPEN UNTIL 5 or

CERRADO LOS DOMINGOS.
Say-RRA-doh los doh-MEEN-gohs.
CLOSED ON SUNDAYS.

También oímos frases como
Tahm-B'YEN oh-EE-mohs FRA-says KO-mo
We also hear phrases like

"Está permitido,"
"Ess-TA pair-mee-TEE-doh,"
"It is permitted,"

"Esto está vendido,"
"ESS-toh ess-TA ven-DEE-doh,"
"This is sold,"

"Está roto" o
"Ess-TA RRO-toh" oh
"It is broken" or

"El vice presidente está ocupado."
"El VEE-say pray-see-DEN-tay ess-TA oh-koo-PA-doh."
"The vice president is busy."

Las palabras *prohibido, abierto, cerrado,*
Lahs pa-LA-brahs *proee-BEE-doh, ah-B'YAIR-toh, say-RRA-doh,*
The words "forbidden," "opened," "closed,"

vendido, roto y *ocupado*
ven-DEE-doh, RO-toh* ee *oh-koo-PA-doh
"sold," "broken" and "busy"

son los participios pasados
sohn lohs par-tee-SEE-p'yohs pa-SA-dohs
are the past participles

de los verbos *prohibir, abrir,*
day los VAIR-bohs *pro-ee-BEER, ah-BREER,*
of the verbs "to prohibit," "to open,"

cerrar, vender, romper y *ocupar.*
sair-RAR, ven-DAIR, rom-PAIR* ee *oh-koo-PAR.
"to close," "to sell," "to break" and " to occupy."

The past participle is formed in the following way: for the 1st conjugation add -ado to the base, for the 2nd and 3rd add -ido.

Here are the principal irregular past participles of the 2nd and 3rd conjugation, and the verbs from which they come: *hecho (hacer), puesto (poner), dicho (decir), visto (ver), escrito*

233

(escribir), abierto (abrir), roto (romper), vuelto
(volver), cubierto (cubrir).

El participio pasado se usa también
El par-tee-SEE-p'yo pa-SA-doh say OO-sa tahm-b'YEN
The past participle is used also

para formar los tiempos compuestos
PA-ra for-MAR lohs T'YEM-pohs kohm-PWESS-tohs
to form the compound tenses

de los verbos.
deh lohs VAIR-bohs.
of the verbs.

Aquí, por ejemplo, tienen el pasado compuesto de *estar:*
Ah-KEE, por ay-HEM-plo T'YAY-nen el pa-SA-doh kohm-PWESS-toh
                                                    day ess-*TAR:*
Here, for example, you have the compound past (the perfect) of "to be":

¿Ha estado Ud. aquí antes?
¿Ah ess-TA-doh oo-STED ah-KEE AHN-tays?
Have you been here before?

No, nunca he estado aquí.
No, NOON-ka ay ess-TA-doh ah-KEE.
No, I've never been here.

Hemos estado esperando mucho tiempo.
AY-mohs ess-TA-doh ess-pair-RAHN-doh MOO-cho T'YEM-po.
We have been waiting a long time.

¿Dónde han estado últimamente?
¿DOHN-day ahn ess-TA-doh OOL-tee-ma-MEN-tay?
Where have you been lately?

El pasado compuesto
The perfect tense corresponds generally to the
English perfect such as "have spoken", "have
seen", "have been",, etc. The present tense of
haber ("to have") is used with the past participle to form the perfect:

he caminado
has caminado

ha caminado
hemos caminado
han caminado

Remember that *haber* meaning "to have" is not used alone, as "to have" is expressed by *tener*.

The only form of *haber* in frequent use in the present tense is *hay* ("there is" or "there are"), a variant of *ha*.

Aquí hay unos ejemplos
Ah-KEE I OO-nohs ay-HEM-plohs
Here are some examples

del pasado compuesto
del pa-SA-doh kohm-PWESS-toh
of the compound past

de los verbos que terminan an -*ar:*
day lohs VAIR-bohs kay tair-MEE-nahn en -*ar:*
of the verbs that end in -*ar:*

Yo nunca he estado aquí antes.
Yo NOON-ka ay ess-TA-doh ah-KEE AHN-tays.
I have never been here before.

¿Has terminado el trabajo?
¿Ahs tair-mee-NA-doh el tra-BA-ho?
Have you finished the work?

¿Ha llamado alguien esta mañana?
¿Ah l'ya-MA-doh AHL-gh'yen ES-ta mahn-YA-na?
Has anyone called this morning?

No hemos llegado todavía.
No AY-mohs l'yay-GA-doh toh-da-VEE-ya.
We haven't arrived yet.

¿Han comprado sus billetes de regreso?
¿Ahn kohm-PRA-doh soos beel-YAY-tays day ray-GRAY-so?
Have you bought your return tickets?

Spanish Step by Step

Para la segunda
PA-ra la say-GOON-da
For the second

y tercera conjugaciones
ee tair-SAIR-ra kohn-hoo-ga-S'YO-nays
and third conjugations

el participio pasado termina en *-ido,*
el par-tee-SEE-p'yo pa-SA-doh tair-MEE-na en *-EE-doh,*
the past participle ends in *-ido,*

excepto algunos verbos
ek-SEP-toh ahl-GOO-nohs VAIR-bohs
except some verbs

como: *hacer, poner, decir, ver,*
KO-mo: *ah-SAIR, po-NAIR, day-SEER, vair,*
such as: "to do," (or) "to make," "to put," "to say," "to see,"

escribir, abrir, y romper,
eh-skree-BEER, ah-BREER ee rohm-PAIR,
"to write," "to open," and "to break,"

cuyos participios pasados son:
KOO-yohs par-tee-SEEP-yohs pa-SA-dohs sohn:
whose past participles are:

hecho, puesto, dicho, visto,
AY-cho, PWESS-toh, DEE-cho, VEES-toh,
"done," (or) "made," "put," "said," "seen,"

escrito, abierto, roto.
eh-SKREE-toh, ahb-YAIR-toh, RRO-toh.
"written," "opened," "broken."

Algunos ejemplos:
Ahl-GOO-nohs ay-HEM-plohs:
Some examples:

¿Cuánto tiempo ha vivido aquí?
¿KWAHN-toh T'YEM-po ah vee-VEE-doh ah-KEE?
How long a time have you lived here?

He vivido aquí ocho meses.
Hay vee-VEE-doh ah-KEE OH-cho MAY-says.
I have lived here eight months.

¿Ha leído *Don Quijote?*
¿Ah lay-EE-doh *Dohn Kee-HO-tay?*
Have you read *Don Quixote?*

Si, lo he leído.
See, lo hay lay-EE-doh.
Yes, I have read it.

Las siguientes frases
Lahs see-GH'YEN-tays FRA-says
The following phrases

pueden ser de utilidad en un viaje:
PWAY-den sair day oo-tee-lee-DAHD en oon V'YA-hay:
may be of use on a trip:

¿Ha venido el auto?
¿Ah vay-NEE-doh el OW-toh?
Has the car come?

¿Ha salido el tren para Rosario?
¿Ah sa-LEE-doh el train PA-ra Ro-SAR-yo?
Has the train for Rosario left?

¿Qué ha sucedido?
¿Kay ah soo-say-DEE-doh?
What has happened?

¿Por qué hemos parado?
¿Por kay AY-mohs pa-RA-doh?
Why have we stopped?

Mi equipaje no ha llegado todavía.
Mee eh-kee-PA-hay no ah l'yay-GA-doh toh-da-VEE-ya.
My baggage hasn't arrived yet.

He perdido una maleta negra.
Ay pair-DEE-doh OO-na ma-LAY-ta NAY-gra.
I have lost a black suitcase.

Alguien se ha llevado mi abrigo
AHL-gh'yen say ah l'yay-VA-doh mee ah-BREE-go
Someone has taken my coat

probablemente por equivocación.
pro-ba-blay-MEN-tay por ay-kee-vo-ka-S'YOHN.
probably by mistake.

El participio pasado también se emplea
El par-tee-SEEP-yo pa-SA-doh tahm-b'YEN say em-PLAY-ah
The past participle is also used

con los verbos *ser* y *estar*.
kohn lohs VAIR-bohs *sair* ee *ess-TAR*.
with the verbs "to be" (description) and "to be" (location).

Estos ejemplos pueden ser útiles
ESS-tohs ay-HEM-plohs PWAY-den sair OO-tee-lays
These examples may be useful

cuando Ud. visita museos
KWAHN-doh oo-STED vee-SEE-ta moo-SAY-ohs
when you visit museums

u otros lugares históricos:
oo OH-trohs loo-GAR-ays ee-STO-ree-kohs:
or other historic places:

¿Está abierto el museo hoy?
¿Ess-TA ahb-YAIR-toh el moo-SAY-oh oy?
Is the museum open today?

¿Cuándo fue construído esto?
¿KWAHN-doh fway kohn-stroo-EE-doh ESS-toh?
When was this built?

¿Fue pintado este cuadro por Murillo?
¿Fway peen-TA-doh ESS-tay KWA-dro por Moo-REEL-yo?
Was this picture painted by Murillo?

¿En qué siglo fue descubierta Suramérica?
¿En kay SEE-glo f'way days-koo-B'YAIR-ta Soor-ah-MAY-ree-ka?
In what century was South America discovered?

238

INSTANT CONVERSATION: WHAT HAPPENED AT THE OFFICE

UNA SECRETARIA:
OO-na say-kray-TAR-ya:
A SECRETARY:
Bienvenido, señor Jaramillo.
B'yen-vay-NEE-doh, sen-YOR Ha-ra-MEEL-yo.
Welcome back, Mr. Jaramillo.

Le hemos extrañado mucho.
Lay AY-mohs ex-trahn-YA-doh MOO-cho.
We have missed you very much.

EL JEFE:
El HEH-feh:
THE BOSS:
Gracias. ¿Qué ha sucedido
Gra-s'yahs. ¿Kay ah soo-say-DEE-doh
Thanks. What has happened

durante mi ausencia?
doo-RAHN-tay mee ow-SEN-s'ya?
during my absence?

LA SECRETARIA:
Bueno, vamos a ver.
BWAY-no, VA-mohs ah vair.
Well, let's see.

Esta semana los vendedores han vendido
ESS-ta say-MA-na lohs ven-day-DOH-rays ahn ven-DEE-doh
This week the salesmen have sold

dos camiones, siete camionetas,
dohs ka-M'YO-nays, S'YAY-tay ka-m'yo-NAY-tahs,
two trucks, seven station wagons,

239

Spanish Step by Step

y una motocicleta.
ee OO-na mo-toh-see-KLAY-ta.
and a motorcycle.

Han pasado el total de ventas
Ahn pa-SA-doh el toh-TAHL day VEN-tahs
They have passed the total of sales

del mes pasado.
del mays pa-SA-doh.
of last month.

EL JEFE:
¡No me diga! ¿Ha completado
¡No may DEE-ga! ¿Ah kohm-play-TA-doh
You don't say! Have you finished

> **You don't say**
> *¡No me diga!* literally "Don't tell me!" is an idiom for "You don't say!" or "You don't tell me!"

todas las facturas
TOH-dahs lahs fahk-TOO-rahs
all the bills

para estas ventas?
PA-ra ESS-tahs VEN-tahs?
for these sales?

LA SECRETARIA:
Desde luego.
DESS-day LWAY-go.
Of course.

También he depositado
Tahm-B'YEN hay day-po-see-TA-doh
I have also deposited

los cheques y el efectivo
lohs CHAY-kays ee el ay-fek-TEE-vo
the checks and the cash

240

en el banco cada día.
en el BAHN-ko KA-da DEE-ya.
in the bank each day.

EL JEFE:
Veo que Ud. ha trabajado bastante
VAY-oh kay oo-STED ah tra-ba-HA-doh bahs-TAHN-tay
I see that you have worked a lot

en estos días.
en ESS-tohs DEE-yahs.
these days.

LA SECRETARIA:
¡Ya lo creo!
¡Ya lo KRAY-oh!
Yes indeed!

> **¡Ya lo creo!**
> The literal meaning of *Ya lo creo* is "I certainly
> think so." and its idiomatic meaning is equiva-
> lent to "Yes, indeed" or "I should say so."

No he salido de la oficina
No hay sa-LEE-doh day la oh-fee-SEE-na
I haven't left the office

hasta las siete o las ocho
AHS-ta lahs S'YAY-tay oh lahs OH-cho
until seven or eight

en toda la semana.
en TOH-da la say-MA-na.
all week long.

EL JEFE:
¿La señorita Hernández
¿La sen-yo-REE-ta Air-NAHN-dayss
Miss Hernandez

no la ha ayudado?
no la ah ah-yoo-DA-doh?
hasn't helped you?

241

LA SECRETARIA:
No, no ha venido
No, no ah vay-NEE-doh
No, she hasn't come for

los tres últimos días.
lohs trayss OOL-tee-mohs DEE-yahs.
the last three days.

Ha estado enferma.
Ah ess-TA-doh en-FAIR-ma.
She has been sick.

EL JEFE:
Lo siento. Dígame,
Lo S'YEN-toh. DEE-ga-may,
I'm sorry. Tell me,

la nueva recepcionista
la NWAY-va ray-sep-s'yo-NEES-ta
the new receptionist

¿ha estado trabajando bien?
¿ah ess-TA-doh tra-ba-HAHN-doh b'yen?
has she been working well?

LA SECRETARIA:
Bueno, a decir verdad,
BWAY-no, ah day-SEER vair-DAHD,
Well, to tell the truth,

ha llegado tarde cada mañana
ah l'yay-GA-doh TAR-day KA-da mahn-YA-na
she has arrived late every morning

y además ha pasado
ee ah-day-MAHS ah pa-SA-doh
and, furthermore, she has spent

la mayor parte del día
la ma-YOR PAR-tay del DEE-ya
most of the day

charlando por teléfono.
char-LAHN-doh por tay-LAY-fo-no.
chatting on the telephone.

EL JEFE:
A propósito, ¿ha habido
Ah pro-PO-see-toh, ¿ah ah-BEE-doh
By the way, have there been

llamadas importantes para mí?
l'ya-MA-dahs eem-por-TAHN-tays PA-ra mee?
important calls for me?

LA SECRETARIA:
Hemos llevado una lista.
AY-mohs l'yay-VA-doh OO-na LEES-ta.
We have kept a list.

Una señorita Gloria
OO-na sen-yo-REE-ta GLO-r'ya
A Miss Gloria

le ha llamado varias veces.
lay ah l'ya-MA-doh VA-r'yahs VAY-says.
has called you several times.

Dejó su número
Day-HO soo NOO-may-ro
She left her number

pero no quiso dejar su apellido.
PAY-ro no KEE-so day-HAR soo ah-pel-YEE-doh.
but she wouldn't leave her last name.

EL JEFE:
¡Ah, sí! Creo que sé quién es.
¡Ah, see! KRAY-oh kay say k'yen ess.
Ah, yes! I believe I know who it is.

¿Dónde ha puesto mis recados?
¿DOHN-day ah PWESS-toh mees reh-KA-dohs?
Where have you put my messages?

LA SECRETARIA:

En la gaveta de su escritorio. Está cerrada con llave.
**En la ga-VAY-ta day soo ess-kree-TOH-r'yo. Ess-TA sair-RRA-da
kohn L'YA-vay.**
In the drawer of your desk. It is locked.

Nadie los ha leído.
NA-d'yay lohs ah lay-EE-doh.
No one has read them.

EL JEFE:

Ha sido Ud. muy discreta, señorita Valdés.
**Ah SEE-doh oo-STED mwee dees-KRAY-ta, sen-yo-REE-ta
Vahl-DAYSS.**
You have been very discreet, Miss Valdes.

Y, como ha trabajado tanto,
Ee, KO-mo ah tra-ba-HA-doh TAHN-toh,
And, as you have worked so much,

he decidido darle
ay day-see-DEE-doh DAR-lay
I have decided to give you

el aumento de sueldo.
el ow-MEN-toh day SWEL-doh.
the raise in salary.

del cual hemos hablado antes.
del kwal AY-mohs ah-BLA-doh AHN-tays.
about which we have spoken before.

LA SECRETARIA:

¿De verdad? Mil gracias, jefe.
¿Day vair-DAHD? Meel GRA-s'yahs, HAY-fay.
Really? Many thanks, chief.

> **El jefe**
> *Jefe*, the word for "chief," is also used colo-
> quially for one's employer or "boss."

TEST YOUR SPANISH

Complete each sentence by translating from English into Spanish. Score 10 points for each correct answer. See answers below.

1. Podemos entrar — la tienda está _____.
   (open)

2. No está _____ fumar aquí.
   (permitted)

3. El cuadro ya está _____.
   (sold)

4. ¿_____ este letrero?
   (Have you seen)

5. No lo conozco — yo _____ allí.
   (have not been)

6. ¿_____ el trabajo?
   (Have they done)

7. El Quijote _____ por Cervantes.
   (was written)

8. ¿Qué _____ aquí?
   (has happened)

9. ¿_____ la lección?
   (Have we finished)

10. No podemos venderlo porque _____.
    (it is broken.)

SCORE _____%

step 21

THE IMPERFECT: A TENSE TO USE WHEN TELLING A STORY

Cuando empleamos expresiones como
KWAN-doh em-play-AH-mohs ess-pray-S'YO-nays KO-mo
When we employ expressions like

Mi padre siempre decía . . .
Mee PA-dray s'YEM-pray day-SEE-ya . . .
My father always used to say . . .

o "Cuando yo era joven . . ."
oh "KWAN-doh yo AY-ra HO-ven . . ."
or "When I was young . . ."

o "Cuando vivíamos en Cuba . . ."
oh "KWAN-doh vee-VEE-ya-mohs en KOO-ba . . ."
or "When we lived in Cuba . . ."

o "Cuando estábamos en el colegio . . ."
oh "KWAN-doh ess-TA-ba-mohs en el ko-LAY-h'yo . . ."
or "When we were in school . . ."

y otras cosas expresando acciones repetidas
**ee OH-trahs KO-sahs ess-pray-SAHN-doh ahk-S'YO-nays
ray-pay-TEE-dahs**
and other things expressing repeated actions

o continuadas en el pasado
oh kohn-tee-NWA-dahs en el pa-SA-doh
or continued in the past

usamos el tiempo imperfecto.
oo-SA-mohs el T'YEM-po eem-pair-FEK-toh.
we use the imperfect tense.

El imperfecto
The imperfect is equivalent to the English "used to" in the sense of a continued action in the past whether or not "used to" is specifically used. For instance, to say you were living somewhere for a period of time, use the imperfect, as this was a continued action. The imperfect is also used for something that was going on at a certain time.

I was singing	*Cantaba*
I used to sing	
You were dancing	*Bailaba*
You used to dance	
They were living	*Vivían*
(or) used to live	

And a repeated action in the past, such as:

Nuestro maestro nos decía,
"Más vale pájaro en la mano que cien volando."
Our teacher used to tell us,
"(A) bird in the hand is worth more than a hundred flying."

Para formar el imperfecto
PA-ra for-MAR el eem-pair-FEK-toh
To form the imperfect

de la primera conjugación
day la pree-MAY-ra kohn-hoo-ga-s'yohn
of the first conjugation

acuérdense de la combinación *-aba*
ah-KWAIR-den-say day la kohm-bee-na-S'YOHN *-aba*
remember the combination -aba

First conjugation ending; -aba
The imperfect endings for the 1st conjugation can be recognized by the *-aba* combination as in the imperfect of *tomar* ("to take"): *tomaba, tomabas, tomábamos* and *tomaban.* Yo, Ud., él, ella have the same form. The verb *ir* "to go" follows the 1st conjugation in the imperfect and becomes *iba, ibas, íbamos, iban.*

247

y para la segunda y tercera conjugaciones
ee PA-ra la say-GOON-da ee tair-SAIR-ra kohn-hoo-ga-S'YO-nays
and for the second and third conjugations

acuérdense de la combinación *-ía.*
ah-KWEHR-den-say day la kohm-bee-na-S'YOHN *-ía.*
remember the combination *-ía.*

> **Second and Third Conjugations: -ía**
> The imperfect endings for the 2nd and 3rd con-
> jugations are the same. The key sound is *-ía*
> which is, you will remember, the same as the
> conditional endings, but this time they go
> directly on the *base* of the verb. The imperfect
> of *vivir*, for example, is *vivía, vivías, vivíamos, vi-*
> *vían.* The only exception in the 2nd conjugation
> is the verb *ser* — "to be" which in the imper-
> fect is: *era, eras, éramos, eran.*

El imperfecto se usa
El eem-pair-FEK-toh say OO-sa
The imperfect is used

para contar cuentos, recuerdos.
PA-ra kohn-TAR KWEN-tohs, reh-KWAIR-dohs.
to tell stories, memories.

Cuando yo era joven
KWAN-doh yo AIR-ra HO-ven
When I was young

y vivíamos en Santa Clara,
ee vee-VEE-yah-mohs en SAHN-ta KLA-ra,
and we lived in Santa Clara,

había una costumbre interesante
ah-BEE-yah OO-na kohs-TOOM-bray een-tay-ray-SAHN-tay
there was an interesting custom

que tenía lugar por las noches
kay tay-NEE-ya loo-GAR por lahs NO-chays
that took place in the evening

en la plaza principal.
en la PLA-sa preen-see-PAHL.
in the main square.

Mientras la banda militar
M'YEN-trahs la BAHN-da mee-lee-TAR
While the military band

tocaba en el centro
toh-KA-ba en el SEN-tro
played in the center

las chicas solían pasear
lahs CHEE-kahs so-LEE-yahn pa-say-AR
the girls would walk

en parejas o en grupos
en pa-RAY-hahs oh en GROO-pohs
in pairs or in groups

alrededor de la plaza
ahl-ray-day-DOR day la PLA-sa
around the square

en un sentido,
en oon sen-TEE-doh,
in one direction,

mientras que los chicos
M'YEN-trahs kay lohs CHEE-kohs
while the boys

daban la vuelta en el sentido contrario
DA-bahn la VWEL-ta en el sen-TEE-doh kohn-TRA-r'yo
went around in the opposite direction

o se quedaban parados
oh say kay-DA-bahn pa-RA-dohs
or they remained standing

mirando a las chicas pasar.
mee-RAHN-doh ah lahs CHEE-kahs pa-SAR.
watching the girls go by.

Así es que en su vuelta
Ah-SEE ess kay en soo VWEL-ta
Thus in their turn

todos los muchachos
TOH-dohs lohs moo-CHA-chohs
all the boys

veían pasar a todas las muchachas
vay-EE-yahn pa-SAR ah TOH-dahs lahs moo-CHA-chahs
would see all the girls pass

> **Habitual action**
> *Veían* is translated here as "would see" al-
> though it could equally well be translated as
> "saw" "used to see" or "were seeing," as
> long as it gives the sense of extended, re-
> peated, or habitual action; which is what the im-
> perfect is.

repetidas veces.
ray-pay-TEE-dahs VAY-says.
repeatedly.

Si una muchacha
See OO-na moo-CHA-cha
If a girl

respondía a una sonrisa o a un saludo
rays-pohn-DEE-yah ah OO-na sohn-REE-sa oh ah oon sa-LOO-doh
responded to a smile or a greeting

el joven cambiaba de rumbo
el HO-ven kahm-B'YA-ba day ROOM-bo
the young man would change direction

y continuaba con esa señorita
ee kohn-tee-NWA-ba kohn ES-sa sen-yo-REE-ta
and would continue with that young lady

paseando en el sentido contrario.
pa-say-AHN-doh en el sen-TEE-doh kohn-TRA-r'yo.
walking in the opposite direction.

Así se formaban parejas
Ah-SEE say for-MA-bahn pa-RAY-hahs
Thus couples were formed

y si las mismas parejas
ee see lahs MEES-mahs pa-RAY-hahs
and if the same couples

continuaban paseando juntas
kohn-tee-NWA-bahn pa-say-AHN-doh HOON-tahs
continued to walk together

varias noches,
VA-r'yahs NO-chays,
several evenings,

la gente consideraba que eran novios.
la HEN-tay kohn-see-day-RA-ba kay EH-rahn NO-v'yohs.
people considered they were engaged.

Novio — novia
The word *novio* (feminine: *novia*) means "fiancée," official or semi-official, as used here. The expression "engaged to be married" is *comprometido* of which the literal translation is "compromised."

Las cosas han cambiado
Lahs KO-sahs ahn kahm-B'YA-doh
Things have changed

An old Spanish custom
Although the old custom described here is no longer as prevalent as before, in many smaller towns it is still followed. ¡Olé! for romance.

desde entonces, ¿verdad?
DES-day en-TOHN-says, ¿vair-DAHD?
since then, haven't they?

El imperfecto se usa para expresar
El eem-pair-FEK-toh say OO-sa PA-ra ess-pray-SAR
The imperfect is used to express

una acción continuada
OO-na ahk-S'YOHN kohn-tee-NWA-da
a continued action

interrumpida por una acción terminada: —
een-tay-rroom-PEE-da por OO-na ahk-S'YOHN tair-mee-NA-da: —
interrupted by a finished action: —

Estaba dormido de lo más tranquilo
Ess-TA-ba dor-MEE-doh day lo mahs trahn-KEE-lo
I was sleeping very quietly

cuando sonó el teléfono.
KWAN-doh so-NO el tay-LAY-fo-no.
when the phone rang.

Era ese idiota de Gómez
EH-ra EH-say ee-D'YO-ta day GO-mayss
It was that idiot Gómez

que quería saber el número
kay kay-REE-yah sa-BAIR el NOO-may-ro
who wanted to know the number

de Gloria Hernández.
day GLO-r'ya Air-NAHN-dayss.
of Gloria Hernandez.

Yo le dije que no me gustaba
Yo lay DEE-hay kay no may goos-TA-ba
I told him that I didn't like

tener que contestar el teléfono
teh-NAIR kay kohn-tess-TAR el tay-LAY-fo-no
to have to answer the telephone

cuando dormía.
KWAN-doh dor-MEE-ya.
when I was sleeping.

Interrupted action
Another important use of the imperfect is to set
the descriptive stage for something that was
going on when something else happened, as in
the above case of a man awakened by the sud-

den intrusion of the telephone, who was already performing one action (sleeping) when another event happened (the sudden ringing of the telephone).

INSTANT CONVERSATION: A FAMILY REUNION — RECALLING THE PAST

ÉL:
El:
HE:

Al visitar a mis abuelos
Ahl vee-see-TAR ah mees ah-BWAY-lohs
When we visit my grandparents

"Al" and the infinitive
The contraction *al* used with the infinitive of the verb can be translated as "when" and the infinitive is then translated by the verb form that would correspond to English usage. *Al visitar* could be translated as "when I (you, he, she, etc.) visited." Here we translate it as the present because the speakers haven't made the visit yet.

La cortesía (politeness)
When you are visiting people, they will usually say at some point *Está Ud. en su casa* — "You are in your (own) home." Also, if you express admiration for something, they will usually say *Es suyo* — "It is yours," and frequently try to give it to you.

sin duda encontrarás
seen DOO-da en-kohn-tra-RAHS
no doubt you will find

que hablarán mucho de mí.
kay ah-bla-RAHN MOO-cho day mee.
that they will talk a lot about me.

Contarán cómo era
Kohn-ta-RAHN KO-mo AIR-ra
They will tell how I was

cuando niño
KWAHN-do NEEN-yo
when a boy

y todo lo que hacía cuando era joven.
ee TOH-doh lo kay ah-SEE-ya KWAHN-doh AIR-ra HO-ven.
and all (that) I used to do when I was young.

ELLA:
El-ya:
SHE:
Eso tendría que ser interesantísimo.
ES-so ten-DREE-ya kay sair een-tay-ray-sahn-TEE-see-mo.
That should be very interesting.

LA ABUELA:
La ah-BWAY-la:
THE GRANDMOTHER:
Pablo siempre pasaba los veranos
PA-blo S'YEM-pray pa-SA-ba lohs vay-RA-nos
Pablo always spent the summers

en nuestra finca.
en NUES-tra FEEN-ka.
at our farm.

> **Finca, rancho, hacienda**
> *Finca* is just one word for "farm" or "country property." Others include *rancho, granja, hacienda,* and *estancia,* the last two suggesting somewhat more lavish and extensive properties.

Era un muchacho buen mozo
AIR-ra oon moo-CHA-cho bwen MO-so
He was a handsome boy

y muy inteligente
ee mwee een-tay-lee-HEN-tay
and very intelligent

pero nos daba mucho que hacer.
PAIR-ro nohs DA-ba MOO-cho kay ah-SAIR.
but he gave us a lot of trouble.

EL ABUELO:
El ah-BWAY-lo:
THE GRANDFATHER:
Salía a caballo
Sa-LEE-ya ah ka-BAHL-yo
He would go horseback riding

sin decirnos adónde iba.
seen day-SEER-nohs ah-DOHN-day EE-ba.
without telling us where he was going.

LA ABUELA:
A veces regresaba
AH VAY-says ray-gray-SA-ba
And sometimes he would return

muy tarde de noche.
mwee TAR-day day NO-chay.
very late at night.

EL ABUELO:
Siempre le encantaban las corridas.
S'YEM-pray lay en-kahn-TA-bahn lahs ko-REE-dahs.
He always was crazy about bullfights.

Decía que quería
Day-SEE-ya kay kay-REE-ya
He used to say that he wanted

llegar a ser matador algún día.
l'yay-GAR ah sair ma-ta-DOR ahl-GOON DEE-ya.
to be a matador some day.

LA ABUELA:
Imagínese, una vez
Ee-ma-HEE-nay-say, OO-na vayss
Just imagine, once

¡Figúrese!
Imaginarse and *figurarse* both mean "to imagine" and they are often used in the exclamations *¡Imagínese!* and *¡Figúrese!*, meaning "Just imagine!"

que lo buscábamos por todas partes
kay lo boos-KA-ba-mohs por TOH-dahs PAR-tays
when we were looking everywhere for him

lo encontramos en el corral.
lo en-kon-TRA-mohs en el ko-RRAHL.
we found him in the corral.

Estaba jugando a torero
Ess-TA-ba hoo-GAHN-doh ah toh-RAY-ro
He was playing bullfighter

The progressive
The imperfect tense, like other tenses, can use the progressive form to make the story more vivid. In this case the verb is in the present participle form and estar is in the imperfect.

con los novillos.
kohn lohs no-VEEL-yohs.
with the calves.

EL ABUELO:
Era muy travieso pero valiente.
AIR-ra mwee tra-V'YAY-so PAIR-ro va-L'YEN-tay.
He was very mischievous but brave.

No tenía miedo de nada.
No tay-NEE-ya M'YAY-doh day NA-da.
He wasn't afraid of anything.

LA ABUELA:
Al salir él para los Estados Unidos
Ahl sa-LEER el PA-ra lohs Ess-TA-dohs Oo-NEE-dohs
When he left for the United States

pensábamos que iba a hacer
pen-SA-ba-mohs kay EE-ba ah ah-SAIR
we thought that he was going to make

sólo una corta visita
SO-lo OO-na KOR-ta vee-SEE-ta
just a short visit

> **Solo-sólo**
> *Solo* without an accent means "alone," but *sólo*
> with an accent means "just" or "only."

y que debía regresar pronto.
ee kay day-BEE-ya ray-gray-SAR PROHN-toh.
and that he was going to come back soon.

Desde luego nosotros no sabíamos
DES-day LWEH-go no-SO-trohs no sa-BEE-ya-mohs
Of course we didn't know

que iba a casarse
kay EE-ba ah ka-SAR-say
that he was going to get married

con una americana.
kohn OO-na ah-may-ree-KA-na.
to an American.

EL ABUELO:

¡Y con una americana tan encantadora!
¡Ee kohn OO-na ah-may-ree-KA-na tahn en-kahn-ta-DOH-ra!
And to so charming an American!

Siempre queríamos conocerla en persona.
S'YEM-pray kair-REE-ya-mohs ko-no-SAIR-la en pair-SO-na.
We always wanted to meet you in person.

LA ABUELA:

Vengan, hijos míos.
VEN-gahn, EE-hohs MEE-yohs.
Come, my children.

Está servida la comida.
Ess-TA sair-VEE-da la ko-MEE-da.
The dinner is served.

Al saber la cocinera
Ahl sa-BAIR la ko-see-NAIR-ra
When the cook learned

que Pablo venía
kay PA-blo vay-NEE-ya
that Pablo was coming

preparó un cabrito guisado.
pray-pa-RO oon ka-BREE-toh ghee-SA-doh.
she prepared a goat stew.

A Pablo le gustaba tanto
Ah PA-blo lay goos-TA-ba TAHN-toh
Pablo used to like it so much

cuando era niño.
KWAN-doh AIR-ra NEEN-yo.
when he was a boy.

———————

ELLA:
Bueno, me enteré de muchas cosas
BWAY-no, may en-tair-RAY day MOO-chahs KO-sahs
Well, I learned many things

acerca de ti y de tus hazañas
ah-SAIR-ka day tee ee day toos ah-SAHN-yahs
about you and your exploits

que no conocía antes.
kay no ko-no-SEE-ya AHN-tayss.
that I didn't know before.

Pero, ¡dime tú!
PAIR-ro, ¡DEE-may too!
But you tell me!

¿Cómo voy a preparar un cabrito guisado?
¿KO-mo voy ah pray-PA-rar oon ka-BREE-toh ghee-SA-doh?
How am I going to prepare a goat stew?

TEST YOUR SPANISH

Match these phrases: Score 10 points for each correct answer. See answers below.

1. I used to sing
—— Vivían aquí.

2. You were dancing.
—— Había una chica allí.

3. They used to live here.
—— Dormía cuando él llamó.

4. We used to go there.
—— Había parejas bailando.

5. I used to know him.
—— Eran las dos cuando llegué.

6. There was a girl there.
—— Cantaba

7. I was sleeping when he called.
—— Tenía cinco años cuando fuí al colegio.

8. It was two o'clock when I arrived.
—— Lo conocía.

9. I was five when I went to school.
—— Bailaba.

10. There were couples dancing.
—— Íbamos allí.

Answers: 3–6–7–10–8–1–9–5–2–4

SCORE ____%

THE PAST PERFECT AND THE FUTURE PERFECT

Las formas del imperfecto de *haber,*
Lahs FOR-mahs del eem-pair-FEK-toh day *ah-BAIR,*
The forms of the imperfect of "to have,"

había, habías, habíamos y *habían.*

se combinan
say kohm-BEE-nahn
are combined

con el participio pasado
kohn el par-tee-SEE-p'yo pa-SA-doh
with the past participle

para formar otro tiempo,
PA-ra for-MAR OH-tro T'YEM-po,
to make another tense,

el pluscuamperfecto.
el ploos-kwahm-pair-FEK-toh.
the pluperfect.

A long name: an easy tense
This tense, the *pluscuamperfecto* (past perfect);
has a name almost longer than the time it takes
to explain how to use it, which is quite simple. It
is equivalent to the English constructions "had
gone," "had seen," "had heard," "had come,"
etc. and is formed with the imperfect of *haber*
plus the past participle of the verb.

Ejemplos:
Ay-HEM-plohs:
Examples:

Cuando llegamos a la estación
KWAN-doh l'yay-GA-mohs a la ess-ta-S'YOHN
When we arrived at the station

el tren ya había partido.
el trayn ya ah-BEE-ya par-TEE-doh.
the train had already left.

Ya nos habíamos acostado
Ya nohs ah-BEE-ya-mohs ah-kohs-TA-doh
We had already gone to bed

cuando Víctor vino de visita.
KWAN-doh VEEK-tor VEE-no day vee-SEE-ta.
when Victor came to visit.

Anoche cuando fui a tu casa
Ah-NO-chay KWAN-doh fwee ah too KA-sa
Last night when I went to your house

me dijeron que habías salido con otro.
may dee-HEH-rohn kay ah-BEE-yahs sa-LEE-doh kohn OH-tro.
they told me you had gone out with someone else.

Antes de ver a los españoles
AHN-tays day vehr ah lohs ess-pahn-YO-lays
Before seeing the Spaniards

los aztecas nunca habían visto
lohs ahs-TEH-kahs NOON-ka ah-BEE-yahn VEES-toh
the Aztecs had never seen

a hombres blancos.
ah OHM-brays BLAHN-kohs.
white men.

La siguiente narración mostrará claramente
La see-GH'YEN-tay na-ra-SYOHN mohs-tra-RA kla-ra-MEN-tay
The following narrative will show clearly

cómo se usa este tiempo
KO-mo say OO-sa ESS-tay T'YEM-po
how this tense is used

en la conversación:
en la kohn-vehr-sa-S'YOHN:
in conversation:

Ya habíamos terminado la cena
Ya ah-BEE-ya-mohs tair-mee-NA-doh la SAY-na
We had already finished dinner

y estábamos en la sala
ee ess-TA-ba-mohs en la SA-la
and we were in the living room

cuando de repente oímos un grito
KWAN-doh day ray-PEN-tay oh-EE-mohs oon GREE-toh
when suddenly we heard a scream

que venía del jardín.
kay veh-NEE-ya del har-DEEN.
which was coming from the garden.

Al salir fuera encontramos
Ahl sa-LEER FWAY-ra en-kohn-TRA-mohs
When we got outside we found

que la sirvienta que estaba allí
kay la seer-V'YEN-ta kay ess-TA-ba ahl-YEE
that the maid who was there

había visto una sombra detrás de un árbol
ah-BEE-ya VEES-toh OO-na SOHM-bra day-TRAHS day oon AR-bol
had seen a shadow behind a tree

y creía que era un intruso
ee kray-EE-ah kay EH-ra oon een-TROO-so
and thought that it was an intruder

que había subido por la pared
kay ah-BEE-ya soo-BEE-doh por la pa-RED
who had climbed the wall

263

y que iba a entrar en la casa.
ee kay EE-ba ah en-TRAR en la KA-sa.
and who was going to enter (inside) the house.

Different stages of action
This little scene illustrates the relationship between the different past tenses: the imperfect sets the stage for what was going on at a certain time; the sudden cry, in that it happened once only, is the regular past; and the fact that the girl *had* thought she had seen someone about whom she *had* read is, of course, in the past perfect.

¡Socorro!
Speaking of emergencies, here are some key words:

Help! — *¡Socorro!*
Fire! — *¡Fuego!*
Look out! — *¡Cuidado!*
Quickly! — *¡Rápido!*
Stop, thief! — *¡Al ladrón!*
There he (she) goes! — *¡Allí va!*
Stop! — *¡Alto!*

La probrecita tenía mucho miedo
La po-bray-SEE-ta teh-NEE-ya MOO-cho M'YAY-doh
The poor girl was very frightened

y aunque le asegurábamos
ee OW'N-kay leh ah-seh-goo-RA-ba-mohs
and although we kept assuring her

que no había nadie allí
kay no ah-BEE-ya NA-d'yay ah-YEE
that there was no one there

seguía de lo más nerviosa.
seh-GHEE-ah day lo mahs nair-V'YO-sa.
she continued to be extremely nervous.

Parece que había leído un artículo
Pa-RAY-say kay ah-BEE-ya lay-EE-doh oon ar-TEE-koo-lo
It appears that she had read an article

en la prensa
en la PREN-sa
in the press

sobre un ladrón que entraba
SO-breh oon la-DROHN kay en-TRA-ba
about a burglar who was in the habit of entering

en las casas de noche
en lahs KA-sahs day NO-chay
houses at night

subiendo por las paredes de los jardines.
soo-B'YEN-doh por lahs pa-RAY-days day lohs har-DEE-nays.
by climbing over the garden walls.

Como el pluscuamperfecto indica
KO-mo el ploos-kwam-pair-FEK-toh een-DEE-ka
As the past perfect indicates

una acción ya terminada en el pasado
OO-na ahk-S'YOHN ya tair-mee-NA-da en el pa-SA-doh
an action already finished in the past

el futuro perfecto indica
el foo-TOO-ro pair-FEK-toh een-DEE-ka
the future perfect indicates

una acción terminada en el futuro.
OO-na ahk-S'YOHN tair-mee-NA-da en el foo-TOO-ro.
an action finished in the future.

Se forma con el futuro de *haber*
Se FOR-ma kohn el foo-TOO-ro day *ah-BAIR*
It is formed with the future of *"to have"*

y el participio pasado. Así:
ee el par-tee-SEE-p'yo pa-SA-doh. Ah-SEE:
and the past participle. Like this:

¿Cree Ud. que ya habrán terminado de comer?
¿Kray oo-STED kay ya ah-BRAHN tair-mee-NA-doh day ko-MAIR?
Do you think they will have already finished dinner?

Para la semana próxima habré recibido
PA-ra la say-MA-na PROHK-see-ma ah-BRAY ray-see-BEE-doh
By next week I will have received

> **An action that will have happened**
> The past participle is used with the future of
> *haber* to form the future perfect. Here are the
> five forms with *recibir* ("to receive"), corre-
> sponding to the concept "will have received":
>
> *habré recibido, habrás recibido, habrá recibido,
> habremos recibido, habrán recibido.*

mis notas de los exámenes finales.
mees NO-tahs day lohs ek-SA-meh-nays fee-NA-lays.
my grades in the final exams.

En su próximo aniversario habrán cumplido
**En soo PROHK-see-mo ah-nee-vair-SA-r'yo ah-BRAHN
koom-PLEE-doh**
On their next anniversary they will have completed

veinte años de casados.
vayn-tay AHN-yohs day ka-SA-dohs.
twenty years of (being) married.

La conversación siguiente muestra
La kohn-vair-sa-S'YOHN see-GH'YEN-tay MWESS-tra
The following conversation shows

cómo este tiempo sirve
KO-mo ESS-tay T'YEM-po SEER-vay
how this tense is used

para expresar cosas que
PA-ra ess-preh-SAR KO-sahs kay
to express things which

habrán ocurrido en el futuro.
ah-BRAHN oh-koo-RREE-doh en el foo-TOO-ro.
will have occurred in the future.

INSTANT CONVERSATION: FUTURE PROGRESS IN SCIENCE

FULANO:

En cien años
En s'yen AHN-yohs
In a hundred years

¿qué cambios habrán ocurrido?
¿kay KAHM-b'yohs ah-BRAHN oh-koo-RREE-doh?
what changes will have occurred?

MENGANO:

Sin duda muchos ya habrán hecho
Seen DOO-da MOO-chohs ya ah-BRAHN AY-cho
Without doubt many will already have made

viajes a la luna.
V'YA-hays ah la LOO-na.
trips to the moon.

Habremos establecido colonias en los otros planetas.
Ah-BRAY-mohs ess-ta-bleh-SEE-doh ko-LO-nee-yahs en lohs
                                      OH-trohs pla-NAY-tahs.
We will have established colonies on the other planets.

Los científicos habrán descubierto
Lohs s'yen-TEE-fee-kohs ah-BRAHN des-koob-YAIR-toh
Scientists will have discovered

nuevos métodos de alimentación.
N'WAY-vohs MAY-toh-dohs day ah-lee-men-ta-S'YOHN.
new methods of nutrition.

El progreso de la medicina
El pro-GRAY-so day la may-dee-SEE-na
Progress in medicine

habrá prolongado la vida.
ah-BRA pro-lohn-GA-doh la VEE-da.
will have prolonged life.

El uso de las computadoras
El OO-so day lahs kohm-poo-ta-DOH-rahs
The use of computers

habrá cambiado el sistema de educación.
ah-BRA kahm-B'YA-doh el sees-TAY-ma day eh-doo-ka-S'YOHN.
will have changed the system of education.

ZUTANO:

Quizá. ¿Pero cree Ud. que habrán encontrado
Kee-SA. ¿Pair-ro kray oo-STED kay ah-BRAHN en-kohn-TRA-doh
Perhaps. But do you think that they will have found

un medio de reducir los impuestos?
oon mayd-yo day ray-doo-SEER lohs eem-PWESS-tohs?
a means of reducing taxes?

Fulano
The three names used in the preceding discussion come from the Spanish version of "Tom, Dick, and Harry" which is *Fulano, Mengano, y Zutano.* And, *when a person's name is unknown, Fulano* is generally used, as in the English expression "What's his name"

Planeta — Planet
Although ending in a *planeta* is masculine since it stems from a Greek masculine word.

TEST YOUR SPANISH

Fill in the past perfect and future perfect verb forms. Score 10 points for each correct answer. See answers below.

1. Cuando llegamos al café él_____.
   (had left)

2. Pensaba que yo_____mi cartera.
   (had lost)

3. Pero un policía me llamó diciéndome que la_____.
   (had found)

4. Cuando llamó a su casa le dijeron que ella_____a Acapulco.
   (had gone)

5. Queríamos conocerlo porque_____ su último libro.
   (we had read)

6. Ellos no sabían que yo_____ en España.
   (had lived)

7. Mañana él_____ el cheque.
   (will have received)

8. Dentro de dos años ellos_____sus diplomas.
   (will have received)

9. En poco tiempo los astronautas_____bases en la luna.
   (will have established)

10. ¿Cuándo cree que nosotros_____ el trabajo?
    (will have finished)

Answers: 1. había partido 2. había perdido 3. había encontrado 4. había ido 5. habíamos leído 6. había vivido 7. habrá recibido 8. habrán recibido 9. habrán establecido 10. habremos terminado.

SCORE _____%

step 23 HOW TO USE THE SUBJUNCTIVE

El subjuntivo es fácil
El soob-hoon-TEE-vo ess FA-seel
The subjunctive is easy

porque ya sabe Ud. cómo se forma,
POR-kay ya SA-be oo-STED KO-mo say FOR-ma,
because you already know how it is formed,

puesto que el verbo tiene la misma forma
PWESS-toh kay el VAIR-bo T'YAY-nay la MEES-ma FOR-ma
since the verb has the same form

que se usa para dar órdenes:
kay say OO-sa PA-ra dar OR-day-nays:
that is used to give orders:

¡Entre! ¡Venga aquí! ¡Siéntese!
¡EN-tray! ¡VEN-ga ah-KEE! ¡S'YEN-tay-say!
Come in! Come here! Sit down!

Tome un cigarrillo. ¡Dígame!
TOH-may oon see-ga-RREEL-yo. ¡DEE-ga-may!
Have a cigarette. Tell me!

El subjuntivo se usa
El soob-hoon-TEE-vo say OO-sa
The subjunctive is used

en frases que expresan deseo.
en FRA-sess kay es-PRAY-sahn day-SAY-oh.
in phrases that express a wish.

Quieren que vayamos a la fiesta.
K'YAIR-ren kay va-YA-mohs ah la F'YESS-ta.
They want us to go to the party.

Espero que no llueva.
Ess-PAY-ro kay no L'WAY-va.
I hope it doesn't rain.

Nos piden que lleguemos temprano
Nohs PEE-den kay yay-GHAY-mohs tem-PRA-no
They ask us to arrive early

y que llevemos la guitarra.
ee kay l'yay-VAY-mohs la ghee-TA-rra.
and to bring the guitar.

El subjuntivo

The subjunctive is not a tense but a mood which includes several tenses. You have really been using the subjunctive since Step 7, since this is the form where the -ar verbs change to -e and the -er and -ir verbs change to -a, or, if they have a -go ending in the first person, to -ga. You first learned these constructions as examples of how to give commands, although they are polite commands, since, when you say Venga it means "May you come."

When the subjunctive is used without a main verb — with the third person — it has the sense of "let . . . !"

"Let him leave!" — ¡Que se vaya!

The reason the subjunctive is important in Spanish is because you must use it in expressions such as "I want you to come," which must be expressed by "I want that you come." In fact, anything that you want, desire, or wish another person to do is put in the subjunctive.

The key word of the subjunctive is que. It is like a sign saying that the following verb must be in the subjunctive, that is; after expressions of wishing, doubt, emotion, uncertainty, and after certain conjunctions.

A further use of the subjunctive is in the case when you are looking for something that you haven't found yet.

271

*Busco a una muchacha que sepa cuidar
niños* — I'm looking for a girl who knows how
to take care of children.

Subjunctive verb endings
Here are examples of the subjunctive endings
for the 1st conjugation:

llevar: lleve, lleves, llevemos, lleven.

We have given only four forms because the first
form is the same for *yo, Ud., él,* and *ella.* The
endings for the 2nd and 3rd conjugations are
the same, as in the case of *aprender:*

aprenda, aprendas, aprendamos, aprendan.

María quiere que yo cante
Ma-REE-ya K'YAIR-ray kay yo KAHN-tay
Maria wants me to sing

y que Ud. toque la guitarra.
ee kay oo-STED TOH-kay la ghee-TA-rra.
and you to play the guitar.

Sound conversion
Tocar changes the *c* to *qu* in the subjunctive as
well as the past in order to keep the sound of
the hard *c.*

No quieren que nos vayamos temprano.
No K'YAIR-ren kay nohs va-YA-mohs tem-PRA-no.
They don't want us to leave early.

Insisten en que nos quedemos hasta el fin.
Een-SEES-ten en kay nohs kay-DAY-mohs AHS-ta el feen.
They insist that we stay until the end.

El subjuntivo se usa con expresiones
El soob-hoon-TEE-vo say OO-sa kohn es-pray-S'YO-nays
The subjunctive is used with expressions

para pedir permiso.
PA-ra pay-DEER pair-MEE-so.
to ask permission.

¿Está bien que yo fume?
¿Ess-TA b'yen kay yo FOO-may?
Is it all right if I smoke?

¿Permite Ud. que tome una foto?
¿Pair-MEE-tay oo-STED kay TOH-may OO-na FO-toh?
Will you permit me to take a photo?

Con expresiones indicando emoción o duda:
**Kohn es-pray-S'YO-nays een-dee-KAHN-doh eh-mo-S'YOHN oh
DOO-da:**
With expressions indicating emotion or doubt:

— Me alegra que haya venido.
May ah-LAY-gra kay AH-ya vay-NEE-doh.
I'm glad you have come.

Siento mucho que su esposa esté enferma.
S'YEN-toh MOO-cho kay soo ess-PO-sa ess-TAY en-FAIR-ma.
I'm very sorry your wife is sick.

Espero que mejore muy pronto.
Ess-PAIR-ro kay may-HO-ray mwee PROHN-toh.
I hope she gets better very soon.

— Gracias; no creo que sea nada grave.
GRA-s'yahs; no KRAY-oh kay SAY-ah NA-da GRA-vay.
Thank you; I don't think it is anything serious.

First person endings in -go
The verbs that end in *go* in the present keep the
g in the present subjunctive.

Tener: tenga, tengas, tengamos, tengan.

Pero temo que tenga que guardar cama.
PAIR-ro TAY-mo kay TEN-ga kay gwar-DAR KA-ma.
But I'm afraid she has to stay in bed.

— Es una lástima que no haya podido acompañarlo.
**Ess OO-na LAHS-tee-ma kay no AH-ya po-DEE-do
ah-kohm-pahn-YAR-lo.**
It is a pity that she is not able to accompany you.

The past subjunctives
Note the difference between "I am sorry she
can't come." — *Siento que no pueda venir.*
And "I am sorry she couldn't come." — *Siento
que no haya podido venir.* The second example
is the past subjunctive which is simply formed
by *haya* (the subjunctive of *haber*) plus the past
participle.

Quizá pueda venir la semana próxima.
Kee-SA PWEH-da veh-NEER la say-MA-na PROHK-see-ma.
Maybe she can come next week.

El subjuntivo se usa
El soob-hoon-TEE-vo say OO-sa
The subjunctive is used

con expresiones impersonales
kohn es-preh-S'YO-nays eem-pair-so-NA-less
with impersonal expressions

y con ciertos adverbios.
ee kohn S'YEHR-tohs ahd-VEHR-b'yohs.
and with certain adverbs.

— Es necesario que nos llamen temprano
Ess nay-say-SA-r'yo kay nohs YA-men tem-PRA-no
It is necessary that they call us early

a fin de que tengamos tiempo
ah feen day kay ten-GA-mohs T'YEM-po
so that we have time

de hacer las maletas.
day ah-SAIR lahs ma-LAY-tahs.
to pack the (our) suitcases.

Es importante que estemos
Ess eem-por-TAHN-tay kay ess-TAY-mohs
It is important that we be

en el aeropuerto
en el ah-ay-ro-PWEHR-toh
at the airport

274

una media hora antes de la hora de salida.
OO-na MAY-d'ya OH-ra AHN-tess day la OH-ra day sa-LEE-da.
a half hour before the time of departure.

Antes de que podamos subir al avión
AHN-tess day kay po-DA-mohs soo-BEER ahl ah-V'YOHN
Before we can board the plane

es menester que pesen el equipaje.
ess may-ness-TAIR kay PAY-sen el ay-kee-PA-hay.
it is necessary that they weigh the luggage.

— Pero ¿para qué tanta prisa?
PAIR-ro ¿PA-ra kay TAHN-ta PREE-sa?
But, why the rush?

Aunque lleguemos tarde
OW'N-kay yay-GHAY-mohs TAR-day
Even if we arrive late

es probable que haya otro vuelo más tarde.
ess pro-BA-blay kay AH-ya OH-tro VWAY-lo mahs TAR-day.
it is probable that there may be another flight later.

— ¿Ud. cree? También es posible que no haya.
¿Oo-STED KRAY-eh? Tahm-B'YEN ess po-SEE-blay kay no AH-ya.
Do you think so? It's also possible that there may not be (any).

El subjuntivo se usa
El soob-hoon-TEE-vo say OO-sa
The subjunctive is used

con expresiones de tiempo indefinido:
kohn es-pray-S'YO-nays day T'YEM-po een-day-fee-NEE-doh:
with expressions of indefinite time:

Cuando vaya a Madrid verá cosas muy bellas.
KWAN-doh VA-ya ah Ma-DREED vay-RA KO-sahs mwee BEL-yahs.
When you go to Madrid you will see very beautiful things.

Cuando vuelva tendrá que contármelo todo.
KWAN-doh VWEL-va ten-DRA kay kohn-TAR-may-lo TOH-doh.
When you return you will have to tell me everything.

El día que regrese, llámeme.
El DEE-ah kay reh-GRAY-say, L'YA-may-may.
The day you return, call me.

¿Por qué se usa el subjuntivo?

Some students of Spanish have difficulty understanding why the subjunctive is used at all, since it is no longer in common use in English. It is quite important in Spanish, however, where the ending of a verb is the key to its precise meaning and the correct use of the subjunctive is a proof of your ability to speak Spanish with style.

INSTANT CONVERSATION: THE GENERATION GAP

EL PADRE:
El PA-dray:
THE FATHER

Me apena que Marcos
May ah-PAY-na kay MAR-kohs
I'm sorry that Marc

no reciba mejores notas
ro ray-SEE-ba may-HO-ress NO-tahs
doesn't receive better grades

en el colegio.
en el ko-LAY-h'yo.
in school.

Tengo miedo de que vaya a tener dificultades
TEN-go M'YAY-doh day kay VA-ya ah tay-NAIR dee-fee-kool-TA-days
I fear that he is going to have difficulties

cuando vengan los exámenes de bachillerato.
**KWAN-doh VEN-gahn lohs ek-SA-may-NAYS day
ba-cheel-yay-RA-toh.**
when the high school examinations come.

Es importante que estudie más
Ess eem-por-TAHN-tay kay es-TOO-d'yay mahs
It is important that he study more

y que no pase todo su tiempo
ee kay no PA-say TOH-doh soo T'YEM-po
and that he not spend all his time

en el cine o yendo a los teatros.
en el SEE-nay oh YEN-doh ah lohs tay-AH-trohs.
at the movies or going to theatres.

Spanish Step by Step

LA MADRE:
La MA-dray:
THE MOTHER:

Pero no es para tanto.
PAIR-ro no ess PA-ra TAHN-toh.
But you're making too much of it.

Yo no dudo de que tenga éxito
Yo no DOO-doh day kay TEN-ga EK-see-toh
I don't doubt that he will be successful

en los exámenes.
en lohs ek-SA-may-nays.
in the examinations.

EL PADRE:

No hay "pero" que valga.
No I "PAIR-ro" kay VAHL-ga.
There are no "buts" about it.

Cuando él regrese a casa
KWAN-doh el ray-GRAY-say ah KA-sa
When he returns home

quiero que tú le digas que quiero verlo
K'YAIR-ro kay too lay DEE-gahs kay K'YAIR-ro VAIR-lo
I want you to tell him that I want to see him

para que me explique su última boleta.
PA-ra kay may es-PLEE-kay soo OOL-tee-ma bo-LAY-ta.
so that he explain his last report card to me.

> **"C" to "qu"**
> *Explicar*, like *tocar*, changes the c to qu to keep
> the hard sound of c.

No puedo permitir que él continúe tan flojo
No PWAY-doh pair-mee-TEER kay el kohn-tee-NOO-ay tahn FLO-ho
I cannot allow that he continue to be so lazy

en sus estudios,
en soos ess-TOO-d'yohs,
in his studies,

278

ni que sea tan negligente.
nee kay SAY-ah tahn nay-glee-HEN-tay.
nor that he be so negligent.

LA MADRE:
Oye, Marcos —
OH-yay, MAR-kohs —
Listen, Marc —

Tu papá está muy enojado
Too pa-PA ess-TA mwee eh-no-HA-doh
Your father is very angry

de que hayas recibido malas notas.
day kay AH-yahs ray-see-BEE-doh MA-lahs NO-tahs.
that you have received bad grades.

Es necesario que vayas a verlo.
Ess nay-say-SA-r'yo kay VA-yahs ah VAIR-lo.
It is necessary that you go see him.

> **The familiar tú**
> Although we have given the *tú* form for the different tenses and moods, it has not been used very often in the examples. Here, however, in a conversation between mother and son, it is the natural form to use when they speak to each other.

EL HIJO:
El EE-ho:
THE SON:
¿Para qué?
¿PA-ra kay?
What for?

Cuando me vea, sin duda me hablará
KWAN-doh may VAY-ah, seen DOO-da may ah-bla-RA
When he sees me he will, without doubt, speak to me

sobre lo que él quiere que yo haga,
SO-bray lo kay el K'YAIR-ray kay yo AH-ga,
about what he wants me to do,

sobre la carrera que él quiere que yo siga,
SO-bray la ka-RRAY-ra kay el K'YAY-ray kay yo SEE-ga,
about the career that he wants me to follow,

sobre la vida que él quiere que yo lleve.
SO-bray la VEE-da kay el K'YAY-ray kay yo l'YAY-vay.
about the life that he wants me to lead.

Mi ambición es llegar a ser
Mee ahm-bee-S'YOHN ess l'yay-GAR ah sair
My ambition is to become

director de cine.
dee-rek-TOR day SEE-nay.
(a) movie director.

En la vida quiero hacer
En la VEE-da K'YAY-ro ah-SAIR
In life I want to do

lo que me dé la gana
lo kay may day la GA-na
what I feel like doing

sin que él siempre me mande.
seen kay el S'YEM-pray may MAHN-day.
without his always ordering me.

LA MADRE:
¡Ay, Dios! No hables así, hijo.
¡I, d'yohs! No AH-blays ah-SEE, EE-ho.
Oh, God! Don't talk like that, son.

> **¡Dios mío!**
> *Dios* — "God" is often used in Spanish as an interjection, and is not considered profane.

Bien sabes que tu padre
B'yen SA-bess kay too PA-dray
You well know that your father

quiere todo para ti
K'YAIR-ray TOH-doh PA-ra tee
wants everything for you

y para Eduardo.
ee PA-ra Ay-DWAR-doh.
and for Edward.

Quiere que Uds. se gradúen,
K'YAIR-ray kay oo-STAY-days say gra-DOO-en,
He wants you to graduate,

> **The plural of "tú"**
> While the plural of *Ud.* is *Uds.* — and the gram-
> matical plural of *tú* is *vosotros*, *vosotros* is sel-
> dom used in most Latin American countries and
> *Uds.* is preferred as the plural of *tú*. A more
> complete explanation of *vosotros* and its use
> will appear in Step 25.

que reciban su grado de bachillerato
kay ray-SEE-bahn soo GRA-doh day ba-cheel-yay-RA-toh
to receive your high school degree

y que sigan a la universidad.
ee kay SEE-gahn ah la oo-nee-vair-see-DAHD.
and to continue to the university.

Tu padre siempre quería que Eduardo llegara a ser médico
Too PA-dray S'YEM-pray kay-REE-ya kay ay-DWAR-doh l'yay-GA-
                                     ra ah sair MAY-dee-ko
Your father always wanted Edward to become a doctor

> **The imperfect subjunctive**
> The subjunctive mood has an imperfect tense.
> This means that when the verb that introduces
> the subjunctive is in a past tense, the subjunc-
> tive must also be in the past (the imperfect
> tense). Compare:
>
> > His father doesn't want him to smoke.
> > *Su padre no quiere que él fume.*
> >
> > His father didn't want him to smoke.
> > *Su padre no quería que él fumara.*
>
> The subjunctive imperfect past uses the same
> base as the regular past tense, and adds either
> *-ase* or *-ara* for the 1st. conjugation and *-iese* or

-iera for the 2nd. and 3rd. conjugations. The meaning and use is the same for alternate ending.

tomar —— (*que*) *tomara, tomaras, tomáramos, tomaran*

aprender —— (*que*) *aprendiera, aprendieras, aprendiéramos, aprendieran.*

You have already seen the imperfect subjunctive of *querer* (*yo quisiera*) which is a polite way of saying "I should like" or "I would like." The same verbs that are irregular in the past are irregular in the imperative subjunctive.

I didn't want him to know.
No quería que él supiera.

Some other examples: saber (*supiera*), *querer* (*quisiera*), *venir* (*viniera*), *poder* (*pudiera*), *poner* (*pusiera*), *tener* (*tuviera*), *estar* (*estuviera*), *haber* (*hubiera*), *decir* (*dijera*), *ser* (or) *ir* (*fuera*), *traer* (*trajera*) (Note that the *i* is dropped from the last three examples.)

All of these can equally be used with the alternate ending and would be *quisiese, viniese,* etc.

y que tú fueras abogado como él.
ee kay too FWAY-rahs ah-bo-GA-doh KO-mo el.
and you to be a lawyer like him.

EL HIJO:
Bien lo sé.
B'yen lo say.
I know it well.

Pero entre lo que yo quiero hacer
PAIR-ro EN-tray lo kay yo K'YAY-ro ah-SAIR
But between what I want to do

y lo que él quiere que yo haga
ee lo kay el K'YAY-ray kay yo AH-ga
and what he wants me to do

hay la mar de diferencia.
i la mar day dee-fay-REN-s'ya.
there is the ocean of difference.

¡Que me deje en paz!
¡Kay may DAY-hay en pahs!
Let him leave me in peace!

LA MADRE:
¡Cielos! ¡Qué cosas!
¡S'YAY-lohs! ¡Kay KO-sahs!
Heavens! What things!

Qué diferente era la vida
Kay dee-fay-REN-tay AY-ra la VEE-da
How different life was

cuando yo era joven.
KWAN-doh yo AY-ra HO-ven.
When I was young.

Nunca les hablaba uno así
NOON-ka lays ah-BLA-ba OO-no ah-SEE
One never spoke like that

a sus padres.
ah soos PA-drays.
to one's parents.

La vida era diferente
At the end of this conversation, relative to the
generation gap, the mother, in her aside, shifts
into the imperfect which is the tense indicated
for speaking of things that were or used to be.

TEST YOUR SPANISH

Fill in the missing verb in each sentence in the subjunctive mood. Score 10 points for each correct answer. See answers below.

1. I hope that he doesn't see me.
   Ojalá que él no me _____.

2. They want us to arrive at eight.
   Quieren que _____ a las ocho.

3. I want him to go.
   Quiero que él _____.

4. He insists that I play.
   Insiste en que yo _____.

5. Do you want me to stay?
   Quiere que me _____?

6. I'm very sorry that you can't go.
   Siento mucho que Ud. no _____ ir.

7. I hope that she comes tomorrow.
   Espero que ella _____ mañana.

8. It is necessary that you study often.
   Es necesario que _____ a menudo.

9. Even if it rains, I'm going.
   Aunque _____, iré.

10. When he comes in, call me.
    Cuando _____, llámeme.

Answers: 1. vea, 2. lleguemos, 3. vaya, 4. toque, 5. quede 6. pueda, 7. venga, 8. estudie, 9. llueva, 10. entre.

SCORE _____ %

284

CONDITIONS AND
SUPPOSITIONS

Frases como:
FRA-says KO-mo:
Sentences like:

> Si llueve mañana no iremos.
> **See L'WAY-vay mahn-YA-na no ee-RAY-mohs.**
> If it rains tomorrow we won't go.

> Si él vino yo no lo vi.
> **See el VEE-no yo no lo vee.**
> If he came I didn't see him.

son condiciones sencillas.
sohn kohn-dee-S'YO-nays sen-SEEL-yahs.
are simple conditions.

Pero hay otras condiciones
PAIR-ro I OH-trahs kohn-dee-S'YO-nays
But there are other conditions

que son suposiciones.
kay sohn soo-po-see-S'YO-nays.
that are suppositions.

En estos casos use el condicional
En ESS-tohs ka-sohs OO-say el kohn-dee-s'yo-NAHL
In these cases use the conditional

con el imperfecto del subjuntivo.
kohn el eem-pehr-FEK-toh del soob-hoon-TEE-vo.
with the imperfect subjunctive.

Por ejemplo:
Por ay-HEM-plo:
For example:

Si Ud. estuviera en mi lugar,
See oo-STED ess-too-V'YAY-ra en mee loo-GAR,
If you were in my place,

> **Suppositions**
> When you say "if you were in my place" or "if I
> were you", you are supposing something that
> isn't true. For this sort of condition, you must
> use the imperfect subjunctive for one clause,
> the one with "if", and the conditional with the
> other clause of the supposition.

¿qué haría?
¿kay ah-REE-ya?
what would you do?

Si you estuviese en su lugar, lo haría.
See yo ess-toov-YAY-say en soo loo-GAR, lo ah-REE-ah.
If I were in your place, I would do it.

Si Ud. me lo dijese,
See oo-STED may lo dee-HEH-seh,
If you told it to me,

yo no se lo diría a nadie.
yo no say lo dee-REE-ya ah NA-d'yay.
I wouldn't tell it to anyone.

Note cómo se usan las condiciones
NO-tay KO-mo say OO-sahn lahs kohn-dee-S'YO-nays
Notice how the conditions are used

en el chiste que sigue:
en el CHEES-tay kay SEE-ghay:
in the joke that follows:

FEDERICO:
Fay-day-REE-ko:
FREDERICK:
  Dime, ¿qué harías tú
  DEE-may, ¿kay ah-REE-yahs too
  Tell me, what would you do

si vieses un tigre en la selva?
see V'YAY-says oon TEE-gray en la SELL-va?
if you saw a tiger in the jungle?

ESTEBAN:
Ess-TAY-bahn:
STEPHEN:
Si lo viese lo mataría con mi rifle.
See lo V'YAY-say lo ma-ta-REE-ya kohn mee REE-flay.
If I saw him I would kill him with my rifle.

FEDERICO:
Pero, si no tuvieras rifle,
PAIR-ro, see no too-V'YAY-rahs REE-flay,
But, if you didn't have a rifle,

¿cómo te defenderías?
¿KO-mo tay day-fen-day-REE-yahs?
how would you defend yourself?

ESTEBAN:
Si no tuviera rifle
See no too-V'YAY-ra REE-flay
If I didn't have a rifle

subiría a un árbol.
soo-bee-REE-ya ah oon AR-bohl.
I would climb up a tree.

FEDERICO:
Y, si no hubiera árbol,
Ee, see no oo-B'YAY-ra AR-bohl,
And, if there were no tree,

¿cómo te escaparías?
¿KO-mo tay ess-ka-pa-REE-yahs?
how would you escape?

ESTEBAN:
Si no hubiera árbol cerca,
See no oo-B'YAY-ra AR-bohl SAIR-ka,
If there were no tree nearby,

tendría que correr.
ten-DREE-ya kay ko-RRAIR.
I would have to run.

FEDERICO:

Hmm . . . Creo que el tigre
Hmm . . . KRAY-oh kay el TEE-gray
Hmm . . . I think that the tiger

te alcanzaría fácilmente.
tay ahl-kahn-sa-REE-ya FA-seel-men-tay.
would get you easily.

ESTEBAN:

¡Pero, hombre! ¡Por Dios! ¿Eres amigo mío,
¡PAIR-ro, OHM-bray! ¡Pohr D'yohs! ¿AIR-ress ah-MEE-go MEE-oh,
But, man! For God's sake! Are you a friend of mine,

o amigo del tigre?
oh ah-MEE-go del TEE-gray?
or a friend of the tiger's?

> The speakers in the above dialogue used the *tú*
> form of the verb throughout, as is customary
> between close friends. Note again how rarely
> the subject pronoun is used as the form of the
> verb indicates who is speaking or who is being
> spoken to.

Además de éstas, hay otras suposiciones
Ah-day-MAHS day ESS-tahs, I OH-trahs soo-po-see-S'YO-nays
Besides these, there are other suppositions

que se refieren a cosas
kay say ray-F'YAIR-ren ah KO-sahs
that refer to things

que nunca sucedieron:
kay NOON-ka soo-say-D'YAIR-rohn:
that never happened:

Si la Reina Isabel
See la RAY-na ee-sa-BEL
If Queen Isabella

no le hubiera ayudado a Colón
no lay oo-B'YAY-ra ah-yoo-DA-doh ah ko-LOHN
had not helped Columbus

¿quién habría descubierto
¿k'yen ah-BREE-ya des-koo-B'YAIR-toh
who would have discovered

el Nuevo Mundo?
el NWAY-vo MOON-doh?
the New World?

¿Qué habría pasado si la Armada Invencible
¿Kay ah-BREE-ya pa-SA-doh see la ar-MA-da een-ven-SEE-blay
What would have happened if the Invincible Armada

hubiera sido victoriosa contra Inglaterra?
**oo-B'YAIR-ra SEE-doh veek-toh-R'YO-sa KOHN-tra
een-gla-TAY-rra?**
had been victorious against England?

Suppositions that never happened
An even more pronounced supposition concerns wondering about how things would have been if something else had happened or never happened. The above example illustrates this because Queen Isabella did help Columbus, and the Spanish Armada, to the chagrin of Philip II (*Felipe Segundo* in Spanish), never did get around to conquering England.

In a case like this, the past conditional — simply the imperfect subjunctive of *haber* with the past participle — is used in the "if" clause and the past conditional — the conditional of *haber* with the past participle, in the other clause.

Compound tenses, despite the difficult names, are really quite easy, as the only changes occur in *haber*, while the past participle remains the same.

INSTANT CONVERSATION: WHAT WOULD YOU DO IF YOU WON THE LOTTERY?

— ¿Qué haría Ud. si ganara
¿Kay ah-REE-ya oo-STED see ga-NA-ra
What would you do if you won

el gran premio de la lotería?
el grahn PRAY-m'yo day la lo-tay-REE-ya?
the big prize in the lottery?

— Lo primero sería mudarnos
Lo pree-MAY-ro say-REE-ya moo-DAR-nohs
The first thing would be to move

a una casa más grande.
ah OO-na KA-sa mahs GRAHN-day.
to a bigger house.

Eso me haría feliz a mí.
ES-so may ah-REE-ya fay-LEESS ah mee.
That would make me happy.

En segundo lugar
En say-GOON-doh loo-GAR
In the second place

compraría un nuevo auto.
kohm-pra-REE-ya oon NWAY-vo OW-toh.
I would buy a new car.

Eso me haría feliz a mí.
ES-so may ah-REE-ya fay-LEESS ah mee.
That would make me happy.

Después iríamos a España,
Dess-PWESS ee-REE-ya-mohs ah Ess-PAHN-ya,
Then we would go to Spain,

y visitaríamos a mis padres.
ee vee-see-ta-REE-ya-mohs ah mees PA-drays.
and we would visit my parents.

Les conseguiría maquinaria moderna
Less kohn-say-ghee-REE-ya ma-kee-NA-r'ya mo-DAIR-na
I would get them modern machinery

para su finca.
PA-ra soo FEEN-ka.
for their farm.

Así no tendrían que trabajar tanto
Ah-SEE no ten-DREE-yahn kay tra-ba-HAR TAHꞃ -toh
This way they wouldn't have to work so much

y la vida les sería más fácil.
ee la VEE-da less say-REE-ya mahs FA-seɛ
and life would be easier for them.

— Y después ¿qué haría?
Ee dess-PWESS ¿kay ah-REE-ya?
And afterwards, what would you do?

— Regresaríamos aquí.
Ray-gray-sa-REE-ya-mohs ah-KEE.
We would return here.

— Y ¿seguiría trabajando?
Eee ¿say-ghee-REE-ya tra-ba-HAHN-doh?
And would you continue working?

— Por supuesto. Tendría que trabajar.
Por soo-PWESS-toh. Ten-DREE-ya kay tra-ba-HAR.
Of course. I would have to work.

El dinero de la lotería
El dee-NAY-ro day la lo-tay-REE-ya
The lottery money

no duraría siempre.
no doo-ra-REE-ya S'YEM-pray.
would not last forever.

Pero sería agradable
PAIR-ro say-REE-ya ah-gra-DA-blay
But it would be agreeable

mientras durase, ¿no?
M'YEN-trahs doo-RA-say, ¿no?
while it lasted, no?

— ¡Seguro! Salgamos ahora
¡Say-GOO-ro! Sahl-GA-mohs ah-OH-ra
Sure! Let's go out now

a comprar un billete.
ah kohm-PRAR oon beel-YAY-tay.
to buy a ticket.

(El domingo siguiente)
(El doh-MEEN-go see-GH'YEN-tay)
(The following Sunday)

— ¡Qué chasco! No gané nada.
¡Kay CHAHS-ko! No ga-NAY NA-da.
What a disappointment! I didn't win anything.

— Menos mal. Si lo hubiese ganado
MAY-nohs mahl. See lo oo-B'YAY-say ga-NA-doh
It's just as well. If you had won it

pronto lo habría gastado todo.
PROHN-toh lo ah-BREE-ya gahs-TA-doh TOH-doh.
you would soon have spent it all.

— Quizá. Pero de todos modos
Kee-SA. PAIR-ro day TOH-dohs MO-dohs
Maybe. But anyway

habría tenido el gusto
ah-BREE-ya tay-NEE-doh el GOOS-toh
I would have had the pleasure

de haberlo gastado.
day ah-BAIR-lo gahs-TA-doh.
of having spent it.

The infinitive with the perfect

Here is an example of the infinitive with the past participle. Compare:

Es un placer hacerlo.
It's a pleasure to do it.
Es un placer haberlo hecho.
It's a pleasure to have done it.

TEST YOUR SPANISH

Fill in the missing words with the proper forms of the conditional or the imperfect subjunctive. You may use the imperfect subjunctive endings -ase or -iese instead of -ara or -iera. Both are correct. Score 10 points for each correct answer. See answers on following page.

1. If I had the money I would buy a new car.
   Si yo tuviera el dinero _____ un nuevo automóvil.

2. If you told it to me I wouldn't tell it to anyone.
   Si Ud. me lo dijese no se lo _____ a nadie.

3. What would you do if you missed the train?
   Qué _____ si perdiera el tren?

4. What would you buy if you won the lottery?
   Qué compraría Ud. si _____ la lotería?

5. If I were able to I would do it.
   Si yo _____ lo haría.

6. He would come with me if you permitted it.
   Vendría conmigo si Ud. lo _____.

7. If I wanted to, I could stop smoking.
   Si quisiera, yo _____ dejar de fumar.

8. If there were no policemen would there be an increase in cri·nes?
   Si no _____ policías, ¿habría un aumento en los crímenes?

9. If I had the time I would go to Spain.
   Si tuviera el tiempo _____ a España.

10. If Napoleon had conquered Spain, would history have been different?
    Si Napoleón hubiera conquistado España _____ _____ diferente la historia?

ANSWERS: 1. compraría, 2. diría, 3. haría, 4. ganara, 5. pudiera, 6. permitiera, 7. podría, 8. hubiera, 9. iría, 10. ¿habría sido.

SCORE _____%

step 25   HOW TO READ SPANISH

Aquí hay unos consejos para hacer más fácil su lectura en español.
Here is some advice to make your reading in Spanish easier.

En las cartas comerciales el conditional
In business letters the condictional

y el subjuntivo se usan mucho. Así:
and the subjunctive are much used. Thus:

Muy señor mío:
(My) dear Sir:

Business greetings
Business letter headings change according to whether the writer or the recipient is one or more than one.

Muy señor mío, Muy señores míos
Muy señor nuestro, Muy señores nuestros

Les agradeceríamos que nos mandasen
We would be grateful if you would send us

su último catálogo
your latest catalog

y su lista de precios.
and your price list.

Les rogamos que nos contesten
We beg you to answer us

a la mayor brevedad posible.
as soon as possible.

Pendientes de sus gratas noticias
Awaiting your pleasant news

quedamos de Uds. muy atentamente ...
we remain very attentively yours ...

La cortesía en la correspondencia

Although they all are equivalent to "very truly yours," a useful ending is *Attos. y Ss. Ss. (atentos y seguros servidores)* — "Faithful and sure servants," or *Q.E.S.M. (que estrecha su mano)* — "who shakes your hand," or, in social correspondence *Q.B.S.M. (que besa su mano)* — "who kisses your hand," or *Q.B.V.M.* (the V. standing for vuestra — another and more formal way of saying "you.")

En los periódicos verá que
In the newspapers you will see that

acostumbran ser muy breves
they are accustumed to being very brief

en los titulares:
in the headlines:

Celoso mató a su mujer.
A jealous man killed his wife.

Huelguistas exigen aumento inmediato.
Strikers demand immediate raise.

Régimen actúa contra amenazas.
Regime acts against threats.

Pepín cortó orejas y rabo en Córdoba.
Pepín cut ears and tail in Cordoba.

Newspaper style

Newspaper headlines and reportorial or radio — TV style, often drops articles and superfluous pronouns. However, as in the case of the last headline, some things you must know by familiarity and association. *Cortó orejas y rabo* means that a bullfighter was given a great honor, in honor of his performance — that of cutting off the ears and tail of the bull. Incidentally, Spanish has two words for "ear" —

oído — the inner ear we hear with, and
oreja — the outer ear.

La literatura española y latinoamericana es riquísima.
Spanish and Latin American literature is very rich.

Aquí les presentamos un ejemplo de poesía
Here we present to you an example of poetry

seleccionado de *Don Juan Tenorio,*
selected from *Don Juan Tenorio,*

una obra maestra del teatro clásico español:
a masterpiece of the Spanish classical theater:

¡Ah! ¿No es cierto, angel de amor,
Ah! Isn't it so, angel of love,

que en esta apartada orilla
that on this remote shore

más pura la luna brilla
the moon shines more purely

y se respira mejor?
and one breathes better?

Esta aura que vaga, llena
This gentle breeze that roves about, filled

de los sencillos olores
with the simple fragrances

de las campesinas flores
of the country flowers

que brota esa orilla amena;
that this pleasant shore gives forth;

esa agua limpia y serena
that clear and serene water

que atraviesa sin temor
that without fear traverses

la barca del pescador
the boat of the fisherman

que espera cantando el día,
who awaits the day singing,

¿no es cierto, paloma mía,
isn't it true, my dove,

que están respirando amor?
that they are breathing love?

En cuanto a prosa *Don Quijote de la Mancha*
As for prose *Don Quixote of the Mancha*

está considerado como una de las grandes obras
is considered as one of the great works

de la literatura mundial.
of world literature.

En ella, tanto como en otras obras clásicas,
In it, as well as in other classical works,

encontrará el uso de *vosotros* y *vos*
you will encounter the use of vosotros and vos

Vosotros

Vosotros is frequently shortened to *vos* and as such is used in literature, even referring to one person, as a very polite form of *Ud.* Besides in books, you will probably hear *vosotros* used in public addresses, as a special mark of honor to the listeners.

Vosotros, another word for "you," uses another set of pronouns and verb forms which you should at least recognize, as you will see them in books and occasionally hear them. *Vosotros* is really the plural of the familiar form *tú* and is used as such especially in Spain. (In Latin America *ustedes* is generally used for the familiar plural.) The endings for *vosotros* are *-áis* for the first conjugation and *-éis* and *-ís for the second and third.*

Vosotros habláis — aprendéis — salís

These endings, in the other tenses and moods, are appended to the base or to the infinitive. The imperative ends in *-d*.

¡hablad! — ¡aprended! — ¡salid!

The possessive form is *vuestro* and the object form is *os*, for both the direct and indirect object.

que hoy día se usa mucho menos que *usted.*
which nowadays is used much less than usted.

Aquí hay unos ejemplos del uso de *vosotros*
Here are some examples of the use of vosotros

en una conferencia pública:
in a public address:

Ha sido para mí un gran honor
It has been a great honor for me

dirigiros la palabra esta noche.
to address you this evening.

Os agradezco vuestra atención
I thank you for your attention

y la hospitalidad que me habéis brindado.
and the hospitality you have offered me.

Ahora me tenéis a vuestra disposición
Now you have me at your disposal

si queréis hacerme preguntas u observaciones.
if you wish to ask me questions or make observations.

Todo lo que Ud. lee en español
All (that) you read in Spanish

aumentará sus conocimientos
will increase your knowledge

y, al mismo tiempo,
and, at the same time,

será una fuente de gusto
will be a source of pleasure

y de diversión.
and of amusement.

Pero lo más importante
But the most important thing

es hablar y escuchar hablar a otros
is to speak and listen to others speak

porque para aprender a hablar un idioma
because in order to learn to speak a language

lo más importante de todo es practicarlo en toda ocasión.
the most important thing of all is to practice at every opportunity.

YOU KNOW MORE SPANISH
THAN YOU THINK

While you have learned up to now the essential elements for speaking Spanish, you will encounter, when reading books, magazines, and newspapers in Spanish, many words not included in this book. You will be aided, however, in your understanding and use of new words by the fact that there are so many words in English which are similar in Spanish, in meaning and *almost* in spelling.

This is because Spanish belongs to the group of Romance languages, meaning it is descended from Latin, the language of ancient Rome, as are Italian, French, Portuguese, and several other languages. A large part of the English language, perhaps more than 40%, comes from Latin and French through the Norman-French conquest of England in 1066 and is, therefore, similar to Spanish in much of its vocabulary. You will find as you learn more and more Spanish that there are thousands of words that are almost the same as English. All you have to do is get used to their Spanish pronunciation.

When you read new material in Spanish or when you hear Spanish spoken, you will constantly encounter many words that you may not have studied but that *you already know*. Therefore, if you have a two-way dictionary, use the English/Spanish part frequently for making up your own sentences, but do not use the Spanish/English section, except in rare cases. Let the meaning and construction become evident to you through context and your own initiative — and, above all, read *aloud* at every chance you get. It is suggested that you read Spanish material onto cassettes, or copy spoken material in your own voice, and compare your entries from day to day. As you progress, you will be surprised at how soon you will sound as if you were speaking your own language.

DICTIONARY
ENGLISH — SPANISH

This dictionary contains numerous words not in the preceding text, but which will complete your ability to use current Spanish. It is an interesting linguistic fact that most people use less than 2,000 words in their daily conversation in any language. In this dictionary, you have over 2,600 words chosen especially for frequency of use.

N.B. 1. Masculine and feminine gender of nouns is shown only when the noun does not end in -o (masc.) or -a (fem.).

2. Adjectives must agree in number and gender with the nouns they describe. Adjectives ending in -o change to -os when masculine plural is used, and to -a for feminine singular and -as for feminine plural.

3. Adjectives ending in a letter other than -o remain the same for masculine and feminine (unless otherwise indicated) and form the plural for both genders by adding -s, -es, or -as as indicated.

4. Only the most important adverbs are given. But remember that most adjectives become adverbs by adding -mente to the feminine form.
    Adjective: *exacto — exact*
    Adverb: *exactamente — exactly*

5. When a choice of meaning is approximately equal between two frequently used words or expressions, both are given, separated by a comma. This will help to increase your comprehension of the words you will hear or see in Spanish.

A

a, an (*m*) un (*f*) una
(*to be*) able poder
about (*concerning*) acerca de
above sobre
absence ausencia
absent ausente (*m & f*)
accent acento
(*to*) accept aceptar
accident accidente (*m*)
according to según
account (*commercial*) cuenta
accurate exacto
(*to*) accuse acusar
ache dolor (*m*)
across a través de
act acto
actor actor (*m*)
actress actriz (*f*)
(*to*) add añadir
address dirección (*f*)
(*to*) admire admirar
admission admisión (*f*)
(*to*) advance avanzar
adventure aventura
advertisement anuncio

advice consejo
affectionate cariñoso
(*to be*) afraid (*of*) tener miedo
    (*de*)
Africa África
African africano
after después
afternoon tarde (*f*)
again otra vez, de nuevo
against contra
age edad (*f*)
agency agencia
agent agente (*m*)
ago hace
agreeable agradable (*m & f*)
(*to*) agree concordar
ahead adelante
air aire (*m*)
air-conditioned aire
    acondicionado
air mail correo aéreo
airplane avión (*m*)
airport aeropuerto
alcohol alcohol (*m*)
all todo
    That's all eso es todo, basta
(*to*) allow permitir

all right está bien
almost casi
alone solo
alphabet alfabeto
already ya
also también
always siempre
(*I*) **am** (*permanent status*) soy
(*I*) **am** (*location or temporary status*) estoy
America América
American americano, norteamericano
among entre
amount cantidad (*f*)
amusing divertido
and y, (*e when the next word begins with i*)
anesthetic anestésico
angry enojado
animal animal (*m*)
ankle tobillo
anniversary aniversario
(*to*) **annoy** molestar
annoying molesto
another otro
answer respuesta, contestación (*f*)
(*to*) **answer** responder, contestar
ant hormiga
antiseptic antiséptico
any cualquier
anyone, anybody alguien
anyone (*at all*) cualquiera
anything algo
anywhere en cualquier parte
apartment apartamento
(*to*) **apologize** disculparse, excusarse

appetite apetito
apple manzana
appointment cita
(*to*) **appreciate** apreciar, estimar
(*to*) **approve** aprobar
April abril
Arab árabe (*m or f*)
Arabic árabe (*m*)
architect arquitecto
architecture arquitectura
are (*permanent status*)
    (*you sg.*) **are** (*Ud.*) es
    (*we*) **are** somos
    (*they, you pl.*) **are** (*ellos, ellas, Uds.*) son
are (*location or temporary status*)
    (*you sg.*) **are** (*Ud.*) está
    (*we*) **are** estamos
    (*they, you pl.*) **are** (*ellos, ellas, Uds.*) están
(*there*) **are** hay
area área (*m*)
Argentinean argentino
argument argumento
arithmetic aritmética
arm brazo
army ejército
around (*surrounding*) alrededor
around (*approximately*) alrededor de
(*to*) **arrange** arreglar
(*to*) **arrest** arrestar, detener
arrival llegada
(*to*) **arrive** llegar
art arte (*m*)
article artículo
artificial artificial (*m & f*)
artist artista (*m or f*)
as como

Asia Asia
(*to*) **ask** (*a question*) preguntar
(*to*) **ask** (*for*) pedir
asleep dormido
asparagus espárrago
aspirin aspirina
ass asno
assortment surtido
astronaut astronauta (*m & f*)
at (*location*) en
at (*time*) a
Atlantic Atlántico
atmosphere atmósfera
atomic atómico
(*to*) **attend** atender
attention atención (*f*)
August agosto
aunt tía
Australia Australia
Australian australiano
Austria Austria
Austrian austriaco
author autor (*m*)
authority autoridad (*f*)
automatic automático
automobile automóvil (*m*)
autumn otoño
avenue avenida
average promedio
(*to*) **avoid** evitar
(*far*) **away** lejos
(*not there*) **away** fuera

B

baby bebé (*m*)
bachelor soltero

back (*part of body*) espalda
bacon tocino
bad malo
bag maleta
baggage equipaje (*m*)
bakery panadería
ballerina bailarina
ballet ballet (*m*)
banana banana
band (*musical*) banda
bandage venda
bank banco
banquet banquete (*m*)
bar bar (*m*)
barber barbero
bargain ganga
basement sótano
basket cesta
bath baño
bathing suit traje de baño (*m*)
bathroom cuarto de baño
battery batería
battle batalla
bay bahía
(*to*) **be** (*permanent status*) ser
(*to*) **be** (*location or temporary status*) estar
beach playa
beans frijoles (*m*)
bear (*animal*) oso
beard barba
beautiful bello
beauty belleza
beauty shop salón de belleza (*m*)
because porque
bed cama
bedroom alcoba
bedspread cubrecama (*m*)

bee abeja
beef carne de res (*f*)
been (*permanent status*) sido
been (*location or temporary status*) estado
beer cerveza
before antes
beggar mendigo
(*to*) begin comenzar
behind detrás
Belgian belga
Belgium Bélgica
(*to*) believe creer
bell campana
(*to*) belong pertenecer
below debajo
belt cinturón (*m*)
bench banco
(*to*) bend doblar
beside al lado
besides además
best (*adj.*) el (*la*) mejor
best (*adv.*) lo mejor
bet apuesta
better mejor
between entre
bicycle bicicleta
big grande (*m & f*)
bill factura, cuenta
bird pájaro
birthday cumpleaños (*m*)
black negro
blanket frazada
blond rubio
blood sangre (*f*)
blouse blusa
(*to*) blow soplar
blue azul

boarding house casa de huéspedes
boat barco
body cuerpo
boiled hervido
Bolivian boliviano
bomb bomba
book libro
bookstore librería
boot bota
border frontera
born nacido
(*to*) borrow pedir prestado
boss jefe (*m*)
both ambos
(*to*) bother molestar
bottle botella
bottom fondo
bought comprado
bowl tazón (*m*)
box caja
boy muchacho
bracelet brazalete (*m*)
brain cerebro
brake freno
brand marca de fábrica
brandy coñac
brass latón (*m*)
brassiere sostén (*m*)
brave valiente
Brazil Brasil
Brazilian brasileño
bread pan (*m*)
(*to*) break romper
breakfast desayuno
breast seno
(*to*) breathe respirar
breeze brisa
(*to*) bribe sobornar

brick ladrillo
bride novia
bridegroom novio
bridge puente (*m*)
brief breve (*m & f*)
briefcase maletín (*m*)
bright brillante (*m & f*)
(*to*) bring traer
(*to*) broil asar
broken roto
broom escoba
brother hermano
brother-in-law cuñado
brown pardo
brunette morena
brush cepillo
brute bruto
(*to*) build construir
building edificio
built construido
bull toro
bullet bala
bullfight corrida de toros
bullfighter torero
bullring plaza de toros
bureau (*furniture*) cómoda
(*to*) burn quemar
bus autobús (*m*)
bus stop parada de autobús
business negocio
businessman hombre de negocio
busy ocupado
but pero
butcher carnicero
butcher shop carnicería
butter mantequilla
button botón (*m*)
to buy comprar

by por
by the way a propósito

C

cab taxi (*m*)
cabaret cabaret (*m*)
cabbage repollo, col
cable cable (*m*)
cake torta
calendar calendario
calf ternero
(*to*) call llamar
call llamada
calm (*adj.*) tranquilo
camera cámara
camp campo
can (*to be able*) poder
can (*container*) lata
can opener abrelatas (*m*)
candle vela
candy bombón (*m*)
cap gorra
capable capaz (*m & f*)
cape capa
capital (*geographic*) capital (*f*)
capital (*financial*) capital (*m*)
captain capitán (*m*)
car automóvil (*m*)
carburetor carburador (*m*)
card tarjeta
(*to take*) care of cuidar
careless descuidado
Caribbean Caribe (*m*)
carpet alfombra
carrot zanahoria
(*to*) carry llevar
case caso

cash efectivo
cashier cajero
castle castillo
cat gato
catalog catálogo
cathedral catedral (*f*)
Catholic católico
cattle ganado
cave cueva
ceiling cielo raso
celebration celebración (*f*)
cellar sótano
cement cemento
cemetery cementerio
cent centavo
center centro
central central (*m & f*)
century siglo
cereal cereal (*m*)
certainly ciertamente, cómo no
certificate of origin (*business*) cer-
  tificado de origen
(*to*) certify certificar
chair silla
chandelier araña
change cambio
(*to*) change cambiar
(*to*) chat conversar
character carácter (*m*)
charming encantador, -a
chauffeur chofer (*m*)
cheap barato
cheaper más barato, más
  económico
check cheque (*m*)
checkroom guardarropa (*m*)
cheerful alegre (*m & f*)
cheese queso

chest pecho
chicken pollo
child niño
children niños
Chilean chileno
chimney chimenea
chin barbilla
China China
Chinese chino
chocolate chocolate (*m*)
(*to*) choose escoger
chop chuleta
Christmas Pascuas (*de Navidad*)
church iglesia
cigar cigarro
cigarette cigarrillo
city ciudad (*f*)
clam almeja
class clase (*f*)
classroom sala de clase (*f*)
(*to*) clean limpiar
clean limpio
clear claro
clerk dependiente (*m*)
clever hábil (*m & f*)
client cliente (*m & f*)
climate clima (*m*)
(*to*) climb subir
clock reloj (*m*)
close cerca
(*to*) close cerrar
closed cerrado
closet armario
clothes ropa
cloud nube (*f*)
club club (*m*)
coast costa
coat abrigo

cocktail coctel (*m*)
coffee café (*m*)
coin moneda
coincidence coincidencia
cold frío
(*to*) collect recoger, coleccionar
college universidad (*f*)
Colombian colombiano
colonel coronel (*m*)
color color (*m*)
comb peine (*m*)
combination combinación (*f*)
(*to*) come venir
(*to*) come back volver, regresar
comedy comedia
comfortable cómodo
comment comentario
commercial comercial (*m & f*)
commercial (*T.V.*) anuncio
commission comisión (*f*)
communist comunista (*m & f*)
company (*business*) compañía, so-
   ciedad (*f*)
(*to*) compare comparar
competition competencia
complete completo
composer compositor (*m*)
computer máquina calculadora
concert concierto
condition condición (*f*)
(*to*) congratulate felicitar
congratulations felicitaciones (*f*)
conservative conservador,-a
consul cónsul (*m*)
contented contento
contest concurso
(*to*) continue continuar
(*to*) control controlar
convenient conveniente (*m & f*)

conversation conversación (*f*)
(*to*) convince convencer
cook cocinero
(*to*) cook cocinar
cookies galletas
cool fresco
copy copia
cork corcho
corkscrew sacacorchos (*m*)
corn maíz (*m*)
corner (*street*) esquina
corner (*room*) rincón (*m*)
corporation corporación (*f*)
correct correcto
(*to*) correspond corresponder
(*to*) cost costar
Costa Rican costarricense (*m & f*)
cotton algodón (*m*)
cough tos (*f*)
(*to*) count contar
country país (*m*)
countryside campo
course curso
courtesy cortesía
court (*law*) corte (*f*)
cousin primo
(*to*) cover cubrir
cow vaca
crab cangrejo
crazy loco
cream crema
credit crédito
crime crimen (*m*)
criminal criminal (*m & f*)
crisis crisis (*f*)
(*to*) criticize criticar
cross cruz (*f*)
(*to*) cross cruzar
crossing cruce (*m*)

crossroads encrucijada
crowd muchedumbre (*f*)
cruel cruel (*m & f*)
(*to*) **cry** llorar
Cuban cubano
cup taza
curve curva
custard flan (*m*)
custom (*habit*) costumbre (*f*)
customer cliente (*m & f*)
customs (*office*) aduana
customs form formulario de
  aduana
(*to*) **cut** cortar

D

daily cotidiano
dairy lechería
damp húmedo
(*to*) **dance** bailar
danger peligro
dangerous peligroso
dark oscuro
darling querido
  (*remember the feminine ends*
  in -a!)
date (*calendar*) fecha
date (*appointment*) cita
daughter hija
daughter-in-law nuera
dawn alba, madrugada
day día (*m*)
dead muerto
dear (*beloved*) querido
dear (*expensive*) caro
debt deuda
(*to*) **deceive** engañar
December diciembre

(*to*) **decide** decidir
deck (*boat*) cubierta
deep hondo
(*to*) **defend** defender
delay demora
delicious delicioso
delighted encantado
(*to*) **deliver** entregar
dentist dentista (*m & f*)
(*to*) **depart** salir
department store gran almacén
(*to*) **deposit** depositar
desert desierto
design diseño
desk escritorio
dessert postre (*m*)
(*to*) **destroy** destruir
detective detective (*m & f*)
detour desvío
dialect dialecto
dialogue diálogo
diamond diamante, brillante (*m*)
dictionary diccionario
(*to*) **die** morir
diet dieta
difference diferencia
different diferente (*m & f*)
difficult difícil (*m & f*)
(*to*) **dine** cenar
dining room comedor (*m*)
dinner comida, cena
dinner jacket smoking (*m*)
direct directo
(*to*) **direct** dirigir
direction dirección (*f*)
directly directamente
dirty sucio
(*to*) **disappear** desaparecer
disappointed desilusionado

discount descuento
(to) discover descubrir
discotheque discoteca
discreet discreto
(to) discuss discutir
dish plato
dishonest ímprobo
(to) disobey desobedecer
(to) distrust desconfiar
(to) disturb molestar
diverse diverso
divine divino
diving (underwater) buceo
divorced divorciado
dizzy mareado
(to) do hacer
dock muelle (m)
doctor médico, doctor
dog perro
doll muñeca
dollar dólar (m)
door puerta
double doble (m & f)
doubt duda
dove paloma
down abajo
downtown centro de la ciudad
dozen docena
drawer gaveta
dream sueño
dress vestido
(to) drink beber
(to) drive conducir
driver conductor
driver's license permiso de
   conducir
(to) drown ahogarse
drugstore farmacia
drunk borracho

dry seco
dry cleaner tintorería
duck pato
during durante
dust polvo

E

each cada
ear (outer) oreja
ear (inner) oído
early temprano
(to) earn ganar
earrings aretes (m)
earth tierra
earthquake terremoto
easily fácilmente
east este (m)
easy fácil (m & f)
(to) eat comer
economical económico
Ecuadorian ecuatoriano
egg huevo
eight ocho
eighteen dieciocho
eighty ochenta
either ... or o ... o
either (one) cualquiera
elderly de edad
election elección (f)
electric eléctrico
electricity electricidad (f)
elegant elegante (m & f)
elephant elefante (m)
elevator ascensor (m)
eleven once
embarrassed apenado
embassy embajada
embroidery bordado

emerald esmeralda
emergency emergencia
emotion emoción (*f*)
employee empleado
employer patrón (*m*)
empty vacío
end fin (*m*)
(*to*) **end** terminar
enemy enemigo
engine máquina
engineer ingeniero
England Inglaterra
English inglés (*m*) inglesa (*f*)
enough bastante
(*to*) **enter** entrar
(*to*) **entertain** hospedar, divertir
entertaining divertido
entertainment diversion (*f*)
entrance entrada
envelope sobre (*m*)
(*to*) **envy** envidiar
equal igual
equator ecuador (*m*)
error error (*m*)
(*to*) **escape** escapar
especially especialmente
Europe Europa
European europeo
even (*adv.*) aun
evening noche (*f*)
ever (*sometime*) alguna vez
every cada
everybody todo el mundo
everything todo
everywhere en todas partes
exact exacto
exactly exactamente
(*to*) **examine** examinar
example ejemplo

excellent excelente (*m & f*)
except excepto
(*to*) **exchange** cambiar
excited excitado, agitado
exercise ejercicio
exhausted agotado
exhibition exhibición (*f*)
exit salida
(*to*) **expect** esperar
expedition expedición (*f*)
expenses gastos
expensive caro
experience experiencia
experiment experimento
expert experto
(*to*) **explain** explicar
explanation explicación (*f*)
(*to*) **explode** explotar, volar
explorer explorador (*m*), explora-
  dora (*f*)
(*to*) **export** exportar
exposition exposición (*f*)
(*to*) **express** expresar
expression expresión (*f*)
exquisite exquisito
(*to*) **extend** extender
extra extra, adicional
eye ojo
eyesight vista

F

fabric tejido, tela
face cara
fact hecho, realidad (*f*)
factory fábrica
failure fracaso
fair (*show*) feria
fall caída

fall (*autumn*) otoño
(*to*) fall caerse
family familia
famous famoso
far lejos
fare tarifa
farm finca
farther más lejos
fashion moda
fast rápido
(*to*) fast ayunar
(*to*) fasten asegurar
fat gordo
fate destino
father padre
father-in-law suegro
fault culpa
favor favor (*m*)
(*to*) fear temer
February febrero
fee honorario
(*to*) feel sentir
feet pies (*m*)
feminine femenino
fence cerca
festival festival (*m*)
fever fiebre (*f*)
few pocos
fewer menos
fiancé novio
field campo
fifteen quince
fifth quinto
fifty cincuenta
fig higo
(*to*) fight pelear
fight pelea
(*to*) fill llenar
film película

final final
finally finalmente
(*to*) find encontrar
(*to*) find out descubrir
finger dedo
(*to*) finish terminar
finished terminado
(*to*) fire (*a shot*) disparar
fire fuego
fireman bombero
first primero
fish (*in the water*) pez (*m*)
fish (*on the plate*) pescado
(*to*) fish pescar
fishmarket pescadería
fist puño
five cinco
(*to*) fix arreglar
flag bandera
flame llama
flashlight linterna
flat llano, plano
flat tire llanta desinflada
flight vuelo
flood inundación (*f*)
floor (*of a room*) suelo
floor (*of a building*) piso
florist floristería
flour harina
flower flor (*f*)
(*to*) fly volar
fly (*insect*) mosca
fog neblina
(*to*) follow seguir
food comida
foot pie (*m*)
for (*sake or purpose*) por, para
for (*use or destination*) para
(*to*) forbid prohibir

314

forbidden prohibido
force fuerza
foreigner extranjero
forest selva
forever siempre
(*to*) forget olvidar
(*to*) forgive perdonar
fork tenedor (*m*)
form forma
(*to*) form formar
formal formal (*m & f*)
formula fórmula
fortunate afortunado
fortunately afortunadamente
fortune fortuna
forty cuarenta
fountain fuente (*f*)
four cuatro
fourteen catorce
fourth cuarto
fox zorro
fragile frágil (*m & f*)
frame (*of picture*) marco
France Francia
free libre (*m & f*)
free (*of charge*) gratis (*m & f*)
freedom libertad (*f*)
French francés (*m*), francesa (*f*)
frequently frecuentemente
fresh fresco
Friday viernes
fried frito
friend amigo
friendly amistoso
frog rana
from de, desde
front frente (*m*)
frozen congelado
fruit fruta

full lleno
fun diversión (*f*)
funny divertido
fur piel (*f*)
furniture muebles (*m*)
fuse fusible (*m*)

G

(*to*) gain ganar
game juego
garage garaje (*m*)
garbage basura
garden jardín (*m*)
garlic ajo
gas gas (*m*)
gasoline gasolina
gas station puesto de gasolina
gate portón (*m*)
gender género
general general (*m*)
generally generalmente
generation generación (*f*)
generous generoso
gentle suave (*m & f*)
gentleman caballero
genuine genuino
geography geografía
German alemán (*m*), alemana
  (*f*)
Germany Alemania
(*to*) get (*obtain*) conseguir
(*to*) get (*become*) ponerse
(*to*) get off bajarse
(*to*) get on subir
(*to*) get out salir
(*to*) get up levantarse·
gift regalo
gin ginebra

girl muchacha
(to) give dar
glad contento
glass (*for windows*) vidrio
glass (*drinking*) vaso
glasses anteojos
glove guante (*m*)
glue cola
(to) go ir
(to) go away irse
(to) go back regresar
(to) go on continuar
(to) go out salir
goat cabra
God Dios
goddaughter ahijada
godfather padrino
godmother madrina
godson ahijado
gold oro
golf golf (*m*)
good bueno
Good afternoon Buenas tardes
Good morning Buenos días
Good night (*or*) **good evening** Buenas noches
Goodbye Adiós
goose ganso
gossip chisme (*m*)
government gobierno
graceful gracioso
gradually poco a poco
grandchild nieto
granddaughter nieta
grandfather abuelo
grandmother abuela
grandson nieto
grapefruit toronja

grape uva
grass hierba
grateful agradecido
gravy salsa
gray gris (*m & f*)
great gran (*m & f*) (*before a noun*)
great grande (*after a noun*)
Greece Grecia
Greek griego
green verde (*m & f*)
greetings saludos
groceries comestibles (*m*)
group grupo
(to) grow crecer
Guatemalan guatemalteco
guest invitado, huésped (*m*)
guide guía (*m & f*)
guilty culpable (*m & f*)
guitar guitarra
gun fusil (*m*)
gypsy gitano

H

habit costumbre (*f*)
hair cabello
hairbrush cepillo
haircut corte de pelo (*m*)
hairdresser peluquero
half mitad (*f*)
ham jamón (*m*)
hammer martillo
hand mano (*f*)
handbag cartera
handmade hecho a mano
handsome buen mozo
(to) happen pasar
happy feliz (*m & f*)

harbor puerto
hard duro
(*to*) **harm** (*a thing*) dañar
(*to*) **harm** (*a person*) hacer daño
  a . . .
hat sombrero
(*to*) **hate** odiar
(*to*) **have** (*possess*) tener
(*to*) **have** (*as aux. verb only*) haber
he él
head cabeza
headache dolor de cabeza (*m*)
(*to*) **heal** sanar
health salud (*f*)
healthy saludable (*m & f*)
(*to*) **hear** oír
heart corazón (*m*)
heat calor (*m*)
heaven cielo
heavy pesado
heel (*foot*) talón (*m*)
heel (*shoe*) tacón (*m*)
heir, heiress heredero, (*a*)
helicopter helicóptero
hell infierno
Hello Hola
(*to*) **help** ayudar
Help! ¡Socorro!
hen gallina
her (*direct object*) la, le
her (*indirect object*) le
her (*adjective*) su
here aquí
hero héroe
heroine heroína
hers el suyo
(*to*) **hesitate** vacilar
(*to*) **hide** esconder

high alto
highway carretera
hill colina
him (*direct object*) lo, le
him (*indirect object*) le
hip cadera
(*to*) **hire** alquilar
his (*adjective*) su
his (*pronoun*) el suyo
historical histórico
history historia
(*to*) **hit** pegar
(*to*) **hold** sostener
hole hueco
holiday día feriado (*m*)
holy santo
home casa
Honduran hondureño
honest honesto
honesty honradez
honey miel (*f*)
honeymoon luna de miel
honor honor (*m*)
(*to*) **hope** esperar
horizon horizonte (*m*)
horrible horrible (*m & f*)
horse caballo
hospital hospital (*m*)
hospitality hospitalidad (*f*)
host anfitrión (*m*)
hostess anfitriona
hot caliente (*m & f*)
hotel hotel (*m*)
hour hora
house casa
how cómo
How far? ¿A qué distancia?
How much? ¿Cuánto?

How much time? ¿Cuánto
   tiempo?
however sin embargo
(to) **hug** abrazar
huge enorme *(m & f)*
human humano
humid húmedo
humorous chistoso
hundred cien
(a) **hundred** *(and)* ... ciento ...
(to be) **hungry** tener hambre
(to) **hunt** cazar
hunter cazador *(m)*, cazadora *(f)*
hurricane huracán *(m)*
(to) **hurry** darse prisa
(to) **hurt** hacer daño
husband esposo

I

I yo
ice hielo
ice box nevera
ice cream helado
idea idea
idiot idiota *(m & f)*
if si
ignorant ignorante *(m & f)*
ill enfermo
illegal ilegal *(m & f)*
illness enfermedad *(f)*
illustration ilustración *(f)*
imagination imaginación *(f)*
(to) **imagine** imaginar
(to) **imitate** imitar
imitation imitación *(f)*
immediately inmediatamente
impatient impaciente *(m & f)*
imperfect imperfecto

importance importancia
important importante *(m & f)*
impossible imposible *(m & f)*
(to) **improve** mejorar
improvement mejoría
in en
(to) **include** incluir
included incluído
income entrada
income tax impuesto sobre la
   renta
inconvenient incómodo
incorrect incorrecto
(to) **increase** aumentar
incredible increíble *(m & f)*
independence independencia
independent independiente
   (m & f)
Indian indio
(to) **indicate** indicar
indigestion indigestión *(f)*
indirect indirecto
indiscreet indiscreto
individual *(n)* individuo
industrial industrial *(m & f)*
industry industria
inefficient ineficiente *(m & f)*
inexpensive barato
infection infección *(f)*
inferior inferior *(m & f)*
infinitive infinitivo
influence influencia
information información *(f)*
inhabitant habitante *(m & f)*
injection inyección *(f)*
ink tinta
in-laws familia política
inn posada, fonda

innocent inocente (*m & f*)
(*to*) **inquire** averiguar
inquiry pregunta
insane loco
insect insecto
inside (*direction*) adentro
inside (*preposition*) dentro de
(*to*) **insist** insistir
(*to*) **inspect** inspeccionar
instead of en vez de
instrument instrumento
intelligent inteligente (*m & f*)
intention intención (*f*)
interested interesado
interesting interesante (*m & f*)
international internacional
  (*m & f*)
interpreter intérprete (*m & f*)
interview entrevista
into dentro
(*to*) **introduce** presentar
invitation invitación (*f*)
(*to*) **invite** invitar
Ireland Irlanda
Irish irlandés (*m*), irlandesa (*f*)
irregular irregular (*m & f*)
is (*permanent status*) es
is (*location or temporary*
  status) está
Israel Israel
Israeli israeli (*m & f*)
island isla
it (*object*) lo, la
Italian italiano
Italy Italia
(*to*) **itch** picar
its su
ivory marfil (*m*)

J

jacket chaqueta
jail cárcel (*f*)
January enero
Japan Japón
Japanese japonés (*m*), japonesa
  (*f*)
jar jarro
jealous celoso
jewelry joyas
Jew, Jewish judío
job empleo
joke chiste (*m*)
journey viaje (*m*)
joy alegría
judge juez (*m*)
(*to*) **judge** juzgar
July julio
(*to*) **jump** saltar
June junio
jungle selva
jury jurado
just (*only*) solamente
just now ahora mismo
justice justicia

K

(*to*) **keep** guardar
key llave (*f*)
kid (*goat*) cabrito
(*to*) **kill** matar
kind (*nice*) amable (*m & f*)
kind (*type*) tipo
king rey
kiss beso
(*to*) **kiss** besar
kitchen cocina
knee rodilla

(*to*) **kneel** arrodillarse
knife cuchillo
(*to*) **knock** tocar
(*to*) **know** (*a person*) conocer
(*to*) **know** (*a fact or how to*) saber

L

label etiqueta
laboratory laboratorio
laborer obrero
lace encaje (*m*)
ladder escalera
ladies room cuarto para señoras
lady dama, señora
lake lago
lamb cordero
lame cojo
lamp lámpara
land tierra
(*to*) **land** (*from ship*) desembar-
car, aterrar
(*to*) **land** (*airplane*) aterrizar
landscape paisaje (*m*)
language idioma (*m*), lengua
lard manteca (*de cerdo*)
large grande (*m & f*)
last último
(*to*) **last** durar
late tarde
later más tarde
(*to*) **laugh** reír
laundry lavandería
law ley (*f*)
lawn césped (*m*)
lawyer abogado
laxative laxante (*m*)
lazy perezoso

leader jefe, guía (*m*)
leaf hoja
(*to*) **leak** gotear
(*to*) **learn** aprender
(*to*) **lease** alquilar
least mínimo
leather cuero
(*to*) **leave** (*something*) dejar
(*to*) **leave** (*depart*) salir
left (*direction*) izquierdo
(*to the*) **left** a la izquierda
leg pierna
legal legal (*m & f*)
leisure ocio
lemon limón (*m*)
lemonade limonada
(*to*) **lend** prestar
leopard leopardo
less menos
lesson lección (*f*)
(*to*) **let** (*permit*) permitir
letter carta
letter (*of alphabet*) letra
lettuce lechuga
liar mentiroso
liberal liberal (*m & f*)
liberty libertad (*f*)
library biblioteca
license permiso
lie (*untruth*) mentira
(*to*) **lie down** acostarse
lieutenant teniente (*m*)
life vida
lifeboat bote salvavidas (*m*)
(*to*) **lift** levantar
light (*weight*) ligero
light (*illumination*) luz (*f*)
light (*color*) claro

lightning relámpago
like (*as*) como
like this así
(*to*) like gustar
likewise igualmente
limit límite (*m*)
linen (*material*) lino
lingerie ropa interior
lion león (*m*)
lip labio
liquor licor (*m*)
list lista
(*to*) listen escuchar
little (*small*) pequeño
(*a*) little un poco
(*to*) live vivir
lively alegre (*m & f*)
liver hígado
living room sala
(*to*) load cargar
(*a*) loan préstamo
lobby vestíbulo, sala
lobster langosta
local local (*m & f*)
(*to*) lock cerrar con llave
logical lógico
lonely solitario
long largo
    a long time mucho tiempo
(*to*) look mirar
(*to*) look for buscar
loose flojo
(*to*) lose perder
losses pérdidas
lost perdido
lot (*much*) mucho
love amor (*m*)
(*in*) love enamorado

(*to*) love querer, amar
lovely lindo, precioso
low bajo
luck suerte (*f*)
luggage equipaje (*m*)
lunch almuerzo
lung pulmón (*m*)
luxury lujo

M

machine máquina
machinery maquinaria
mad loco
madam señora
made hecho
magazine revista
magic (*n*) magia
magic (*adj*) mágico
maid criada
mail correo
mailbox buzón (*m*)
mailman cartero
main (*principal*) mayor, principal
main course plato principal
(*to*) make hacer
male macho
man hombre
manager gerente (*m & f*)
manicure manicura
(*to*) manufacture fabricar
many muchos
marble mármol (*m*)
March marzo
market mercado
married casado
masculine masculino
mass (*religious*) misa

321

massage masaje (*m*)
match fósforo
(*to*) matter importar
    It doesn't matter No
    importa
    What's the matter? ¿Qué
    pasa?
May mayo
    May one? ¿Se puede?
maybe quizás
me me
    with me conmigo
meal comida
(*to*) mean significar
(*to*) measure medir
meat carne (*f*)
mechanic mecánico
medicine medicina
Mediterranean Mediterráneo
(*to*) meet encontrar
meeting reunión (*f*)
member miembro
men hombres
(*to*) mend remendar
men's room cuarto para
    caballeros
menu menú (*m*), lista de platos
message recado, mensaje (*m*)
metal metal (*m*)
meter (*measure*) metro
Mexican mexicano
middle medio
midnight medianoche (*f*)
mile milla
milk leche (*f*)
million millón (*m*)
mine mío
mineral water agua mineral (*m*)
minister ministro

mink visón (*m*)
minus menos
minute minuto
mirror espejo
misfortune desgracia
Miss señorita (*Srta.*)
(*to*) miss (*a train, etc.*) perder
(*to*) miss (*sentiment*) echar de
    menos
mistake error (*m*)
misunderstanding malentendido
(*to*) mix mezclar
mixture mezcla
model modelo (*m. or f.*)
modern moderno
moment momento
Monday lunes
money dinero
monkey mono
month mes (*m*)
monument monumento
moon luna
more más
more or less más o menos
morning mañana
mortgage hipoteca
mosquito mosquito
most of la mayor parte
mother madre
mother-in-law suegra
motor motor (*m*)
motorcycle motocicleta
mountain montaña
mouse ratón (*m*)
mouth boca
(*to*) move mover
movie película
movies cine (*m*)
Mr. señor (*Sr.*)

Mrs. señora (*Sra.*)
much mucho
mud barro
museum museo
mushroom hongo
music música
musician músico
must hay que, deber
mustache bigote (*m*)
mustard mostaza
my mi
mystery misterio

N

nail (*metal*) clavo
naked desnudo
name (*first*) nombre (*m*)
name (*last*) apellido
narrow angosto
national nacional (*m & f*)
nationality nacionalidad (*f*)
natural natural (*m & f*)
naturally naturalmente
navy marina
near cerca
necessary necesario
neck cuello
necklace collar (*m*)
necktie corbata
(*to*) **need** necesitar
(*to*) **neglect** descuidar
neighborhood vecindario
nephew sobrino
nervous nervioso
neutral neutral (*m & f*)
never nunca
new nuevo
news noticias

newspaper periódico
New Year Año Nuevo
next próximo
Nicaraguan nicaragüense (*m & f*)
nice simpático
niece sobrina
night noche (*f*)
nightclub club nocturno
nightgown camisa de dormir
nine nueve
nineteen diecinueve
ninety noventa
ninth noveno
no no
nobody nadie
noise ruido
none ninguno, nada
nonsense tontería
noon mediodía (*m*)
normal normal (*m & f*)
north norte (*m*)
nose nariz (*f*)
not no
    not yet todavía no
note nota
(*to*) **note** notar
nothing nada
notice aviso
(*to*) **notice** notar
noun nombre (*m*)
novel novela
November noviembre
now ahora
nowhere en ninguna parte
number número
numerous numeroso
nurse enfermera
nut (*food*) nuez (*f*), nueces (*pl*)

O

oak roble (*m*)
(*to*) obey obedecer
object objeto
(*to*) oblige obligar
obvious obvio
occasion ocasión (*f*)
occupation ocupación (*f*)
occupied ocupado
(*to*) occupy ocupár
ocean océano
October octubre
of de
    of course ¡cómo no! desde
    luego
(*to*) offer ofrecer
office oficina
officer oficial (*m*)
often a menudo
oil aceite (*m*)
oil (*for industry*) petróleo
o.k. está bien, de acuerdo
old viejo
olive aceituna
olive oil aceite de oliva (*m*)
omelet tortilla de huevos
on en, sobre
    on time a tiempo
once una vez
(*at*) once en seguida
one uno
one-way (*street*) vía única
onion cebolla
only solamente
open abierto
(*to*) open abrir
open air aire libre
opera ópera

operation operación (*f*)
operator telefonista (*m* & *f*)
opinion opinión (*f*)
opportunity oportunidad (*f*)
opposite opuesto
or o
orange naranja
orchestra orquesta
orchid orquídea
order orden (*f*)
(*to*) order ordenar
(*in*) order to para
ordinary ordinario
organization organización (*m*)
original original (*m* & *f*)
other otro
ought to debería
our nuestro
ours el nuestro
outdoors el aire libre
outside afuera
over encima (*de*)
over (*finished*) terminado
overcoat abrigo
over there allá
overweight sobrepeso
(*to*) owe deber
own propio
owner dueño
ox buey
oxygen oxígeno
oyster ostra

P

(*to*) pack empacar
package paquete (*m*)
page página
paid pagado

pail cubo
pain dolor (*m*)
painful doloroso
(*to*) **paint** pintar
painter pintor
painting cuadro
pair pareja
palace palacio
pan cacerola
pants pantalones (*m pl*)
Panamanian panameño
paper papel (*m*)
parade desfile (*m*)
Paraguayan paraguayo
Pardon me perdón
parents padres
park parque (*m*)
(*to*) **park** estacionar
part parte (*f*)
participle participio
partner (*business*) socio
party fiesta
party (*polit.*) partido
(*to*) **pass** pasar
passenger pasajero
passport pasaporte (*m*)
past pasado
pastry pastel (*m*)
(*to*) **pay** pagar
(*to*) **pay cash** pagar al contado
peace paz (*f*)
peach durazno
peas guisantes (*m*)
pen pluma
pencil lápiz (*m*)
people gente (*f*)
pepper pimienta
percent por ciento
perfect perfecto

perfume perfume (*m*)
perhaps quizás
permanent permanente (*f*)
permission permiso
(*to*) **permit** permitir
permitted permitido
person persona
Peruvian peruano
phone teléfono
photo foto (*f*)
piano piano
(*to*) **pick up** recoger
picture cuadro
picture (*movie*) película
piece pedazo
pier muelle (*m*)
pig puerco
pill píldora
pillow almohada
pilot piloto
pin alfiler (*m*)
pineapple piña
pink rosado
pipe (*smoking*) pipa
pipe (*plumbing*) tubo
pistol pistola
place lugar (*m*)
plain (*simple*) sencillo
plan plan (*m*)
plane avión (*m*)
planet planeta (*m*)
plant (*garden*) planta
plant (*factory*) fábrica
plastic plástico
plate plato
platinum platino
play (*theater*) pieza
(*to*) **play** (*games*) jugar
(*to*) **play** (*piano, etc.*) tocar

pleasant agradable (*m & f*)
please por favor
(*to*) **please** gustar (*a*)
pleasure placer (*m*)
plum ciruela
plural plural (*m*)
pocket bolsillo
poet poeta (*m*)
poetry poesía
(*to*) **point** señalar
poisonous venenoso
police policía (*f*)
policeman policía (*m*)
police station cuartel de
  policía (*m*)
(*to*) **polish** pulir
polite cortés
pool piscina
poor pobre (*m & f*)
Pope papa (*m*)
popular popular (*m & f*)
pork cerdo
portrait retrato
Portuguese portugués (*m*), portu-
  guesa (*f*)
position (*job*) puesto
possible posible (*m & f*)
postcard tarjeta postal
post office correo
pot olla
potato papa, patata
pottery alfarería
pound (*weight*) libra
(*to*) **pour** verter
power poder
practical práctico
(*to*) **practice** practicar
precious precioso
(*to*) **prefer** preferir

pregnant embarazada
(*to*) **prepare** preparar
present (*time*) presente
present (*gift*) regalo
(*to*) **present** presentar
president presidente (*m*)
(*to*) **press** (*clothes*) planchar
pretty bonito
(*to*) **prevent** prevenir
previously previamente
price precio
priest sacerdote (*m*)
prince príncipe (*m*)
princess princesa
principal principal
prison cárcel (*f*)
private privado
prize premio
probably probablemente
problem problema (*m*)
(*to*) **produce** producir
production producción (*f*)
profession profesión (*f*)
professor profesor (*m*)
profits beneficios, ganancias
program programa (*m*)
(*to*) **promise** prometer
promised prometido
pronoun pronombre (*m*)
(*to*) **pronounce** pronunciar
pronunciation pronunciación (*f*)
propaganda advertising,
  propaganda
property propiedad (*f*)
(*to*) **protect** proteger
(*to*) **protest** protestar
Protestant protestante (*m & f*)
proud orgulloso
(*to*) **prove** probar

psychiatrist psiquiatra
public público
publicity publicidad (*f*)
publisher editor (*m*)
(*to*) **pull** halar, tirar
(*to*) **punish** castigar
punishment castigo
(*to*) **purchase** comprar
pure puro
purple morado
purse bolsa
(*to*) **push** empujar
(*to*) **put** poner
(*to*) **put on** ponerse

Q

quality calidad (*f*)
quantity cantidad (*f*)
quarter cuarto
queen reina
question pregunta
quick rápido
quickly rápidamente
quiet quieto
quite bastante

R

rabbi rabino
rabbit conejo
race (*human*) raza
race (*contest*) carrera
radio radio (*f*)
railroad ferrocarril (*m*)
rain lluvia
raincoat impermeable (*m*)
raise aumento
rapid rápido
rapidly rápidamente

rare (*uncommon*) raro
rarely rara vez
rat rata
rather más bien
raw crudo
razor navaja de afeitar
(*to*) **reach** alcanzar
(*to*) **read** leer
ready listo
(*to*) **realize** darse cuenta (*de*)
really? ¿de veras?
really verdaderamente
reason razón (*f*)
receipt recibo
(*to*) **receive** recibir
recently recientemente
reception recepción (*f*)
recipe receta
(*to*) **recognize** reconocer
(*to*) **recommend** recomendar
record (*phono*) disco
record (*account*) archivo
record player tocadiscos
red rojo
(*to*) **refund** reembolsar
(*to*) **refuse** rehusar
registration patente (*f*)
(*to*) **regret** sentir, lamentar
regular regular (*m & f*)
relatives parientes (*m*)
religion religión (*f*)
(*to*) **remain** quedarse
(*to*) **remember** recordar
(*to*) **rent** alquilar
(*to*) **repair** reparar
repairs reparaciones
(*to*) **repeat** repetir
(*to*) **reply** contestar
report reporte (*m*)

(*to*) **report** reportar
reporter reportero
(*to*) **represent** representar
representative representante (*m*)
reputation reputación (*f*)
(*to*) **request** pedir
(*to*) **resemble** parecerse a
resident residente (*m & f*)
(*to*) **resist** resistir
rest (*remainder*) resto
(*to*) **rest** descansar
restaurant restaurante (*m*)
result resultado
(*to*) **retire** retirarse
(*to*) **return** (*to a place*) regresar
(*to*) **return** (*give back*) devolver
(*to*) **review** revisar
revolution revolución (*f*)
reward recompensa
rice arroz (*m*)
rich rico
rifle rifle (*m*)
right (*direction*) derecho
right (*correct*) correcto
right away en seguida
right now ahora mismo
ring anillo
riot tumulto
risk riesgo
river río
road camino
roasted asado
(*to*) **rob** robar
roll (*bread*) panecillo
roof techo
room cuarto
room (*space*) espacio
room service servicio de comedor
root raíz (*f*)

rope soga
rose rosa
rough áspero
round redondo
round trip ida y vuelta
route ruta
rubber caucho
ruby rubí (*m*)
ruin ruina
rum ron (*m*)
(*to*) **run** correr
Russia Rusia
Russian ruso

S

sack saco
sad triste (*m & f*)
safe seguro
safety pin imperdible (*m*)
said dicho
sail vela
(*to*) **sail** navegar
sailor marinero
saint santo
salad ensalada
salary sueldo
sale venta
salt sal (*f*)
Salvador El Salvador
Salvadorian salvadoreño
same mismo
sandwich emparedado
satisfied satisfecho
Saturday sábado
sauce salsa
savage salvaje (*m & f*)
saw (*tool*) sierra
(*to*) **say** decir

scarf pañuelo, bufanda
scene escena
scenery paisaje (*m*)
school escuela
science ciencia
scientist científico
scissors tijeras
Scotch escocés (*m*), escocesa (*f*)
Scotland Escocia
(*to*) scratch rascar
(*to*) scream gritar
sea mar (*m*)
seafood mariscos
(*to*) search for buscar
seasickness mareo
season estación (*f*)
seat asiento
second segundo
secret secreto
secretary secretaria, o
section sección (*f*)
security seguridad (*f*)
(*to*) see ver
seed semilla
(*to*) seem parecer
seen visto
seldom rara vez
(*to*) select seleccionar
selfish egoísta (*m* & *f*)
(*to*) sell vender
(*to*) send mandar
(*to*) send for enviar por
sensation sensación (*f*)
separate separado
September septiembre
serious serio
set juego
(*to*) set the table poner la mesa
servant criada, o

service servicio
seven siete
seventeen diecisiete
seventy setenta
several varios
shampoo champú (*m*)
shape forma
shark tiburón (*m*)
sharp agudo
she ella
sheep oveja, carnero
sheet (*bed*) sábana
(*to*) shine brillar
ship nave (*f*)
shipment envío
shirt camisa
shoe zapato
shop tienda
shopkeeper tendero
short corto
shoulder hombro
(*to*) shout gritar
shovel pala
show espectáculo
(*to*) show mostrar
shower (*bath*) ducha
shrimps camarones (*m*)
shut cerrado
(*to*) shut cerrar
sick enfermo
side lado
(*to*) sign firmar
signature firma
silence silencio
silk seda
silver plata
simple sencillo
since desde
sincerely sinceramente

(*to*) **sing** cantar
singer cantante (*m or f*)
single (*only*) único
single (*unmarried*) soltero
sir señor
sister hermana
sister-in-law cuñada
(*to*) **sit down** sentarse
situation situación (*f*)
six seis
sixteen dieciséis
sixty sesenta
size tamaño
(*to*) **skate** patinar
(*to*) **ski** esquiar
skin piel (*f*)
skirt falda
sky cielo
slave esclavo
(*to*) **sleep** dormir
sleeve manga
slippers chancletas
slowly despacio
small pequeño
(*to*) **smell** oler
smile sonrisa
(*to*) **smile** sonreír
smoke humo
(*to*) **smoke** fumar
snail caracol
snake culebra
snow nieve (*f*)
so (*thus*) asi
soap jabón (*m*)
sock calcetín (*m*)
sofa sofá (*m*)
soft blando
soldier soldado
some (*adv.*) un poco de

some (*adj.*) algunos
somebody alguien
something algo
  something else algo más
sometimes algunas veces
somewhere en alguna parte
son hijo
son-in-law yerno
song canción (*f*)
soon pronto
sore adolorido
sorrow tristeza
(*I am*) **sorry** Lo siento
soul alma (*el*)
sour agrio
south sur
South America América del Sur
souvenir recuerdo
space espacio
Spain España
Spanish español (*m*), española (*f*)
(*to*) **speak** hablar
special especial (*m & f*)
speed velocidad (*f*)
(*to*) **spend** gastar
spoon cuchara
sport deporte (*m*)
spot (*stain*) mancha
sprained torcido
spring (*season*) primavera
(*to*) **stab** apuñalar
stain mancha
stairs escalera
stamp estampilla (*in Spain, sello*)
(*to*) **stand** pararse
star estrella
(*to*) **start** (*begin*) empezar

state estado

station estación (*f*)

    gas station puesto de gasolina

station wagon camioneta

statue estatua

(*to*) stay quedarse

steak biftec (*m*)

(*to*) steal robar

steel acero

stenographer taquígrafa, o

stew guisado

still (*adv.*) todavía

stocking media

stockmarket bolsa

stocks (*shares*) acciones (*f*)

stomach estómago

stone piedra

(*to*) stop parar

store tienda

storm tormenta

story cuento

story (*of a building*) piso

straight derecho

strange extraño

stranger extraño

street calle (*f*)

strike (*labor*) huelga

string cuerda

strong fuerte (*m & f*)

student estudiante (*m or f*)

studio estudio

(*to*) study estudiar

stupid estúpido

style estilo

subject asunto

submarine submarino

subway metro

success éxito

such tal

suddenly de repente

suede gamuza

(*to*) suffer sufrir

sugar azúcar (*f*)

suit (*clothes*) traje (*m*)

suitcase maleta

(*to*) sum up sumar

summer verano

summons citación (*f*)

sun sol (*m*)

Sunday domingo

sure seguro

surely seguramente

surprise sorpresa

(*to*) surround rodear

surroundings alrededores (*m*)

sweater suéter (*m*)

sweet dulce (*m & f*)

(*to*) swim nadar

swimming pool piscina

Swiss suizo

Switzerland Suiza

swollen hinchado

symptom síntoma (*m*)

system sistema (*m*)

T

table mesa

tablecloth mantel (*m*)

tail cola

tailor sastre (*m*)

(*to*) take tomar

(*to*) take away llevarse

(*to*) take a walk (*a ride*) dar un paseo

talent talento
(*to*) **talk** hablar
tall alto
tame manso
tank tanque (*m*)
tape cinta
tape recorder grabador (*m*)
taste gusto
tax impuesto
tea té (*m*)
(*to*) **teach** enseñar
teacher maestro
team equipo
tear lágrima
telegram telegrama (*m*)
telephone teléfono
television televisión (*f*)
(*to*) **tell** decir
temperature temperatura
temple templo
temporary temporario
ten diez
tenant inquilino
tennis tenis (*m*)
(*past*) **tense** tiempo pasado
(*future*) **tense** tiempo futuro
tenth décimo
terrace terraza
terrible terrible (*m & f*)
(*to*) **test** probar
than que
(*to*) **thank** agradecer
thanks gracias
that que
the el, la, los, las
theater teatro
their su
theirs suyo

them los, las
then entonces
there allí, allá
there is, there are hay
these (*pronoun*) éstos, éstas
these (*adjective*) estos, estas
they ellos, ellas
thick grueso
thief ladrón (*m*)
thin delgado
thing cosa
(*to*) **think** pensar
third tercero
(*to be*) **thirsty** tener sed
thirteen trece
thirty treinta
this (*pronoun*) esto, éste, ésta
this (*adj.*) este, esta
those (*pronoun*) ésos, ésas
those (*adj.*) esos, esas
thousand mil
thread hilo
three tres
throat garganta
through (*prep*) por
through (*over*) terminado
(*to*) **throw** tirar
thunder trueno
Thursday jueves
ticket billete (*m*)
ticket window taquilla
tie corbata
tiger tigre (*m*)
tight apretado
till hasta
time tiempo
   what time is it? ¿Qué
   hora es?

time of arrival hora de llegada
time of departure hora de salida
tin estaño
tip (*gratuity*) propina
tire llanta
tired cansado
to (*direction*) a
to (*in order to*) para
toast (*bread*) tostada
(*to*) toast (*drinking*) brindar
tobacco tabaco
today hoy
toe dedo del pie
together juntos
toilet excusado, retrete
tomato tomate (*m*)
tomb tumba
tomorrow mañana
tongue lengua
tonight esta noche
too (*also*) también
too (*excessive*) demasiado
tool herramienta
tooth diente (*m*)
toothbrush cepillo de dientes
toothpaste pasta de dientes
torn roto
total total
(*to*) touch tocar
tour jira
tourist turista (*m or f*)
(*to*) tow remolcar
towards hacia
towel toalla
tower torre (*f*)
town pueblo

toy juguete (*m*)
traffic tránsito
tragedy tragedia
train tren (*m*)
(*to*) translate traducir
translation traducción (*f*)
(*to*) travel viajar
traveler viajero
treasure tesoro
treasurer tesorero
tree árbol (*m*)
trial (*legal*) juicio
trip viaje (*m*)
trouble problema (*m*)
trousers pantalones (*m*)
truck camión (*m*)
true verdadero
truth verdad (*f*)
(*to*) try tratar
(*to*) try on probarse
Tuesday martes
tune tonada
tunnel túnel (*m*)
Turk, Turkish turco
Turkey Turquía
turkey pavo
(*to*) turn voltear
(*to*) turn around volverse dar vuelta
(*to*) turn off apagar
(*to*) turn on poner
turtle tortuga
twelve doce
twenty veinte
twice dos veces
twin gemelo
(*to*) twist torcer
two dos

type tipo
typewriter máquina de escribir
typical típico
typist mecanógrafa, o

useful útil (*m & f*)
useless inútil (*m & f*)
usually usualmente

U

ugly feo
umbrella paraguas (*m*)
uncle tío
uncomfortable incómodo
unconscious inconsciente
under debajo de
underneath debajo
undershirt camiseta
(*to*) understand comprender
(*to*) undertake emprender
underwear ropa interior
(*to*) undress desvestirse
unemployed desocupado
unfortunately desgraciadamente
uniform uniforme (*m*)
unit unidad (*f*)
(*to*) unite unir
United Nations Naciones
  Unidas (*f*)
United States Estados Unidos
university universidad (*f*)
unless a menos que
until hasta
up arriba
urgent urgente (*m & f*)
Uruguayan uruguayo
us nos, nosotros (*after a
  preposition*)
use uso
(*to*) use usar
(*to be*) used to (*in habit of*) estar
  acostumbrado a

V

vacant desocupado
vacation vacación (*f*)
vaccination vacuna
valid válido
valley valle (*m*)
valuable valioso
value valor (*m*)
variety variedad (*f*)
various varios
veal ternera
vegetable vegetal (*m*)
Venezuelan venezolano
verb verbo
very muy
  very well muy bien
vest chaleco
vicinity alrededores
victory victoria
view vista
village aldea
vinegar vinagre (*m*)
violent violento
violet violeta
violin violín (*m*)
visa visa
visit visita
(*to*) visit visitar
visiting de visita
vivid vívido
voice voz (*f*)
volcano volcán (*m*)
voyage viaje (*m*)

W

waist cintura
(*to*) **wait** esperar
waiter camarero
waitress camarera
(*to*) **wake up** despertarse
(*a*) **walk** paseo
(*to*) **walk** caminar
wall pared (*f*)
wallet cartera
(*to*) **want** querer
war guerra
warm caliente (*m & f*)
(*to*) **wash** lavar
washable lavable (*m & f*)
(*to*) **waste** malgastar
watch reloj (*m*)
(*to*) **watch** mirar
Watch out! ¡Cuidado!
water agua (*m*)
water color acuarela
waterproof impermeable (*m & f*)
way (*manner*) modo
way (*road*) camino
we nosotros
weak débil (*m & f*)
weapon arma
(*to*) **wear** llevar
weather tiempo
wedding boda
Wednesday miércoles
week semana
weekend fin de semana (*m*)
(*to*) **weigh** pesar
weight peso
Welcome! ¡Bienvenido!
you are welcome de nada
well bien

Well, . . . pues, . . .
west oeste
West Indies las Antillas
West Indian antillano
wet mojado, húmedo
what que
what (*that which*) lo que
wheat trigo
wheel rueda
when cuando
where donde
where to? ¿a dónde?
wherever dondequiera
whether si
which cual
while mientras
(*a*) **while** un rato
white blanco
who quien
whole entero
whom? ¿a quién?
why? ¿por qué?
why not? ¿por qué no?
wide ancho
widow viuda
widower viudo
wife esposa
wig peluca
wild salvaje (*m & f*)
will (*see step 17*)
willing dispuesto
(*to*) **win** ganar
wind viento
window ventana
wine vino
wing ala
wise sabio
(*to*) **wish** desear
with con

without sin
witness testigo (*m & f*)
wolf lobo
woman mujer
(*to*) **wonder** preguntarse
wonderful maravilloso
won't (*see Step 17*)
wood madera
woods bosque (*m*)
wool lana
word palabra
work trabajo
(*to*) **work** trabajar
world mundo
(*to*) **worry** preocuparse
worse peor (*m & f*)
would (*see Steps 19, 21 & 24*)
(*to*) **wrap** envolver
wrist muñeca
(*to*) **write** escribir
writer escritor (*m*), escritora (*f*)
wrong (*not right*) equivocado

X

X-ray rayos X

Y

yacht yate (*m*)
year año
yellow amarillo
yes sí
yesterday ayer
yet todavía
you usted (*singular*), ustedes (*pl.*)
you tú (*familiar*), vosotros (*pl.*)
    as object le, lo, la (*sing*) les,
    los, las (*pl.*) te (*fam.*) os (*pl.*)
young joven (*m or f*)
your su
yours el suyo
yourself, yourselves Ud. mismo,
    Uds. mismos, se (*as reflexive*)
youth juventud (*f*)

Z

zero cero
zipper cierre (*m*)
zone zona
zoo zoológico